Studies in Applied Econometrics

Contributions to Economics

Albrecht Ritschl
Prices and Production
- Elements of a System - Theoretic Perspective -
1989. 159pp. Softcover DM 59,-
ISBN 3-7908-0429-0

Arnulf Grübler
The Rise and Fall of Infrastructures
- Dynamics of Evolution and Technological Change in Transport -
1990. 305pp. Softcover DM 85,-
ISBN 3-7908-0479-7

Peter R. Haiss
Cultural Influences on Strategic Planning
1990. 188pp. Softcover DM 65,-
ISBN 3-7908-0481-9

Manfred Kremer/Marion Weber (Eds.)
Transforming Economic Systems: The Case of Poland
1992. 179pp. Softcover DM 69,-
ISBN 3-7908-91415-3

Marcel F. van Marion
Liberal Trade and Japan
1993. 298pp. Softcover DM 90,-
ISBN 3-7908-0699-4

Michael Carlberg
Open Economy Dynamics
1993. 203 pp. Softcover DM 75,-
ISBN 3-7908-0708-7

Hans Schneeweiß
Klaus F. Zimmermann (Eds.)

Studies in Applied Econometrics

With 1 Figure

Physica-Verlag
A Springer-Verlag Company

Series Editor
Werner A. Müller
Peter Schuster

Editors
Professor Dr. Hans Schneeweiß
University of Munich
Akademiestraße 1/I
D-80799 München, Germany

Professor Dr. Klaus F. Zimmermann
SELAPO, University of Munich
Ludwigstraße 28 RG
D-80539 München, Germany

ISBN 978-3-7908-0716-5 ISBN 978-3-642-51514-9 (eBook)
DOI 10.1007/978-3-642-51514-9

CIP-Titelaufnahme der Deutschen Bibliothek
Studies in applied econometrics / Hans Schneeweiss; Klaus F.
Zimmermann (Eds.). - Heidelberg : Physica-Verl., 1993
(Contributions to economics)

NE: Schneeweiss, Hans [Hrsg.]

7100/7130-543210 - Printed on acid-free paper

Contents

Introduction

This book reports new developments in applied econometrics. All papers originated in two international workshops that were organized in the University of Munich on July 6-7, 1989, and on January 11 - 12, 1990. Financial support for these conferences by the University of Munich and the Thyssen Foundation is gratefully acknowledged. Since then all papers were substantially revised and updated. We wish to thank all authors for their patience with the revisions and Thomas Bauer, Lucie Merkle and Gisela Loos for editorial help.

The first section of the book collects contributions that address new "Methodological Developments". Two of them deal with problems in microeconometrics, the other two consider multi-equation systems. Martin Kukuk and Gerd Ronning treat "Ordinal Variables in Microeconometric Models". They especially deal with the case of limited-dependent variable models where some exogenous variables are either measured on an interval scale or a nominal scale. They discuss and compare two methods to deal with the problem. In his paper on "Goodness of Fit in Qualitative Choice Models: Review and Evaluation", Klaus F. Zimmermann investigates methods to summarize the predictive quality of models that deal with discrete alternatives. For these models, a widely accepted measure for evaluation like the R^2, as in the case of ordinary least squares, does not exist. The paper summarizes the literature and suggests reasonable choices for evaluation on the basis of large-scale Monte Carlo investigations.

A vector-autoregressive process is the model under investigation in Helmut Lütkepohl's paper on "Testing for Causation Between Two Variables in

Higher Dimensional VAR Models". He studies the concept of a causal relation of one variable with respect to another one when still other variables are present in the autoregressive system. Tests for this kind of causality can be developed by considering the response of the first variable on an innovation of the second one. The hypothesis to be tested is then a hypothesis about certain zero restrictions in the impulse response coefficients. Lütkepohl studies the properties of tests for this hypothesis. Another kind of multiequation systems, i.e. recursive systems, where causility is built right into the model, is dealt with by Schneeweiß in his paper on "The Reduced Form of Recursive Models: Asymptotic Properties". The reduced form of such a model can be estimated in two different ways; either by OLS applied to the reduced form or by OLS applied to the structural form with subsequent transformation into the reduced form. It is shown that the latter procedure yields asymptotically more precise estimates than the former, whereby necessary and sufficient conditions are given for their being asymptotically equivalent.

The second section of the book studies "Economic Applications". The paper by Christoph M. Schmidt on "Testing the Stationary Search Model" uses duration analysis to model individual unemployment histories and confronts the resulting structural form with data from West Germany. One important finding is that the reservation wage affects the length of individual unemployment, and that there is a relationship between the duration of a spell and the chosen reservation wage that one cannot control for in a reduced form approach. Gebhard Flaig and Viktor Steiner contribute a paper on "Markup Differentials, Cost Flexibility, and Capacity Utilization in West German Manufacturing". Based on the modern theory of production and costs, they study the relationship between pricing behavior and market structure. They account for both a non-homothetic production function incorporating non-constant returns to scale and the quasi-fixity of factors of production. In explaining industry markups, they use the concepts of short-run and long-run cost flexibility. One important finding is that most prices behave procyclically.

The paper by Franz C. Palm and Gerard A. Pfann on "Empirical Analysis of Optimal Firm Behavior: Asymmetric Adjustment in Labour and Capital Demand in the Manufacturing Sector in the Netherlands and UK" overcomes one of the shortcomings of the linear rational expectations model for labour and capital demand. The dynamics of these models are often the result of the assumption of quadratic adjustment costs which is questionable. The paper uses the more general asymmetric functional form under uncertainty and profit maximisation of the firm. They conclude that the asymmetric adjustment costs model is more appropriate for the data they use than the linear quadratic model. Gebhard Kirchgässner and Jürgen Wolters ask the question "Are Real Interest Rates Stable?". Using unit root tests they find that not only nominal, but also ex post real interest rates seem to be nonstationary, at least for the period under investigation (January 1980 to December 1988) and for the money market rates of Switzerland, Germany, the U.S., France, and the U.K. Inflation rates are also found to be nonstationary. There is hardly any evidence that they are cointegrated with nominal interest rates, implying that the Fisher hypothesis seems not to hold as a long run relationship.

Munich, March 1993

Hans Schneeweiß

Klaus F. Zimmermann

Part I: Methodological Developments

Ordinal Variables in Microeconometric Models*

Martin Kukuk
(University of Konstanz)
and
Gerd Ronning
(University of Konstanz)

1 Introduction

Microeconometric models have become an important tool of econometric analysis since micro data were made available and computer programs gave the necessary computing assistance. In particular probit, Tobit, and duration models have been successfully applied to problems in many fields of economic research. [1] As in linear regression models the distribution of the dependent variable usually depends on some exogenous variables, that is, we consider a conditional distribution. If the exogenous variables are measured either on an interval scale or on a nominal scale, the corresponding econometric methods are well established. However, for

*Results in this paper are related to a project which is financially supported by the Thyssen-Stiftung. We thank Gerhard Arminger and Francois Laisney for helpful comments on an earlier version of this paper.

[1] See Maddala(1983), Amemiya (1985) Pudney(1989) for an overview.

ordinal exogenous variables no specific approach has been offered. Very often such variables have been treated as nominal.[2] Alternatively the *joint* distribution of endogenous and exogenous variables has been considered. This will be a major point in the following presentation. The discussion of proper treatment of ordinal variables in econometric models was initiated by Nerlove (1988). He noted that *polychoric* correlation [3] provides the proper framework. This approach estimates the covariance structure of a latent model from the observed ordinal varables assuming a threshold model for the observed ordinal variables. Ross (1987) has suggested an alternative approach which is much easier to estimate but has some severe shortcomings. In this paper we will discuss both approaches and illustrate them by an empirical example. Section 2 describes the two methods and compares them to each other whereas section 3 presents an empirical example. Some concluding remarks are added in section 4.

2 Alternative Approaches

2.1 General Remarks

We start from the linear model

$$\eta = \alpha + \beta \xi + \varepsilon \quad . \qquad (2-1)$$

[2]See, for example, Kawasaki, McMillan and Zimmermann (1982,1983) and König and Nerlove (1986). Sometimes this procedures might provide a more flexible specification, especially if nonmonotonic relations exist. See the discussion in Hsiao and Mountain (1985).

[3]Below we also consider the closely related case of *polyserial* correlation which applies if only one of the observed variables is ordinal. See Olsson (1979).

Both η and ξ are latent variables and ε is the random error with (conditional) expected value of zero and (conditional) variance $\sigma_\varepsilon{}^2$ which is distributed independently of ξ. Observations related to η are given by the variable y and those related to ξ are given by x. If $y = \eta$ and $x = \xi$, then we have the linear regression model for which all three parameters (α, β and $\sigma_\varepsilon{}^2$) are identified. For further reference we also state the specific structure of the parameters if bivariate normality for η and ξ is assumed. Then we obtain in an obvious notation

$$\begin{aligned} \alpha &= \mu_\eta - \rho \frac{\sigma_\eta}{\sigma_\xi} \mu_\xi \\ \beta &= \rho \frac{\sigma_\eta}{\sigma_\xi} \\ \sigma_\varepsilon^2 &= 1 - \rho^2 \end{aligned} \tag{2-2}$$

If $x = \xi$ and η is observed as an ordinal variable, that is

$$y = i \quad \text{if } a_{i-1} < \eta \leq a_i \quad , i = 1, \ldots, k_\eta \quad , \tag{2-3}$$

then for normally distributed η (given ξ) we arrive at the *standard probit* model with normalizing restrictions $\alpha = 0$ and $\sigma_\varepsilon{}^2 = 1$. This model is well-known and needs no further discussion.[4]

Now asume the reversed situation, that is, the dependent variable η is perfectly observable, $y = \eta$, and for the exogenous variable ξ we have only ordered categories:

$$x = j \quad \text{if } b_{j-1} < \xi \leq b_j \quad , j = 1, \ldots, k_\xi \quad . \tag{2-4}$$

For this case we have to consider the conditional density of η given x. If the joint density of η and ξ is denoted by $f(\eta, \xi)$, then this density has

[4]See, for example, Maddala (1983, chapter 2).

the form[5]

$$g(\eta \mid x = j) = \frac{1}{\pi_{\bullet j}} \int_{b_{j-1}}^{b_j} f(\eta, \xi)\, d\xi \quad , \qquad (2-5)$$

where

$$\pi_{\bullet j} = \int_{-\infty}^{\infty} \int_{b_{j-1}}^{b_j} f(u, v)\ dv\, du \qquad (2-6)$$

is the marginal probability of $x = j$. Hsiao and Mountain (1985) consider this model under the assumption that the thresholds in (2-4) are known. Such a situation arises in applied research if data for the exogenous variable are grouped. However in our model the thresholds are unknown.[6] Let $\delta_{tj} = 1$ if the t-th observation belongs to category j. Then the likelihood function is given by

$$\mathcal{L}_B = \prod_t \prod_j g(\eta_t \mid x_t = j)^{\delta_{tj}} \qquad (2-7)$$

Finally we consider the case which will receive most attention in the following: Both η and ξ are observed as ordinal variables, that is both (2-3) and (2-4) hold. Again assuming a joint density f for the two random variables we arrive at the following probability of $y = i$ given $x = j$:

$$\pi_{i|j} = \frac{\pi_{ij}}{\pi_{\bullet j}} \qquad (2-8)$$

with

$$\pi_{ij} = \int_{a_{i-1}}^{a_i} \int_{b_{j-1}}^{b_j} f(\eta, \xi)\ d\xi\ d\eta \quad . \qquad (2-9)$$

This implies the likelihood function

$$\mathcal{L}_C = \prod_t \prod_i \prod_j \pi_{i|j}^{\delta_{tij}} \qquad (2-10)$$

[5]Note that this density is *not* normal if bivariate normality is assumed for η and ξ.

[6]Identifiability of parameters for this model will not be discussed. See however the next subsection.

with $\delta_{tij} = 1$ if the t-th observation belongs to category (i, j). Note that (2-10) can also be written as follows:

$$\begin{aligned} \mathcal{L}_C &= \prod_t \prod_i \prod_j \pi_{ij}^{\delta_{tij}} \left[\prod_t \prod_j \pi_{\bullet j}^{\delta_{tj}} \right]^{-1} \\ &= \prod_i \prod_j \pi_{ij}^{n_{ij}} \left[\prod_j \pi_{\bullet j}^{n_{\bullet j}} \right]^{-1} \end{aligned} \qquad (2\text{-}11)$$

where n_{ij} and $n_{\bullet j}$ denote the number of observations from category (i, j) and j, respectively.

2.2 Polychoric Correlation

When both η and ξ are ordinal observed variables the estimation of parameters is usually discussed under the heading *polychoric correlation* which has a long tradition in psychometry.[7] However discussion always starts from the *joint* distribution of η and ξ instead of the *conditional* distribution as discussed above. We first state the most relevant results for this approach and then discuss the differences which arise if the conditional distribution is considered.

We assume that η and ξ are jointly *normally* distributed. Since both random variables are not observed their means and variances are arbitrary. We choose

$$\mu_\eta = \mu_\xi = 0 \quad , \quad \sigma_\eta^2 = \sigma_\xi^2 = 1$$

which leads to a bivariate standard normal distribution with correlation coefficient ρ as the only unknown parameter besides the $k_\eta + k_\xi - 2$ thresholds from (2-3) and (2-4) which have to be estimated. Note that

[7]See Olsson (1979) as the most important contribution.

this model is the bivariate probit model without any explanatory variables. The likelihood function for this model is given by

$$\mathcal{L}_J = \prod_{i=1}^{k_\eta} \prod_{j=1}^{k_\xi} \pi_{ij}^{n_{ij}} \quad , \qquad (2-12)$$

where the joint probabilities π_{ij} are now determined under the normal distribution, that is

$$\pi_{ij} = \Phi_2(a_i, b_j) - \Phi_2(a_{i-1}, b_j) - \Phi_2(a_i, b_{j-1}) + \Phi_2(a_{i-1}, b_{j-1}) \quad (2-13)$$

with Φ_2 being the distribution function of the bivariate normal distribution.[8] Note the difference between (2-11) and (2-12) to which we come back later on. However we already remark at this point that the second right hand side term in (2-11) depends only on the thresholds b_j.

First derivatives of the log-likelihood function $L_J \equiv \log(\mathcal{L}_J)$ with respect to the unknown parameters are as follows:[9]

$$\frac{\partial L}{\partial \rho} = \sum_{i=1}^{k_\eta} \sum_{j=1}^{k_\xi} \frac{n_{ij}}{\pi_{ij}} \{\phi_2(a_i, b_j) - \phi_2(a_{i-1}, b_j) - \phi_2(a_i, b_{j-1}) + \phi_2(a_{i-1}, b_{j-1})\} \qquad (2-14)$$

$$\frac{\partial L}{\partial a_k} = \sum_{j=1}^{k_\eta} \left(\frac{n_{kj}}{\pi_{kj}} - \frac{n_{k+1;j}}{\pi_{k+1;j}} \right) \phi(a_k) \left[\Phi \left\{ \frac{b_j - \rho a_k}{(1-\rho^2)^{\frac{1}{2}}} \right\} - \Phi \left\{ \frac{b_{j-1} - \rho a_k}{(1-\rho^2)^{\frac{1}{2}}} \right\} \right] \qquad (2-15)$$

for $k = 1, \ldots, k_\eta - 1$. Correspondingly,

$$\frac{\partial L}{\partial b_h} = \sum_{i=1}^{k_\xi} \left(\frac{n_{ih}}{\pi_{ih}} - \frac{n_{i;h+1}}{\pi_{i;h+1}} \right) \phi(b_h) \left[\Phi \left\{ \frac{a_i - \rho b_h}{(1-\rho^2)^{\frac{1}{2}}} \right\} - \Phi \left\{ \frac{a_{i-1} - \rho b_h}{(1-\rho^2)^{\frac{1}{2}}} \right\} \right] \qquad (2-16)$$

for $h = 1, \ldots, k_\xi - 1$. Here ϕ_2 denotes the density of the bivariate standard normal and ϕ and Φ denote the density and the distribution function, respectively, of the univariate normal.

---

[8]Our notation does not show the dependence on ρ.

[9]See Olsson (1979) or Ronning and Kukuk (1990) for details.

For convenience, in the following let θ denote the vector of all parameters, that is

$$\theta' = (\rho, a_1, a_2, \cdots, a_{k_\eta - 1}, b_1, b_2, \cdots, b_{k_\xi - 1}) \quad .$$

The above results allow us to determine the maximum likelihood estimate of θ and also to compute a consistent estimate of the asymptotic covariance matrix. However, the following two-step procedure suggested by Olsson (1979) simplifies the computations considerably: In a first step we estimate the thresholds from the marginal frequencies and then in a second step we determine ρ from (2-14). More specifically, we use the relative frequencies $p_{i\bullet} = n_{i\bullet}/n$ and $p_{\bullet j} = n_{\bullet j}/n$ where n is the total number of observations. Estimates for the thresholds are then given by

$$\hat{a}_i = \Phi^{-1}(\sum_{k=1}^{i} p_{k\bullet}) \quad , \qquad (2-17)$$

and

$$\hat{b}_j = \Phi^{-1}(\sum_{h=1}^{j} p_{\bullet j}) \quad . \qquad (2-18)$$

The equation (2-14) set equal to zero is then solved for ρ with thresholds a and b replaced by these estimates. Quite a few simulation studies[10] have shown that this procedure works quite well. However, standard errors have to be modified in order to take account of the two-step procedure.[11]

2.3 The conditional model

We now return to the conditional model of subsection 2.1 which is related to likelihood function (2-10) or (2-11). Under bivariate normality π_{ij} is

[10]See Olsson (1979), Lee (1985), Poon and Lee (1987), Kukuk(1990) and Ronning and Kukuk (1990).

[11]See Lee and Poon (1987).

given by (2-13) and $\pi_{\bullet j}$ satisfies

$$\pi_{\bullet j} = \Phi(b_j) - \Phi(b_{j-1}) \quad .$$

For the log-likelihood function (2-11) we can write

$$L_C = L_J - L_M \tag{2-19}$$

where L_J is the logarithm of the likelihood function (2-12) and L_M is the "marginal" log-likelihood

$$L_M = \sum_j n_{\bullet j} \log(\pi_{\bullet j}) \tag{2-20}$$

which depends only on the thresholds b_j. Therefore (full information) maximum likelihood estimates of θ for this model will be obtained by setting equal to zero (2-13), (2-14) together with

$$\frac{\partial L_C}{\partial b_h} = \frac{\partial L}{\partial b_h} - \frac{\partial L_M}{\partial b_h} = 0 \tag{2-21}$$

where $\frac{\partial L}{\partial b_h}$ is taken from (2-15) and $\frac{\partial L_M}{\partial b_h}$ is given by

$$\begin{aligned} \frac{\partial L_M}{\partial b_h} &= \frac{\partial}{\partial b_h} \sum_j n_{\bullet j} \log([\Phi(b_j) - \Phi(b_{j-1})) \qquad \text{(2-22)} \\ &= \phi(b_h)[\frac{n_{\bullet h}}{\Phi(b_h) - \Phi(b_{h-1})} - \frac{n_{\bullet,h+1}}{\Phi(b_{h+1}) - \Phi(b_h)}] \quad . \end{aligned}$$

Therefore the estimate from the conditional model will differ from the one for the joint model as discussed in the last subsection. However our experience is that the differences are negligible. We were so far unable to show formally that the differences from the maximization of the two likelihood functions are zero. At least they seem to converge to zero for large sample size. This conjecture is based on the observation that (2-23) is in fact zero if we use the two-step procedure as described above: Then insertion of (2-18) in (2-23) provides the stated result. On the other hand (2-18) gives consistent estimates of the thresholds.

2.4 Conditional Means as Explanatory Variables

Ross (1987) suggested - in a more general setting to be discussed below - that for the case in which both the dependent and the explanatory variable are ordinally observed the conditional means

$$m_j \equiv E(\xi \mid x = j)$$

should be used as values of the explanatory variable ξ.[12] Under assumption of bivariate normality for η and ξ we obtain

$$m_j = \frac{\phi(b_{j-1}) - \phi(b_j)}{\Phi(b_j) - \Phi(b_{j-1})} \qquad (2-23)$$

and the corresponding variance is given by[13]

$$Var(\xi \mid x = j) = 1 + \frac{b_{j-1}\,\phi(b_{j-1}) - b_j\,\phi(b_j)}{\Phi(b_j) - \Phi(b_{j-1})} - m_j^2 \qquad (2-24)$$

which will be used later on. The m_j's are easily estimated if the thresholds b_j are obtained from the marginals $n_{\bullet j}$. See (2-18).

Note the difference from the models which were discussed in subsection 2.1: There we considered the conditional density

$$g(\eta \mid x = j)$$

and the conditional probability

$$\pi_{i|j} \equiv P\{y = i \mid x = j\}$$

whereas Hsiao and Mountain consider

$$g^*(\eta \mid m_j)$$

---

[12]This was first suggested by Hsiao and Mountain (1985) for the model with likelihood function $\mathcal{L}_B$ as given in (2-7).

[13]For both formulae see, for example, Maddala (1983 ,appendix).

and Ross uses

$$\pi^{\star}_{i|j} \equiv P\{y = i \mid m_j\} \quad .$$

where the condition "m_j" indicates that this variable is taken as the explanatory variable. Both specifications lead to heteroskedastic errors as can be seen from (2-1) which we now write as

$$\begin{aligned} \eta &= \alpha + \beta\, m_j + \beta\,(\xi - m_j) + \varepsilon \\ &= \alpha + \beta\, m_j + \omega_j \end{aligned} \tag{2-25}$$

with

$$\omega_j = \beta\,(\xi - m_j) + \varepsilon \quad . \tag{2-26}$$

Since the new error term ω_j applies only to those values for which $x = j$ holds it follows that $E(\omega_j) = E(\omega_j \mid x = j) = 0$ and its variance is given by

$$var(\omega_j) = \beta^2\, Var(\xi \mid x = j) + {\sigma_\varepsilon}^2 \tag{2-27}$$

Clearly this is then also the variance of η given $x = j$. Therefore under assumption of normality this variance is given by (2-3) and (2-24) , that is, for given j we have

$$var(\omega_j) = \rho^2\;[1 + \frac{b_{j-1}\,\phi\,(b_{j-1}) - b_j\,\phi\,(b_j)}{\Phi\,(b_j) - \Phi\,(b_{j-1})} - m_j^2] + [1 - \rho^2]$$

since

$$\alpha = 0 \quad \text{and} \quad \beta = \rho \quad .$$

From this result we can construct estimators of θ for continuous y (Hsiao and Mountain's (1985) case) and for ordinal y (the case of Ross(1987)). Note that the (conditional) distribution of ω_j is *not normal* since the first summand in (2-26) is truncated. Nevertheless for the case of an *ordinal* observed dependent variable Ross (1987) assumes normality and estimates the parameters from a *probit model with heteroskedastic errors* involving the unknown β . The implied the (pseudo-)log-likelihood function and first derivatives can be found in his paper.[14] Table 1 presents an simulated example which shows that for this simple model (model I) the method of polychoric correlation and the one suggested by Ross (1987) give almost identical results.

Table 1 — Simulation Results

Model I: $\eta = 1.5\xi + \epsilon$		
TRUE	1.5	
ROSS	1.4748777	
STANDARD PROBIT	1.2194417	
POLYCHORIC *	1.4999708	
Model II: $\eta = 1.5\xi_1 - 1.2\xi_2 + \epsilon$, $\text{corr}(\xi_1, \xi_2) = 0$		
TRUE	1.5	−1.2
ROSS	1.5590851	−1.2056827
STANDARD PROBIT	1.1671827	−0.8999806
POLYCHORIC *	1.5257853	−1.1765843
Model III: $\eta = 1.5\xi_1 - 1.5\xi_2 + \epsilon$, $\text{corr}(\xi_1, \xi_2) = -0.6$		
TRUE	1.5	−1.2
ROSS	1.6150022	−1.3776738
STANDARD PROBIT	1.1773290	−0.9905720
POLYCHORIC *	1.5136025	−1.1865422
REMARKS: 1000 observations, 20 iterations. Results from polychoric correlation (marked by *) have been rescaled in order to be comparable to other results.		

Neglection of the heteroskedastic structure leads to estimated coefficients which are *biased towards zero.* See the estimation results under the "standard probit" assumption in table 1. The theoretical derivation of the

[14]Since the explanatory variable has only k_ξ distinct values maximum likelihood estimates will frequently not exist for high correlation between η and ξ.

implied bias is difficult for the general case. However, assume that x is trichotomous with thresholds b_1 and b_2 such that $var(\omega_j)$ is constant over all three categories.[15] Then from Yatchew and Griliches (1985, p. 135) it follows that the standard probit estimate of β will converge to

$$\frac{\beta}{\sqrt{\beta^2 Var(\xi \mid x = j) + \sigma_\varepsilon{}^2}} \tag{2-28}$$

which is always smaller than the theoretical value $\beta/\sigma_\varepsilon^2$. For the general case with variances varying over the categories (2-28) no longer holds exactly although we can argue that the additional error term in (2-26) which appears in the denominator of the standardized variable will always bias the estimate towards zero.[16]

2.5 More than one explanatory variable

2.5.1 Two ordinal explanatory variables

We now consider shortly the more general case

$$\eta = \beta_1 \xi_1 + \beta_2 \xi_2 + \varepsilon \quad . \tag{2-29}$$

[15]From the symmetry of the normal distribution it is clear that this condition is only satisfied for symmetrical thresholds, that is, $b_2 = -b_1$. Therefore only equality of variances for two (adjoining) intervals has to be considered. After some manipulations we obtain the following condition for b_1:

$$2\phi(b_1)\Phi(b_1) - b_1\phi(b_1) - \phi(b_1) = 0 \quad .$$

This leads to $b_1 = -0.848465$ and the variance $Var(\xi \mid x = j)$ is 0.2178 in all three categories.

[16]Note that this kind of bias does not exist if we use the ordinary least squares estimator in Hsiao and Mountain's (1985) model. See Hsiao and Mountain (1985 p. 260) who point out consistency of this estimator.

that is we have two latent explanatory variables which both are observed as ordinal variables. Maximum likelihood estimation of parameters now involves *trivariate* distribution functions. Simulation studies[17] show that two-step and three-step procedures which avoid computation of three-dimensional integrals provide reasonable estimates. Again we can alternatively consider the *joint* or the *conditional* distribution with presumably very little differences in the two estimation approaches.[18] However Ross' (1987) method now is no longer acceptable since the conditional means computed from the marginals disregard the correlation between the two explanatory variables. Therefore this procedure performs very poorly for high 'multicollinearity' among the explanatory variables. See the results for models II and III, respectively, in table 1.

2.5.2 Continuous explanatory variables and dummy variables

If we add another explanatory variable z which may be either a dummy or continuous to (2-1) we obtain:

$$\eta = \beta\xi + \gamma z + \varepsilon \quad . \qquad (2-30)$$

In the latter case polychoric correlation methods have to be extended to the case of polyserial correlation when starting from a joint distribution of η, ξ and z. See the discussion in Olsson (1979). But z is observable so that its marginal distribution is non-informative with respect to unknown parameters.[19] Therefore we could as well use the conditional density

[17] See in particular Lee and Poon (1987).

[18] Again the estimates are identical if the thresholds are estimated from the marginals. See the discussion in section 2.3.

[19] See the discussion in Küsters (1987 p. 20).

given z. If however we consider the conditional density given z *and* ξ we meet the same problems as in section 2.3. The method as suggested by Ross (1987) again faces a problem in (2-30) since use of conditional means disregards the correlation between ξ and z. The same remarks apply to the case where z is a dummy variable: As Arminger pointed out in his discussion of an earlier version of this paper, we can always consider a density for given z. This corrrects earlier statements[20] that the method of polychoric correlation could not be applied to models including qualitative explanatory variables. Kukuk (1990) discusses an alternative estimation procedure when dummy variables are specified.

3 Empirical example

Kawasaki, McMillan and Zimmermann (1983) considered a model in which price and production jointly depend on lagged demand. In their empirical analysis they used qualitative (trichotomous) survey data from the Ifo business test. We will use the same kind of data in our empirical example. However instead of the loglinear probability model as used by those authors we employ our own approach which starts from a model in latent variables as given by (2-26) which we now write as follows:

$$Q_t = \beta_1 P_t + \beta_2 D_{t-1} + \varepsilon_t \qquad (3-31)$$

where Q_t denotes production, P_t denotes price and D_{t-1} denotes lagged demand. Note that our model considers production as a function of both price and demand and therefore differs from the model of Kawasaki et

[20]See, for example, Ross (1987 p.3).

al. (1983). Our data set contains a panel of 575 firms for 23 quarters[21] during the time interval 1/1983 to 3/1989. Table 2 contains the estimation results from polychoric correlation and from the Ross-procedure. Since the estimated correlation between the two explanatory variables is very low (est corr(P,D_{-1} = 0.113) the two procedures give very similar results. Both explanatory variables indicate a positive influence on production. Since we use standardized (latent) explanatory variables the magnitude of the two coefficients can be directly compared: lagged demand has higher influence than price on output of firms. Note that we use "own" prices which we here interprete as reactions to market conditions and not as decision variables. The table also shows (approximate) t-ratios which indicate that both estimated coefficients are significantly different from zero.

Table 2 — Empirical Example, Estimation Results

Dependent Variable: Production				
A. Polychoric Correlation				
Q	$=$	$0.12637P$	$+$	$0.16828D_1$
		(14.808)		(19.717)
B. Ross Method				
Q	$=$	$0.13389P$	$+$	$0.18014D_1$
		(8.885)		(14.841)
REMARKS:				
P = price, D_1 = lagged demand,				
approximate t-ratios in parentheses				

[21] We use the results from the second month of each quarter, that is for the first quarter we use results from February.

4 Concluding remarks

The paper discusses the role of ordinal variables in microeconeometric models with special emphasis on the case that both endogenous and exogenous variables show this property. Under assumption of joint normality of all latent variables maximum likelihod estimation is feasible when two-step procedures are used. Ross (1987) suggested an alternative method which we compared to the polychoric correlation procedure both by means of simulations and an empirical example. It seems that the use of information from the *marginal* distribution of the exogenous variables is the main objection against this procedure since in economic research we cannot control the correlation between explanatory variables. We have not discussed extensions of the methods to the case of simultaneous equations. It is not clear how the Ross-method should be defined in that case. For the polychoric correlation procedure Arminger and Ronning (1991) present results from a model in which the joint adjustment of firms with respect to output, price and inventory is considered.[22].

References

Amemiya, T. (1985). *Advanced Econometrics.* Basil Blackwell.

Arminger, G., and G. Ronning (1991). "Ein Strukturmodell für Preis–, Produktions– und Lagerhaltungsentscheidungen von Firmen". *Ifo-Studien 25* (1991), 229 - 254.

Hsiao, C., and D. Mountain (1985). "Estimating the Short-Run Income Elasticity of Demand for Electricity by Using Cross-Sectional Categorized Data". *Journal of The Americal Statistical Association* 80, 259-265.

[22]The authors use a slightly modified version ofthe model as considered by König and Seitz (1989) who use classical econometric procedures.

Kawasaki, S., J. McMillan and K.F. Zimmermann (1982). "Disequilibrium Dynamics: An Empirical Study."*American Economic Review 72*, 992-1004.

Kawasaki, S., J. McMillan and K.F. Zimmermann (1983). "Inventories and Price Inflexibility." *Econometrica 51*, 599-610.

König, H., and M. Nerlove (1986). "Price Flexibility, Inventory Behavior, and Production Responses". in: W.P. Heller, R.M. Starr and D.A. Starrett (editors). *Equilibrium Analysis - Essays in Honor of Kenneth J. Arrow.* Volume II. Cambridge University Press, 179-218.

König, H., and H. Seitz (1991). "Production and Price Smoothing by Inventory Adjustment". *Empirical Economics 16*, 233-252.

Küsters, U. (1987). *Hierarchische Mittelwert- und Kovarianzstrukturmodelle mit nichtmetrischen endogenen Variablen.* Physica-Verlag.

Kukuk, M. (1990). "Estimating Linear Models Using Polychoric Correlation". Diskussionbeiträge No. 119/s (January 1990), Universität Konstanz.

Lee, S.Y. (1985). "Maximum Likelihood Estimation of Polychoric Correlations in $r \times s \times t$ Contingency Tables". *Journal of Statistical Computation and Simulation 23*, 53-67.

Lee, S.Y., and W.Y. Poon (1987). "Two-Step Estimation of Multivariate Polychoric Correlation". *Communications of Statistics. Theory Meth. 16*,307-320.

Maddala, G.S. (1983). *Limited-dependent and Qualitative Variables.* Cambridge: Cambridge University Press.

Nerlove, M. (1988). "Analysis of Business Test Survey Data by Means of Latent Variable Models". in :W. Franz, W. Gaab und J. Wolters (editors). *Theoretische und Angewandte Wirtschaftsforschung . Heinz König zum 60. Geburtstag.* Berlin, 241-259.

Olsson, U. (1979). "Maximum Likelihood Estimation of the Polychoric Correlation Coefficient". *Psychometrika* 44, 443-460.

Poon, W.Y., and S.Y. Lee (1987). "Maximum Likelihood Estimation of Multivariate Polyserial and Polychoric Correlation Coefficient". *Psychometrika* 52,409-430.

Pudney, S.(1989). *Modelling Individual Choice. The Econometrics of Corners, Kinks and Holes.* Basil Blackwell.

Ronning, G., and M. Kukuk(1990). "Econometric Models Based on Polychoric Correlation. A New Approach to the Analysis of Business Test Data". *Methods of Operations Research 60*, 653-669. .

Ross, D.R. (1987). "Estimating Linear Models Using Categorical Indicators". Mimeo, Williams College, August 1987.

Yatchew, A., and Z. Griliches (1985). "Specification Error In Probit Models". *The Review of Economics and Statistics 67*, 134-139.

Goodness of Fit in Qualitative Choice Models: Review and Evaluation*

Klaus F. Zimmermann
(SELAPO, University of Munich and CEPR, London)

1. Introduction

Qualitative choice models are now widely used in economics. However, widely accepted measures evaluating the goodness of fit, predictive quality, or overall-success of such models do not exist, although many approaches have been suggested. Some measures are based on the likelihood-ratio test statistic, while others evaluate the residuals of the qualitative choice regressions, or use prediction-realization tables for analysis. Some measures are discussed in

---

* A research draft on methods for the binary probit model covered by this paper was given at the First Munich Applied Econometrics Workshop in July 1989. This paper is an extended and completely revised version of it. I wish to thank Gerhard Arminger, Gebhard Flaig and François Laisney for many useful comments, John De New for excellent research assistance, and the German Science Foundation (DFG) for financial support. The paper was completed when I was visiting CentER, Tilburg University, in April 1990.

Amemiya (1981), Maddala (1983), Aldrich and Nelson (1984), Judge, Griffiths, Hill, Lütkepohl and Lee (1985) and Greene (1990), but these reviews are far from being complete.

The organization of the paper is as follows: Section 2 suggests and analyses a set of statistics based on the prediction-realization table and gives an application. The measures can be used in any qualitative choice model, if one is willing to accept its discrete nature. However, if there is an underlying continuous (latent) variable, one may be interested in Pseudo-R^2's and their relationship with the standard OLS-R^2. This issue is investigated in Section 3 for the probit model, and a survey of extensive Monte Carlo work is given. Section 4 contains a summary.

2. Model Evaluations Based on the Prediction-Realization Table[1)]

2.1 Prediction Success and Discrete Choices

Prediction-realization tables have played an important role in the evaluation of forecasts with microeconomic anticipations data. This kind of analysis has a long tradition ever since these data have been collected. (For the German business survey data collected by the Ifo-Institut, Munich, see Anderson, Bauer, and Fels (1954), Theil (1966), Zimmermann (1986a), Kawasaki and Zimmermann (1986), for instance.) In sociology, these questions have been studied in the context of contingency table analysis. (See - among others -

1) Section 2. draws heavily on Zimmermann (1986b). For a different approach see Veall and Zimmermann (1992b).

Hildebrand, Laing and Rosenthal (1974a) and Goodman and Kruskal (1974a). This paper makes an attempt to link these results to the evaluation of qualitative choice models. Throughout the paper, the availability of a set of conditional probabilities between the endogenous and the exogenous variables will be assumed where all variables are qualitative. These probabilities can be based on any qualitative response model and can be generated by various classes of economic models. Whereas there are several methodological approaches for qualitative choice (see Amemiya (1981), the conditional log-linear probability model is used in section 2.3).

Table 1 serves as a basis for the discussion of various approaches to analyze prediction realization tables. It contains time-aggregated cross-classifications of anticipations concerning price changes and their subsequent realizations. The data have been collected from firms in the German textile industry between January 1975 and September 1978. Both variables have three categories: namely, increase (+), no change (=), and decrease (-).

The material used is business test data collected by the Ifo-Institut, Munich. Define $p_{ij}(i, j = 1, 2, \dots, n)$ as the probability of the event that one forecasts category j and realizes category i out of n possible states of an endogenous variable. Then $p_{i.}$ is the marginal probability of realizing i and $p_{.j}$ is the marginal probability of forecasting j. For the special nature of the data in Table 1 (and "+" = 1, "=" = 2, and "-" = 3), one may use concepts for measuring and analyzing prediction success and errors, which have been suggested by Jochems (1962, cited in Theil (1966), p. 363):

The probability of correct forecasts in this table is $p_{11}+p_{22}+p_{33}=$ 0.67723, which is the sum of the diagonal elements of the prediction realization table. One may define $p_{12}+p_{32}=$ 0.23265 as underestimation of change and $p_{21}+p_{23}=$ 0.07804 as overestimation of change, because one forecasts "no change" and realizes "change" in the former and forecasts "change" and realizes "no change" in the latter case. Finally, $p_{31}+p_{13}=$ 0.01208 can be interpreted as the probability of turning point errors.

Most ot these concepts of summarizing success and errors are valid only for the type of data used in Table 1. These data are ordinal and the categories ("increase", "no change", "decrease") classify the information of the underlying latent continuos variable in an easily interpretable way. But this advantage vanishes, if one has no information other than the possible ordering of these categories (e.g.: 1, 2, 3). (Some variables do not even have an underlying latent continuous variable). For nominal data (e.g. colour: green, red, blue), one may only be able to calculate the rate of correct forecasts.

Correspondingly, data-situations are considered, in which the only available information is that the categories are ordered. Two important questions can be answered from the prediction-realization table: To what extent are predictions accurate and unbiased? One can define (i, j = 1, 2, ..., I) measures of correct estimation (CE), overestimation (OE) and underestimation (UE)

$$(1) \qquad CE = \sum_{\substack{i,j \\ i=j}} p_{ij} \; ; \quad OE = \sum_{\substack{i,j \\ i>j}} p_{ij} \; ; \quad UE = \sum_{\substack{i,j \\ i<j}} p_{ij} \; ,$$

where CE is again the sum of the diagonal elements of the prediction-realization table, but the other concepts differ from the measures discussed above. The question of accuracy can be answered by CE and the question of biasedness by comparing OE and UE. In Table 1, OE = 0.20360 and UE = 0.11917. In contrast to the measures suggested by Jochems, which indicate a tendency for underestimation, OE is now greater than UE. Of course, both concepts have different aims: The former measures the underestimation of change with no indication of the direction, and can be interpreted as a measure of conservative prediction, but the latter is the percentage of forecasting a higher category than realized.

In most empirical applications, the marginal distribution of predictions is rather unequal. A concentration of observations in some categories may simply increase forecast errors, because they are more likely than in other categories. E. g., in Table 1 the error probability p_{21}= 0.06155 and p_{32}= 0.13174, but $p_{.1}$ = 0.20615 and $p_{.2}$= 0.70305. Consequently, $p_{32} > p_{21}$ can result from $p_{.2} > p_{.1}$. One possible solution is to normalize the probabilities by giving the elements in each row equal weight (Goodman and Kruskal (1974a), p. 191) to eliminate these and similar effects. In fact, in the above discussed example $p_{32} / p_{.2}$ = 0.18738 < $p_{21}/p_{.1}$ = 0.29857. Taking this into account, one can define (i, j = 1, 2, ... , I) normalized correct estimation (NCE), normalized overestimation (NOE), and normalized underestimation (NUE)

$$(2) \qquad NCE = \frac{1}{I} \sum_{\substack{i,j \\ i=j}} \frac{p_{ij}}{p_{\cdot j}} \; , \quad NOE = \frac{2}{I(I-1)} \sum_{\substack{i,j \\ i>j}} \frac{p_{ij}}{p_{\cdot j}} \; , \quad NUE = \frac{2}{I(I-1)} \sum_{\substack{i,j \\ i<j}} \frac{p_{ij}}{p_{\cdot j}} \; .$$

In Table 1, NCE = 0.70647 (CE = 0.67723), NOE = 0.17865 (OE = 0.20360), and NUE = 0.11488 (UE = 0.11917). Other methods than these have been suggested by Theil (1966) and Hildebrand, Laing and Rosenthal (1974a). Theil (1966, pp. 289, pp. 364) proposed an index of information gain of forecasts based on information theory, whereas the measure used by Hildebrand, Laing and Rosenthal (1974a, pp. 169) fits in the proportionate-reduction-in-error framework. But these measures are more appropriate for purposes of measuring association than in evaluating prediction success.[2)]

In the further discussion, only concepts based on (1) and (2) are used. These measures can be applied to determine forecast success and bias in an easily interpretable way. They vary between 0 and 1 and the greater they are the larger is the

2) See also the discussion between Goodman and Kruskal (1974a, 1974b) and Hildebrand, Laing and Rosenthal (1974b). The arguments of the former apply also to the approach of Theil (1966). The measures by Theil and Hildebrand, Laing and Rosenthal determine, whether the researcher can improve his knowledge about the forecasting success of the estimated model (or the individuals), when he knows the structure of the table instead of the marginals of predictions and realizations alone. This seems to be an artificial question in this context, because prediction is done and one wants to know how accurate it is.

concentration in the corresponding group of cells. For detecting a bias, one has to compare OE and NE or NOE and NUE. In doing so, one can calculate bias (B) and normalized bias (NB) as

(3) $B = OE/(OE + UE); \; NB = NOE/(NOE + NUE)$

with the interval [0, 1]. In both cases .5 means no bias. If B or NB is reasonably greater (smaller) than .5, one detects overestimation (underestimation) of categories. Alternatively one may use

(4) $D = OE - UE \; ; \quad DN = NOE - NUE$.

For all measures, test statistics are easily available. This is examined using D and DN. To derive a valuable test statistic for H_o: $D = 0$ and H_o: $DN = 0$, one needs the asymptotic variance of both measures. By use of the delta method, this derivation is straightforward. For the sake of simplicity I define $p := (p_m) \equiv (p_{11} p_{12} \ldots p_{II})$ as the vector of probabilities with m = 1, 2, ..., M and $M = I^2$ and $\Sigma = \{(\sigma_{mm'} - \tilde{p}_{m'}) \tilde{p}_m\}$ is the (mxm)-covariance matrix of $\sqrt{N}\,(p - \tilde{p})$, $\sigma_{mm'}$ the Kronecker Delta, N the number of observations and $\tilde{p}$ are the population values. Let g be a well-behaved function of the probabilities (D or DN) and Z the vector of the partial derivations $Z: = \partial g/\partial \tilde{p}$. Then by use of the delta method (Cramer (1946), pp. 366) the term $\sqrt{N}\,(G(p) - g(\tilde{p}))$ is asymptotically normally distributed with zero mean and variance $\sigma_g^2 = Z \, \Sigma \, Z'$. Let

(5) $$D = \sum_{\substack{i,j \\ i>j}} p_{ij} - \sum_{\substack{i,j \\ i<j}} p_{ij} = \sum_{i,j} R_{ij}\, p_{ij} \quad \text{and}$$

(6) $$DN = \frac{2}{I(I-1)} \Big(\sum_{\substack{i,j \\ i>j}} \frac{p_{ij}}{p_{.j}} - \sum_{\substack{i,j \\ i<j}} \frac{p_{ij}}{p_{.j}} \Big) = \frac{2}{I(I-1)} \sum_{i,j} R_{ij} \frac{p_{ij}}{p_{.j}},$$

where R_{ij}= (1, if i>j; 0, if i=j; −1, if i<j). Then $Z_D = \{R_m\}$ and $Z_{ND} = \{\partial DN/\partial p_m\}$, where

$$\frac{\partial DN}{\partial p_{i'j'}} = \frac{2}{I(I-1)} \sum_i R_{ij'} \frac{\delta_{ii'}\, p_{.j'} - p_{ij'}}{p_{.j'}^2}$$

i′, j′ = 1, 2, ..., I and the Kronecker Delta $\delta_{ii'}$.

2.2 Analyzing the Prediction Success of Multivariate Models

Consider first the construction of a multivariate prediction-realization table by use of a 1, 2, ..., I_l; k_1 = 1, 2, ..., K_1; k_2 = 1, 2, ..., K_2; ..., qualitative choice model. Let $p_{i_1 i_2 \dots i_l k_1 k_2 \dots k_K} = p_{ik}$ (i_1 = 1, 2, ..., I_1; i_2 = 1, 2, ..., I_2; ..., $i_l = k_K$ = 1, 2, ..., K_K) be the probabilities of the observed multivariate contingency table with I endogenous and K exogenous variables and $i = i_1 i_2 \dots i_l$ ($k = k_1 k_2 \dots k_K$). Let $\Pi_{i|k}$ be the corresponding conditional probabilities generated by the qualitative choice model. To obtain a two-way table between the categories of the endogenous and the exogenous variables, one possibility is to order the indices i and k lexicographically such that i —> i and $\underset{\sim}{k}$ —> k, more detailed (11 ... 1, 11 ... 2, ... ,$I_1 I_2$ ... I_l) —> (1, 2, 3, ... , $I_1 \times I_2 \times\times\times I_l$) and (11 ... 1, 11 ... 2, ..., $K_1 K_2$ ... K_K) —> (1, 2, 3, ... , $K_1 \times K_2 \times\times\times K_K$). The result is $\underset{\sim}{p} = \{p_{\underline{ik}}\}$ and $\underset{\sim}{\Pi} = \{\Pi_{\underline{i|k}}\}$, which are both $(I_1 \times I_2 \times\times\times I_I) \times (K_1 \times K_2 \times\times\times K_K)$ - matrices. Then one may define $\underset{\sim}{q} = \{q_{\underline{i}\underline{i}'}\} = \underset{\sim}{p}\underset{\sim}{\Pi}'$ the basic matrix of the prediction-realization table, where $\underline{i}$ is the index of the realized and $\underline{i}'$ the index of the forecasted categories.

To explain the underlying concept assume that one randomly selects individuals from the population and forecasts their categories for the endogenous variables by use of $\Pi_{i|k}$ and knowledge of their categories for the exogenous variables. Suppose $\underline{k}$ is the index of the categories of a selected individual. Then there are $\prod_{j=1}^{I} I_j$ possible classifications $\underline{i}$ with conditional probabilities $\Pi_{\underline{i}|\underline{k}}$. Classify each selected individual randomly with these conditional probabilities. The probability that an individual with exogenous categories with $\underline{k}$ and with endogenous categories with index $\underline{i}$ is observed and that for the same individual the endogenous categories with index $\underline{i}'$ are predicted is given by $p_{\underline{i}\underline{k}}\Pi_{i'|k'}$ because given $\underline{k}$, the prediction of i' and the occurrence of $\underline{i}$ are independent events. It follows that the probability of predicting $\underline{i}'$ and having $\underline{i}$ realized is $q_{\underline{i}\underline{i}'} = \sum_{\underline{k}} p_{\underline{i}\underline{k}} \Pi_{\underline{i}'|\underline{k}}$ or in matrix notation $\underset{\sim}{q} = \underset{\sim}{p}\,\underset{\sim}{\Pi}'$.

As a simple illustration take the table of realized probabilities (p_{ik}) (a) between an endogenous and an exogenous variable and a table of the conditional probabilities $\Pi_{i'|k}$ of a qualitative model (b):

		k	
		1	2
i	1	0.15	0.35
	2	0.35	0.15

(a)

		i	
		1	2
k	1	0.2	0.8
	2	0.8	0.2

(b)

Then the probability of forecasting 1 and realizing 1 is q_{11} = $0.15 \cdot 0.2 + 0.35 \cdot 0.8 = 0.31$ and the probability of forecasting 2 but realizing 1 is $q_{12} = 0.8 \cdot 0.15 + 0.35 \cdot 0.2 = 0.19$. Similarly, $q_{21} = 0.19$ and $q_{22} = 0.31$.

The proposed method of forecasting has a long tradition in the literature of association measurement. (See the seminal paper by Goodmann and Kruskal (1954), p. 750.) The measure τ, which is based on this logic, is viewed as a qualitative analogue to the coefficient of determination for continous data (Bishop, Fienberg and Holland (1975), pp. 387-388). The 'classical' alternative (see again Goodman and Kruskal (1954), p. 741) is to choose the element of a column of Π $(k=k')$ with the largest proportion and to classify all individuals $(k=k')$ to the corresponding category $i=i'$. In the above example, the forecasting rule would be $k=1 \rightarrow i=2$, and $k=2 \rightarrow i=1$. Thus, the prediction-realization table $(Q_{ll'})$ is $Q_{11} = Q_{22} = 0.35$ and $Q_{12} = Q_{21} = 0.15$. The percentage of correct forecasts is higher (0.70) than for the method described above (0.62), and this result holds in general.

One aim of this study is to compare the predictive quality of different models given a certain rule of predicting, and for this purpose, both methods seem to be equally well suited. (However, one may wish to normalize the measures based on a model with the measures calculated with the observed conditional probabilities.) Nevertheless, some researchers may prefer the rule with higher accuracy. While such forecasting leads to the lowest average probability of error, the resulting distribution of forecasted categories will usually be very different from the original distribution in the population (Goodman and Kruskal (1954), p. 759). Furthermore, this method is usually creating a systematic bias with special nature depending on the data set under study.

Let p_{ik} $(i, k = 1, 2)$ be the probabilities and $\Pi_{j|k} = p_{i|k}$ (the model consists of the observed conditional probabilities), for simplicity. If one takes i′ based on $p_{i'|k'} = \max p_{i|k'}$ for all individuals in $k=k'$, the bias $(D = Q_{21} - Q_{12})$ is $-p_{11} - p_{12}$ if $p_{11} < p_{21}$ and $p_{12} < p_{22}$, $p_{21} + p_{22}$ if $p_{11} > p_{21}$ and $p_{22} < p_{12}$), $p_{21} - p_{12}$ if $p_{11} > p_{21}$ and $p_{12} < p_{22}$, and $p_{22} - p_{11}$ if $p_{11} < p_{21}$ and $p_{12} > p_{22}$. For larger tables, the analysis would be even more complex. Instead, it is easy to prove that $\underset{\sim}{q} = \underset{\sim}{p}\,\underset{\sim}{\Pi}'$ is symmetric and $D = 0$, as long as $\underset{\sim}{\Pi}$ is calculated on the basis of the observed contingency table. Evaluating $\underset{\sim}{q}$ instead of the alternative table, one avoids the creation of an artificial bias which is data-specific and due to the chosen prediction-rule, not to the estimated model.

To evaluate the prediction success, one can analyze $\underset{\sim}{q}$ for the whole model or for each variable alone. For the following analysis, it seems to be easier to look at the table $\{q_{ii'}\}$ instead at $\{q_{\underline{i}\,\underline{i}'}\}$. Considering first the evaluation of the complete model, perfect correct estimation (PCE), perfect overestimation (POE), and perfect underestimation (PUE) is defined as

$$(7) \qquad PCE = \sum_{\substack{i,\,i' \\ i=i'}} q_{ii'}\,; \quad POE = \sum_{\substack{i,\,i' \\ i>i'}} q_{ii'}\,; \quad PUE = \sum_{\substack{i,\,i' \\ i<i'}} q_{ii'}\,,$$

where $i > i'$, for instance, means that $i_1 > i_1'$, $i_2 > i_2'$..., $i_I > i_I'$.

The formulas (7) include only cases, where <u>all</u> corresponding elements of $\underline{i}$ and $\underline{i}'$ fulfill the given restriction, but there are many cases, where this is only partly so. Under the assumption that all variables have equal weights, one may modify the analysis of the forecast pattern by weighting these events and calculating weighted correct estimation (WCE), weighted overestimation (WOE), and weighted underestimation (WUE).

(8) $$WCE = \frac{1}{I} \sum_{i,i'} I^{a}_{ii'} \, q_{ii'} \; , \quad WOE = \frac{1}{I} \sum_{i,i'} I^{b}_{ii'} \, q_{ii'} \; ,$$

$$WUE = \frac{1}{I} \sum_{i,i'} I^{c}_{ii'} \, q_{ii'}$$

$I^{a}_{ii'}$ is the number of cases, where $i_j = i_j'$ ($i = i_1 i_2 \dots i_j \dots I_I$; $i' = i_1' i_2' \dots i_j' \dots i_I'$), $I^{b}_{ii'}$ the number of cases, where $i_j > i_j'$, and $I^{c}_{ii'}$ the number of cases, where $i_j < i_j'$.

As discussed, it may be desired to normalize the probabilities of the prediction-realization table by the marginals of the predictions $q_{\cdot i'}$. This leads to normalized PCE (NPCE) and normalized WCE (NWCE)

(9) $$NPCE = \frac{1}{J} \sum_{\substack{i,i' \\ i=i'}} \frac{q_{ii'}}{\cdot i'} \; , \quad NWCE = \frac{1}{J \cdot I} \sum_{i,i'} I^{a} \frac{q_{ii'}}{q_{\cdot i'}} \; ,$$

$$J = \prod_{j=1}^{1} I_j$$

and similarly defined statistics NPOE, NPUE, NWOE and NWUE. As methods for detecting bias, one can calculate weighted bias (WB) = WOE / (WOE + WUE) and normalized weighted bias (NWB) = NWOE / (NWOE + NWUE) with similar interpretations as in the previous section and a difference-statistics DW = WOE - WUE and DWN = NWOE - NWUE.

Finally, one may want to evaluate the predictive behavior of the model for each variable separately. In doing so, one has first to construct the bivariate prediction-realization table

$$(10) \qquad q^{(j')}_{i_{j'} i'_{j'}} = \sum_{\substack{i \,,\, i' \\ i_j \neq i_{j'} \\ i'_j \neq i'_{j'}}} q_{ii'}$$

between predictions and realizations of the variable j, recalling that $i = i_1 i_2 \ldots i_j \ldots i_l$ and $i' = i'_1 i'_2 \ldots i'_j \ldots i'_l$. Then one can apply measures derived in Section 2.1.

2.3 Predicting Changes of Firm's Price and Output: An Empirical Example

Kawasaki, McMillan and Zimmermann (1983) discussed an economic model of firm's price and output decisions with the testable hypothesis that a firm will change the price it charges in response to a demand change only if it perceives the demand change to be permanent, but it will change its output in response to any change, temporary or permanent, in the previous period's demand. They studied this question for several German industries separately, whereas in this case, a model is considered for all industries together. The data-set is based on the business-survey of the Ifo-Institut, Munich, consisting here of two years monthly observations in the German manufacturing industries from 1977 to 1978. The variables used are the change in price from the previous month (P_t), the change in production level from the previous month (Q_t), the change in incoming orders from the previous month (D_t; a proxy of short-run change in demand), and the expected change in the business conditions for the product of the firm over the next six-month period (G^*; a proxy for the change in long-run demand). All variables are qualitative and have three categories; increase (+), no change (=), and decrease (-). Following the theory, two subsamples have been constructed for the model $Pr(P_t, Q_t | D_{t-1})$: Firstly, in 63,763 cases G^* = "=" (indicating that demand changes are transitory: submodel I) and secondly in 14,648 cases $G^* = D$ and D was equal to "increase" (indicating permanent demand changes: submodel II), so one can expect different behavior of the firms in both subsamples. Both data-sets have been explored by the log-linear probability model

$$(11) \quad \log p_{ij|k} = \mu_k + u_i^P + u_j^Q + u_{ij}^{PK} + u_{i|k}^{PD} + u_{j|k}^{QD}$$

with the overall mean μ, and the specific parameter configurations, the main effects of the endogenous variables u^P and u^Q, and the interaction effects u^{PK}, u^{PD} and u^{QD} measuring the association between the categories of both exogenous and endogenous variables. u^{PK} covers the correlation between the endogenous variables. Note that the ANOVA-type restrictions

$$(12)\quad \sum_{i=1}^{I} u_i = \sum_{j=1}^{J} u_j = \sum_{i=1}^{I} u_{ij} = \sum_{j=1}^{J} u_{ij} = \sum_{i=1}^{I} u_{ik} = \sum_{k=1}^{K} u_{ik} = \sum_{j=1}^{J} u_{jk} = \sum_{k=1}^{K} u_{jk}$$

are valid. For further details see Kawasaki, McMillan and Zimmermann (1983).

Consider first Table 2, which contains the typical prediction-realization table for both submodels. Elements marked with — are perfect correct forecasts, ∩ perfect overestimation and ∪ perfect underestimation, but the other cases are more complex. Note that in the case of q_{24} one underestimates variable 1 and overestimates variable two. In q_{71} variable 2 is correctly forecasted, but there is an overestimation of variable 1; in q_{78} variable 1 is correctly forecasted, but there is an underestimation of variable 2, etc.

Table 3 gives measures to evaluate the micro prediction quality of the complete submodels, whereas Table 4 contains results for each single variable. It turns out that the question of normalization of the elements of the prediction-realization table has some empirical importance. Consider Table 3: The predictive quality of both submodels seems to be quite good. In submodel I (II) in 47% (32%) of the cases, all variables are correctly forecasted and the index of weighted correct estimation is 0.67 (0.61). This also indicates a superiority of submodel I, but this is not supported by the normalized measures NPCE and NWCE, which give more credit to the second submodel. Analyzing the cases where all variables were predicted wrong, one finds no bias in both models comparing POE and PUE, but one detects a tendency to underestimate in submodel I and to overestimate in submodel II taking the normalized results NPOE and NPUE into account. Evaluating all sorts of error cases, submodel II overestimates the variables (WB=0.54; NWB=0.67), whereas in submodel I the result depends on whether or not the events are normalized (WB=0.46; NWB=0.59). Similar conclusions can be drawn from Table 4. Again, normalization plays a crucial role in the evaluation process. As a whole, without normalization submodel I predicts better than submodel II for both variables and the success is higher for prices, but after normalization these results are reversed. Without normalization there is no bias for both variables in both submodels, but NB indicates underestimation for P in submodel I and overestimation for P and Q in submodel II.

3. Measures Based on Individual Data[3)]

3. 1 Pseudo-R^2's: Theory

This section concentrates on a selection of widely used measures for individual data which vary in the [0, 1] interval, comparable to the OLS-R^2. Although, these Pseudo-R^2's also attempt to measure the accuracy with which a model approximates the observed data,

3) This section draws from Veall and Zimmermann (1990a, 1992a).

these measures are different in many ways. None of them is widely accepted nor seems to be straightforward. Though many of these measures have been used in recent years, Veall and Zimmermann (1990a, 1992a, 1992b) have recently compared them within a unique framework by means of Monte Carlo work.

The emphasis here is on measures that can be applied in a binary choice framework, e. g. the probit or logit model, though most of them can also be used if the data is ordinal or multinominal. Measures specifically developed for grouped data are surveyed by Amemiya (1981) and Maddala (1983). There is no review of methods used for the Poisson model or duration and tobit models (see however Veall and Zimmermann, 1990b, for the Tobit model), but the last two approaches for limited dependend variables are beyond the scope of this review. The measures studied in this section are based on residuals of qualitative choice models as of likelihood-values of the ML approach.

In the context of an OLS-framework, the coefficient of determination R^2 has at least three useful interpretations (Dhrymes, 1986, p. 1579): (i) there is a direct analogue to the F-statistic for a test that all coefficients of the explanatory variables are zero[4)], (ii) it measures the reduction of the variability of the dependent variable caused by the exogenous variables, and (iii) it is the squared correlation coefficient between predicted and actual values of the endogenous variable. These are attractive features, though R^2 has been critized for the purpose of selecting regressors (see Amemiya, 1980). Here, the selection of regressors issue is not

4) See also Amemiya (1981), footnote 12.

considered. A qualitative choice model was specified based on some theory and estimated, and now the overall fit of the model is evaluated.

Assume an underlying (continous) response variable Y_i^* and

$$(13) \quad Y_i^* = \alpha + \beta X_i + \eta_i , \quad i = 1, 2, \ldots, N,$$

where X is an exogenous variable and α and β are parameters (of course, β and X will be in general vectors); i is the index of the individual, η a random error term and N the sample size. Y_i^* is unobserved in practice. Instead of Y_i^*, a dummy variable Y_i defined as

$$(14) \quad Y_i = 1 \text{ if } Y^* > 0, \text{ and } Y_i = 0 \text{ otherwise}$$

is observed. Equations (1) and (2) imply

$$(15) \quad \Pr(Y_i = 1) = \Pr(\eta_i > -\alpha - \beta X_i) = F(\alpha + \beta X_i),$$

where F is the cumulative distribution function CDF for η and the CDF has been assumed to be symmetric. The log-likelihood function is

$$(16) \quad l = \sum_{i=1}^{N} Y_i \log F(\cdot) + \sum_{i=1}^{N} (1 - Y_i) \log [1 - F(\cdot)].$$

In the probit model, it is assumed that the η's are identically distributed and standard normal with zero expectation and variance

1, whereas in the standard logit, the variance is $\pi^2/3$.

Some goodness-of-fit measures are based on the value of the likelihood function L and the likelihood-ratio test statistic

$$(17) \quad LRT = 2(l_M - l_0),$$

where l_M is the log-likelihood value of the model and l_0 is the log-likelihood value of a model with a constant only. A measure suggested by Aldrich and Nelson (1984) is

$$(18) \quad R^2_{AN} = LRT/(LRT + N),$$

where the likelihood-ratio test statistic (LRT) is normalized by the number of observations (N). Because the residuals in the probit-model are by assumption standard normal, the unexplained variance is N. Taking LRT as something similar to the explained variance, equation (18) does have intuitive appeal. Equation (18) is also easy to calculate.

Unfortunately, the Aldrich and Nelson measure clearly has an upper bound, which depends an category size of the endogenous variable and the distribution of these categories. (This was first noted by Veall and Zimmermann, 1990a and 1992a.) For $l_M \rightarrow l_{max} = 0$, the Pseudo-$R^2$ is $-l_0/(N-l_0)$. However, $l_0 = \sum_{k=1}^{K} N_k \log (N_k/N)$, where k refers to category number, K is the number of categories and N_k is the number of observations in category k. Hence, the limit is

(19) R^2_{AN} (limit) $= - RS/(1 - RS)$

and $RS = 2 \sum_{k=1}^{K} \frac{N_k}{N} \log \frac{N_k}{N}$. We obtain a maximum of R^2_{AN}(limit), if N_k/N is equal for all k. Under this assumption, RS = −2 log K. Then, the Pseudo-R^2 for an equal distribution across categories is 0.581 for k=2, 0.687 for k=3, and 0.735 for k=4. However, if the observed distribution of the categories is unequal, R^2_{AN}(limit) can be much smaller. For instance, in the two-category case with distribution [0.1, 0.9] or [0.9, 0.1] for the N_k/N's, a maximum possible Pseudo-R^2 of 0.394 is obtained. For k=3, the distribution [0.05, 0.9, 0.05] or any permutation yields a maximum possible Pseudo-R^2 of 0.441. Further note that

(20) R^2_{AN} (limit, equally distributed k's) $= \dfrac{2\log K}{1 + 2\log K}$

approaches 1, if K is sufficiently large.

This suggests a normalization, for which we recommend

(21) $$R^2_{VZ} = \frac{LRT}{LRT + N} \Big/ \frac{-2l_0}{N - 2l_0}$$

$$= \frac{-(l_M - l_0)/l_0}{[2(l_M - l_0) + N]/(N - 2l_0)}$$

$$= \frac{LRT(1 - RS)}{-(LRT + N)RS}$$

Another Pseudo-R^2 is given in McFadden (1973, p. 121) as

(22) $R^2_{MF} = 1 - l_M / l_O$.

This measure is recommended in many econometric textbooks like Fomby, Hill and Johnson (1984, p. 352), Judge, Griffiths, Hill, Lütkepohl and Lee (1985, p. 767), Dhrymes (1986, p. 1585), and Greene (1990, p. 602). Also Hauser (1977) shows that R^2_{MF} has a clear meaning in an information-theoretic context in that it measures the percentage of uncertainty in the data which can be explained by the regressors. This measure is popular because it approaches 0 if l_M is close to l_O, and 1 if $l_M = 0$, the maximum possible log-likelihood value. It also is clearly related to the chi-square statistic for testing the hypothesis that the coefficients of the exogenous variables (without the constant) are zero. Under H_O one obtains $-2\ l_O R^2_{MF} = LRT \sim X^2_{K-1}$, where K is the number of categories estimated. Dhrymes (1986, p. 1585) finds it desirable, in empirical practice, that a statistic like (22) is given, and a constant be routinely included in the specification of the linear model. Greene (1990, p. 682) states that R^2_{MF} hardly ever will be equal to one: Even if F_i is a good CDF, the model will not fit perfectly unless $\alpha + \beta X_i$ explodes to plus or minus infinity. This, however, should not be taken as an indication of a good fit, but a defect in the model specification.

A similar concept as R^2_{MF} is (see Maddala, 1983, p. 39)

$$(23) \quad R^2_M = 1 - (L_O/L_M)^{2/N},$$

where the upper case L's denote the likelihood as opposed to the log likelihood. As the maximum value for L is 1, the R^2_M from equation (23) must lie in the range

$$(24) \quad 0 \le R^2_M \le 1 - (L_O)^{2/N}.$$

Cragg and Uhler (1970) have, therefore, suggested a normalization to the [0,1]-range by

$$(25) \quad R^2_{CU} = \frac{1 - (L_O/L_M)^{2/N}}{1 - (L_O/L_{max})^{2/N}}$$

and $L_{max} = 1$.

Another popular suggestion to measure goodness-of-fit has been the squared correlation coefficient between Y and F (Neter and Maynes, 1970; Lave, 1970; Efron, 1978; Morrison, 1972; Goldberger, 1973)

$$(26) \quad R^2_C = \frac{[\text{cov }(Y,F)]^2}{\text{var }(Y) \cdot \text{var }(F)}.$$

Morrison (1972) claimed that this measure has an upper bound below 1, whereas Goldberger showed that the upper bound is one. $E(Y) = E(F)$ and $E(YF) = E(F^2)$. Hence $\text{cov }(Y,F) = E(YF) - E(Y) \cdot E(F) = E(F^2) - E^2(F) = \text{var }(F)$. Thus,

$$(27) \quad R^2_{RV} = \frac{\text{var }(F)}{\text{var }(Y)} .$$

This is identical to a version proposed by Lave (1970)

$$(28) \quad R^2_L = 1 - \frac{\sum_{i=1}^{N} (Y_i - F_i)^2}{\sum_{i=1}^{N} (Y_i - \overline{Y})^2} ,$$

where $\overline{Y} = \frac{1}{N} \sum_{i=1}^{N} Y_i$. If R^2_C, R^2_{RV} and R^2_L are implemented by replacing F_i with $\hat{F}_i$, all three are not identical in qualitative response models. (See also Amemiya, 1981, p. 1504.) However, this difference disappears if the sample size becomes large and $\hat{F}_i \rightarrow F_i$. Monte Carlo experiments with the binary probit model show that the differences are negligible at least if $N \geq 50$. Because smaller samples than 50 will hardly be of interest, it is unimportant which measure is taken.

Finally, McKelvey and Zavoina (1975, p. 111) have suggested an alternative measure which is not commonly used, even though it has attractive properties. They propose a Pseudo-R^2, that gives an estimate of the R^2 of the underlying regression model: namely the portion of the original variance of the dependent variable explained by the probit analysis. Because the error term in equation (1) is standard normal, an estimate of the sum of squared disturbances is N. The explained sum of squares (EV) can ba computed as usual by

$$(29) \quad EV = \sum_{i=1}^{N} (\hat{Y}_i^* - \hat{\bar{Y}}^*)^2 ,$$

where $\hat{Y}_i^*$ is the conditional expectation of Y_i from equation (1) based on the probit estimates of equation (3) and

$$(30) \quad \hat{\bar{Y}}^* = \frac{1}{N} \sum_{i=1}^{N} Y_i^* = \frac{1}{N} \sum_{i=1}^{N} \hat{Y}_i^* .$$

From this follows a Pseudo-R^2

$$(31) \quad R^2_{MZ} = \frac{\sum_{i=1}^{N} (\hat{Y}_i^* - \hat{\bar{Y}}^*)^2}{\sum_{i=1}^{N} (\hat{Y}_i^* - \hat{\bar{Y}}^*)^2 + N} .$$

The estimated sum of squares disturbances N is not a sum of squared residuals as would be usual in an R^2 measure, but the difference will not affect (28) asymptotically.

3.2. Pseudo - R^2's : Monte Carlo Evidence

To evaluate the various proposed Pseudo-R^2's, Veall and Zimmermann (1990a, 1992a) carried out a number of Monte Carlo experiments. They compared the Pseudo-R^2's and attempted to select the one that is "best" able to mimic the R^2 of the continuous case. Continuous data on the endogenous variable were simulated based on a sequence of true models generating R^2's in the [0,1]-range.They then explored which Pseudo-R^2, calculated from the probit of the corresponding classified binary or ordinal data, is (i) closest to OLS-R^2 and/or is (ii) the best predictor of OLS-R^2.

The Monte Carlo study consisted of 100 experiments, each with sample size 1000. The design followed equation (13). The X's were initially generated as standard normal and were thereafter kept fixed. Also, the U's were drawn from a standard normal distribution for each individual in each sample. Therefore, 100 times 1000 random errors were generated. Given a value for parameter δ, a continuous variable Y_i^* was generated for each individual in the sample, setting ξ=0 for simplicity. These continuous data were transformed to binary or ordinal data according to equation (14) or according to a similar classification scheme for the ordinal 3 and 4 category case.Then 100 probit models were estimated (using Y) as well as the corresponding 100 OLS regressions (using Y^*). Then 100 estimates of R^2's for the continuous case as well as 100 estimates for each suggested Pseudo-R^2 were available. Furthermore, the true OLS-R^2 was varied in the [0,1] intervall to investigate the performance of the Pseudo-R^2's for different sizes of the true goodness of fit. All experiments were carried out using GAUSS.

The results of Veall and Zimmermann (1990a, 1992a) are surprisingly clear: the measure suggested by McKelvey and Zavoina performs the best under the criterion that a Pseudo should best mimic the OLS-R^2. (See also Veall and Zimmermann, 1990b, for a McKelvey and Zavoina analogue in the Tobit case.) However, in the more likely case of low Pseudo-R^2's, the normalization of the

Aldrich and Nelson measure which was suggested by Veall and Zimmermann (1990a, 1992a) is almost as good as the McKelvey and Zavoina, and is in general easier to calculate. All other Pseudo-R^2's severely underestimate the OLS-R^2. Veal and Zimmermann (1990a, 1992a) also show that if the underlying R^2 is predicted using cubic regressions given the Pseudo-R^2, all measures perform much better. They also offer conversion tables between Pseudo-R^2's and the underlying OLS-R^2 which may give an applied researcher some idea as to what a given Pseudo-R^2 value may imply about the underlying OLS-R^2.

Here, the issue is studied from a different angle. Veall and Zimmermann (1990a, 1992a) only considered large cases with sample sizes 200 or 1000. Here, also small samples of 50 and 100 are investigated and the means and variances of the various measures given a certain true R^2 (0.2, 0.5, and 0.8) and experiment size of 100 are more carefully analyzed. However, only the bivariate probit case is investigated.

Tables 5 - 7 contain means and standard deviations for the binary probit Pseudo`s and the OLS-R^2 for given true R^2 (0.2, 0.5, 0.8) and different sample sizes (50, 100, 200, 1000) for experiment size 100. Means and standard deviations for the measures Lave, correlation coefficient and relative variance are very close for all sample sizes and values of the true R^2. These measures and the measures proposed by Aldrich and Nelson, McFadden and Cragg and Uhler severely underestimate the true R^2. For a low true R^2

(0.2 or 0.5), the OLS-R^2, the McKelvey and Zavoina, and the Aldrich and Nelson normalized are broadly similar in the means. (For a true R^2 of 0.8 the Aldrich and Nelson normalized measure is somewhat but not largely underestimating.) In many cases, the Aldrich and Nelson normalized is even closer to the true R^2 than the McKelvey and Zavoina and the OLS-R^2. However, the standard deviations of the OLS-R^2 are always smallest although the differences are converging with larger sample size. The standard deviations of the Aldrich an Nelson normalized are always smaller than the standard deviations of the McKelvey and Zavoina. Given the simplicity of the calculation of the Aldrich and Nelson normalized, this is a very interesting finding.

Tables 8 - 10 investigate the predictive quality of the various Pseudo-R^2's for the true R^2 and the OLS-R^2 given different true R^2's of 0.2, 0.5 and 0.8. Results for the average error term squared, the average error term, as the standard deviation of the error term are given whereas errors are calculated as difference between true R^2 or OLS-R^2, respectively. Using the quadratic loss-function, the OLS-R^2 as predictor of the true R^2 mostly places first. The McKelvey and Zavoina is only superior to the Aldrich and Nelson normalized for a true R^2 of 0.8 and marginally better for sample size 1000 and a true R^2 of 0.2 and 0.5.

Table 11 finally contains an investigation of the predictive quality of the Pseudo-R^2's for their OLS analogues in those cases, where the OLS analogue is different from the OLS-R^2. By comparing Table 11 to Table 8 - 10 it can then be studied whether these Pseudo's are closer associated to their OLS analogue than to OLS-R^2, or than to McKelvey and Zavoina to OLS-R^2. Only the McFadden measure gets better grades in this comparison: for true R^2's of 0.2 and 0.5 and sample sizes smaller than 1000, the McFadden Pseudo predicts the OLS analogue not even better than the OLS-R^2, but also better than the McKelvey and Zavoina predicts the OLS-R^2.

4. Summary

The paper contains a survey of various approaches to analyze goodness of various fit in qualitative choice models, namely measures based on the likelihood-function, residuals of qualitative choice regressions, or frequency measures on the basis of prediction-realization tables. Measures based on prediction-realization tables should be normalized to avoid a frequency bias in the predictions. For individual data, a measure proposed by McKelvey and Zavoina (1975)· and a normalization of measure suggested by Aldrich and Nelson (1984) were shown to be superior.

Table 1

Price Anticipations and Realizations. German Textile Industry (1975-1978). Cross-Classifications of Probabilities.

	Price Anticipation			
Price Realization	increase (+) (1)	no change (=) (2)	decrease (-) (3)	Marginals
increase (+) (1)	0.13429	0.10091	0.00177	0.23697
no change (=) (2)	0.06155	0.47040	0.01649	0.54844
decrease (-) (3)	0.01031	0.13174	0.07254	0.21459
Marginals	0.20615	0.70305	0.09080	1

Total number of observations: 10187. Aggregated monthly data.

Table 2

The Multivariate Prediction-Realization Table

		Prediction									
Realization		$\underline{i}'$	1	2	3	4	5	6	7	8	9
$\underline{i}$	$i_1 i_2$	$i_1' i_2'$	11	12	13	21	22	23	31	32	33
1	11		$\underline{q_{11}}$	q_{12}	q_{13}	q_{14}	$\underset{\smile}{q_{15}}$	$\underset{\smile}{q_{16}}$	q_{17}	$\underset{\smile}{q_{18}}$	$\underset{\smile}{q_{19}}$
2	12		q_{21}	$\underline{q_{22}}$	q_{23}	q_{24}	q_{25}	$\underset{\smile}{q_{26}}$	q_{27}	q_{28}	$\underset{\smile}{q_{29}}$
3	13		q_{31}	q_{32}	$\underline{q_{33}}$	q_{34}	q_{35}	q_{36}	q_{37}	q_{38}	q_{39}
4	21		q_{41}	q_{42}	q_{43}	$\underline{q_{44}}$	q_{45}	q_{46}	q_{47}	$\underset{\smile}{q_{48}}$	$\underset{\smile}{q_{49}}$
5	22		$\overset{\frown}{q_{51}}$	q_{52}	q_{53}	q_{54}	$\underline{q_{55}}$	q_{56}	q_{57}	q_{58}	$\underset{\smile}{q_{59}}$
6	23		$\overset{\frown}{q_{61}}$	$\overset{\frown}{q_{62}}$	q_{63}	q_{64}	q_{65}	$\underline{q_{66}}$	q_{67}	q_{68}	q_{69}
7	31		q_{71}	q_{72}	q_{73}	q_{74}	q_{75}	q_{76}	$\underline{q_{77}}$	q_{78}	q_{79}
8	32		$\overset{\frown}{q_{81}}$	q_{82}	q_{83}	$\overset{\frown}{q_{84}}$	q_{85}	q_{86}	q_{87}	$\underline{q_{88}}$	q_{89}
9	33		$\overset{\frown}{q_{91}}$	$\overset{\frown}{q_{92}}$	q_{93}	$\overset{\frown}{q_{94}}$	$\overset{\frown}{q_{95}}$	q_{96}	q_{97}	q_{98}	$\underline{q_{99}}$

— perfect correct estimation

∩ perfect overestimation

∪ perfect underestimation

Table 3

Evaluation of the Complete Models

	Submodel I	Submodel II
Perfect correct estimation (PCE)	0.46803	0.31770
Normalized perfect correct estimation (NPCE)	0.11727	0.13328
Perfect overestimation (POE)	0.02847	0.05166
Normalized perfect overestimation (NPOE)	0.10459	0.11550
Perfect underestimation (PUE)	0.02938	0.05172
Normalized perfect underestimation (NPUE)	0.11107	0.07447
Weighted correct estimation (WCE)	0.66983	0.60712
Normalized weighted correct estimation (NWCE	0.45079	0.47163
Weighted overestimation (WOE)	0.15344	0.21330
Normalized weighted overestimation (NWOE)	0.32376	0.35425
Weighted Bias (WB)	0.46473	0.54291
Normalized weighted Bias (NWB)	0.58950	0.67046
Weighted bias (DW)	-0.02329	0.03372
Normalized weighted bias (DWN)	0.09831	0.18013

Table 4

Evaluation for the Variables Price (P) and Quantity (Q)

	Submodel I	
	P	Q
Correct estimation (CE)	0.76961	0.60488
Normalized correct estimation (NCE)	0.33465	0.35114
Overestimation (OE)	0.11472	0.19424
Normalized overestimation (NOE)	0.31511	0.32986
Bias (B)	0.49794	0.49160
Normalized Bias (NB)	0.47360	0.50837
Test of no Bias (D)	-0.00095	-0.00664
Test of no normalized Bias (DN)	-0.03513	0.01086

Table 4 continued

	Submodel II	
	P	Q
Correct estimation (CE)	0.68675	0.46000
Normalized correct estimation (NCE)	0.34138	0.39513
Overestimation (OE)	0.15661	0.27001
Normalized overestimation (NOE)	0.33779	0.36309
Bias (B)	0.49995	0.50002
Normalized Bias (NB)	0.51288	0.60028
Test of no Bias (D)	-0.00003	0.00002
Test of no normalized Bias (DN)	0.01696	0.12131

Table 5

Binary Probit Pseudo's, OLS-R^2 and True R^2: Means and Standard Deviations (in Parentheses)

	True R^2 = 0.2	
	50	100
OLS-R^2	0.22408 (0.10281)	0.21681 (0.07482)
McKelvey/Zavoina	0.22376 (0.13350)	0.21181 (0.09916)
Aldrich/Nelson	0.12847 (0.07300)	0.12464 (0.05554)
Aldrich/Nelson Normalized	0.22289 (0.12670)	0.21511 (0.09584)
McFadden	0.11446 (0.07443)	0.10669 (0.05342)
Cragg/Uhler	0.18829 (0.11308)	0.17972 (0.08428)
Lave	0.14120 (0.08858)	0.13527 (0.06466)
Correlation	0.14144 (0.08873)	0.13538 (0.06471)
Relative Variance	0.14302 (0.08790)	0.13687 (0.06532)

Table 5 continued

	True R^2 = 0.2	
	200	1000
OLS-R^2	0.21181 (0.04899)	0.19723 (0.02104)
McKelvey/Zavoina	0.20601 (0.06364)	0.19843 (0.02586)
Aldrich/Nelson	0.12208 (0.03536)	0.11923 (0.01474)
Aldrich/Nelson Normalized	0.21039 (0.06091)	0.20531 (0.02537)
McFadden	0.10192 (0.03338)	0.09796 (0.01375)
Cragg/Uhler	0.17424 (0.05332)	0.16904 (0.02215)
Lave	0.13079 (0.03996)	0.12775 (0.01712)
Correlation	0.13084 (0.03997)	0.12776 (0.01717)
Relative Variance	0.13176 (0.04116)	0.12754 (0.01687)

Table 6

Binary Probit Pseudo's, OLS-R^2 and True R^2: Means and Standard Deviations (in Parentheses)

	True R^2 = 0.5	
	50	100
OLS-R^2	0.52224 (0.08713)	0.51867 (0.06497)
McKelvey/Zavoina	0.54159 (0.13350)	0.52848 (0.09203)
Aldrich/Nelson	0.29410 (0.06825)	0.29225 (0.04583)
Aldrich/Nelson Normalized	0.51131 (0.11801)	0.50422 (0.07898)
McFadden	0.31770 (0.10571)	0.30380 (0.06740)
Cragg/Uhler	0.46265 (0.12151)	0.45371 (0.08086)
Lave	0.36709 (0.11247)	0.35815 (0.07177)
Correlation	0.36764 (0.11257)	0.35856 (0.07188)
Relative Variance	0.36626 (0.11086)	0.35893 (0.07125)

Table 6 continued

	True R^2 = 0.5	
	200	1000
OLS-R^2	0.51413 (0.04192)	0.49811 (0.01885)
McKelvey/Zavoina	0.51752 (0.06769)	0.50026 (0.03075)
Aldrich/Nelson	0.28372 (0.03268)	0.27892 (0.01535)
Aldrich/Nelson Normalized	0.48890 (0.05633)	0.48028 (0.02645)
McFadden	0.28854 (0.04624)	0.27969 (0.02144)
Cragg/Uhler	0.43737 (0.05715)	0.42803 (0.02679)
Lave	0.34060 (0.04906)	0.33374 (0.02330)
Correlation	0.34076 (0.04908)	0.33377 (0.02331)
Relative Variance	0.34115 (0.04868)	0.33358 (0.02244)

Table 7

Binary Probit Pseudo's, OLS-R^2 and True R^2: Means and Standard Deviations (in Parentheses)

	True R^2 = 0.8	
	50	100
OLS-R^2	0.81407 (0.03412)	0.81175 (0.02682)
McKelvey/Zavoina	0.82099 (0.07521)	0.82030 (0.05843)
Aldrich/Nelson	0.43861 (0.04120)	0.43915 (0.03034)
Aldrich/Nelson Normalized	0.76278 (0.07072)	0.75728 (0.05239)
McFadden	0.58428 (0.09550)	0.57095 (0.06965)
Cragg/Uhler	0.73179 (0.07927)	0.72574 (0.05871)
Lave	0.62502 (0.09031)	0.61686 (0.06555)
Correlation	0.62545 (0.09034)	0.61708 (0.06563)
Relative Variance	0.62398 (0.08880)	0.62122 (0.06292)

Table 7 continued

	True R^2 = 0.8	
	200	1000
OLS-R^2	0.80845 (0.01856)	0.79973 (0.00876)
McKelvey/Zavoina	0.81671 (0.03501)	0.79952 (0.01780)
Aldrich/Nelson	0.42840 (0.01793)	0.42495 (0.00920)
Aldrich/Nelson Normalized	0.73795 (0.03087)	0.73183 (0.01580)
McFadden	0.54279 (0.04009)	0.53398 (0.02003)
Cragg/Uhler	0.70386 (0.03459)	0.69693 (0.01768)
Lave	0.58974 (0.03932)	0.58455 (0.02124)
Correlation	0.58990 (0.03937)	0.58458 (0.02124)
Relative Variance	0.59148 (0.03754)	0.58312 (0.01803)

Table 8

Predictive Quality of Pseudo-R^2's for True and OLS-R^2 with True R^2 = 0.2[a]

Measure	True R^2			
N=	50	100	200	1000
OLS-R^2	0.01104	0.00582	0.00252	0.00045
	-0.02408	-0.01681	-0.01181	0.00277
	0.10281	0.07482	0.04899	0.02104
McKelvey/Zavoina	0.01821	0.00987	0.00405	0.00066
	-0.02376	-0.01181	-0.00601	0.00157
	0.13350	0.09916	0.06364	0.02586
Aldrich/Nelson	0.01039	0.00873	0.00731	0.00674
	0.07153	0.07536	0.07792	0.08077
	0.07300	0.05554	0.03536	0.01474
Aldrich/Nelson Normalized	0.01642	0.00932	0.00378	0.00067
	-0.02289	-0.01511	-0.01039	-0.00531
	0.12670	0.09584	0.06091	0.02537
McFadden	0.01280	0.01153	0.01072	0.01060
	0.08554	0.09331	0.09808	0.10204
	0.07443	0.05342	0.03338	0.01375
Cragg/Uhler	0.01280	0.00744	0.00348	0.00144
	0.01171	0.02028	0.02576	0.03096
	0.11308	0.08428	0.05332	0.02215
Lave	0.01123	0.00833	0.00637	0.00551
	0.05881	0.06473	0.06921	0.07225
	0.08858	0.06466	0.03996	0.01717
Correlation	0.01122	0.00832	0.00637	0.00551
	0.05856	0.06462	0.06916	0.07224
	0.08873	0.06471	0.03997	0.01717
Relative Variance	0.01091	0.00822	0.00635	0.00553
	0.05632	0.06337	0.06840	0.07246
	0.08842	0.06514	0.04104	0.01687

Table 8 continued

Measure	N=	OLS-R^2 50	100	200	1000
OLS-R^2					
McKelvey/Zavoina		0.00820	0.00423	0.00187	0.00032
		0.00031	0.00500	0.00580	-0.00120
		0.09102	0.06520	0.04305	0.01782
Aldrich/Nelson		0.01390	0.01087	0.00914	0.00629
		0.09560	0.09217	0.08973	0.07800
		0.06935	0.04899	0.03315	0.01440
Aldrich/Nelson Normalized		0.00730	0.00390	0.00170	0.00037
		0.00119	0.00170	0.00141	-0.00808
		0.08586	0.06277	0.04141	0.01754
McFadden		0.01715	0.01459	0.01317	0.01006
		0.10961	0.11012	0.10988	0.09927
		0.07200	0.04990	0.03326	0.01448
Cragg/Uhler		0.00760	0.00456	0.00279	0.00105
		0.03579	0.03709	0.03757	0.02820
		0.07987	0.05672	0.03735	0.01591
Lave		0.01212	0.00923	0.00769	0.00504
		0.08288	0.08155	0.08102	0.06948
		0.07284	0.05103	0.03366	0.01462
Correlation		0.01209	0.00921	0.00768	0.00504
		0.08264	0.08143	0.08096	0.06947
		0.07292	0.05104	0.03366	0.01462
Relative Variance		0.01165	0.00890	0.00754	0.00506
		0.08039	0.08019	0.08020	0.06969
		0.07238	0.05000	0.03346	0.01446

[a] The basic calculation is the error term (D) connected with each measure. The three numbers for the measures are mean of D^2, mean of D and standard deviation of D.

Table 9

Predictive Quality of Pseudo-R^2's for True and OLS-R^2 with True R^2 = 0.5[a]

Measure	N=	True R^2 50	100	200	1000
OLS-R^2		0.00801	0.00453	0.00194	0.00036
		-0.02224	-0.01867	-0.01413	0.00189
		0.08713	0.06498	0.04192	0.01885
McKelvey/Zavoina		0.01937	0.00920	0.00484	0.00094
		-0.04159	-0.02848	-0.01752	-0.00026
		0.13351	0.09203	0.06769	0.03075
Aldrich/Nelson		0.04701	0.04524	0.04783	0.04911
		0.20590	0.20775	0.21628	0.22108
		0.06825	0.04583	0.03268	0.01535
Aldrich/Nelson		0.01391	0.00619	0.00326	0.00108
Normalized		-0.01131	-0.00422	0.01110	0.01972
		0.11801	0.07898	0.05633	0.02645
McFadden		0.04430	0.04299	0.04683	0.04899
		0.18230	0.19620	0.21146	0.22031
		0.10571	0.06740	0.04624	0.02144
Cragg/Uhler		0.01601	0.00862	0.00716	0.00589
		0.03735	0.04629	0.06263	0.07197
		0.12151	0.08086	0.05715	0.02679
Lave		0.03019	0.02522	0.02779	0.02818
		0.13291	0.14185	0.15940	0.16626
		0.11247	0.07177	0.04906	0.02330
Correlation		0.03007	0.02512	0.02774	0.02817
		0.13236	0.14144	0.15924	0.16623
		0.11257	0.07188	0.04908	0.02331
Relative Variance		0.02879	0.02512	0.02774	0.02819
		0.12964	0.14203	0.15939	0.16642
		0.11003	0.07068	0.04851	0.02244

Table 9 continued

Measure N=	OLS-R^2 50	100	200	1000
OLS-R^2				
McKelvey/Zavoina	0.01151	0.00593	0.00316	0.00049
	-0.01935	-0.00981	-0.00339	-0.00215
	0.10606	0.07678	0.05636	0.02224
Aldrich/Nelson	0.05703	0.05415	0.05436	0.04823
	0.22814	0.22642	0.23041	0.21919
	0.07095	0.05397	0.03586	0.01360
Aldrich/Nelson Normalized	0.00898	0.00475	0.00290	0.00067
	0.01093	0.01444	0.02523	0.01784
	0.09462	0.06770	0.04780	0.01885
McFadden	0.04978	0.04993	0.05260	0.04795
	0.20454	0.21486	0.22560	0.21842
	0.08955	0.06169	0.04151	0.01571
Cragg/Uhler	0.01302	0.00893	0.00821	0.00527
	0.05959	0.06496	0.07676	0.07008
	0.09778	0.06900	0.04835	0.01908
Lave	0.03253	0.02995	0.03200	0.02730
	0.15515	0.16051	0.17353	0.16438
	0.09242	0.06503	0.04361	0.01670
Correlation	0.03238	0.02985	0.03194	0.02729
	0.15461	0.16011	0.17337	0.16435
	0.09254	0.06522	0.04363	0.01671
Relative Variance	0.03137	0.02978	0.03193	0.02734
	0.15188	0.16070	0.17352	0.16453
	0.09158	0.06323	0.04284	0.01646

[a] The basic calculation is the error term (D) connected with each measure. The three numbers for the measures are mean of D^2, mean of D and standard deviation of D.

Table 10

Predictive Quality of Pseudo-R^2's for True and OLS-R^2 with True R^2 = 0.8[a]

Measure N=	True R^2 50	100	200	1000
OLS-R^2	0.00135	0.00085	0.00041	0.00008
	-0.01407	-0.01175	-0.00845	0.00027
	0.03412	0.02682	0.01856	0.00876
McKelvey/Zavoina	0.00604	0.00379	0.00149	0.00031
	-0.02099	-0.02030	-0.01671	0.00048
	0.07521	0.05843	0.03501	0.01780
Aldrich/Nelson	0.13228	0.13113	0.13841	0.14075
	0.36139	0.36085	0.37160	0.37505
	0.04120	0.03034	0.01793	0.00920
Aldrich/Nelson Normalized	0.00634	0.00454	0.00479	0.00489
	0.03722	0.04272	0.06205	0.06817
	0.07072	0.05239	0.03087	0.01580
McFadden	0.05556	0.05727	0.06775	0.07116
	0.21572	0.22905	0.25721	0.26602
	0.09550	0.06965	0.04009	0.02003
Cragg/Uhler	0.01087	0.00893	0.01043	0.01093
	0.06821	0.07426	0.09614	0.10307
	0.07927	0.05871	0.03459	0.01768
Lave	0.03869	0.03779	0.04574	0.04686
	0.17498	0.18314	0.21026	0.21545
	0.09031	0.06555	0.03932	0.02124
Correlation	0.03855	0.03772	0.04568	0.04685
	0.17455	0.18292	0.21010	0.21542
	0.09034	0.06563	0.03937	0.02124
Relative Variance	0.03565	0.03690	0.04566	0.04736
	0.16844	0.18174	0.21043	0.21688
	0.08576	0.06254	0.03739	0.01803

Table 10 continued

Predictive Quality of Pseudo-R^2's for True and OLS-R^2 with True R^2 = 0.8[a]

Measure N=	OLS-R^2 50	100	200	1000
OLS-R^2				
McKelvey/Zavoina	0.00417	0.00263	0.00112	0.00026
	-0.00693	-0.00855	-0.00826	0.00021
	0.06454	0.05086	0.03257	0.01607
Aldrich/Nelson	0.14242	0.13969	0.14486	0.14055
	0.37546	0.37260	0.38006	0.37478
	0.03825	0.02945	0.02041	0.00956
Aldrich/Nelson Normalized	0.00634	0.00507	0.00583	0.00481
	0.05129	0.05446	0.07050	0.06789
	0.06121	0.04612	0.02945	0.01436
McFadden	0.05981	0.06178	0.07196	0.07094
	0.22979	0.24080	0.26566	0.26574
	0.08417	0.06191	0.03739	0.01804
Cragg/Uhler	0.01146	0.01004	0.01199	0.01082
	0.08228	0.08600	0.10459	0.10279
	0.06884	0.05167	0.03255	0.01596
Lave	0.04223	0.04149	0.04926	0.04667
	0.18905	0.19488	0.21871	0.21517
	0.08094	0.05956	0.03796	0.01935
Correlation	0.04208	0.04142	0.04919	0.04666
	0.18862	0.19466	0.21855	0.21514
	0.08101	0.05966	0.03802	0.01936
Relative Variance	0.03878	0.04042	0.04911	0.04718
	0.18251	0.19348	0.21888	0.21661
	0.07435	0.05487	0.03481	0.01627

[a] The basic calculation is the error term (D) connected with each measure. The three numbers for the measures are mean of D^2, mean of D and standard deviation of D.

Table 11

Predictive Quality of Pseudo-R^2's for OLS Analogues[a]

Measure	N	Aldrich/Nelson	Aldrich/Nelson Normalized	McFadden
	50	0.01281	0.03850	0.00322
		0.08609	0.14937	0.02243
		0.07382	0.12787	0.05242
	100	0.01132	0.03371	0.00166
True R^2		0.08979	0.15498	0.01747
= 0.2		0.05736	0.09894	0.03697
	200	0.01049	0.03118	0.00082
		0.09119	0.15719	0.01482
		0.04689	0.08088	0.02471
	1000	0.00676	0.02005	0.00043
		0.07969	0.13722	0.01788
		0.02043	0.03517	0.01033
	50	0.05329	0.16169	0.00964
		0.21313	0.37103	0.04286
		0.08916	0.15578	0.08878
	100	0.05479	0.16316	0.00456
True R^2		0.22327	0.38527	0.02861
= 0.5		0.07063	0.12197	0.06146
	200	0.05665	0.16823	0.00224
		0.23102	0.39806	0.01633
		0.05759	0.09928	0.04465
	1000	0.04969	0.14732	0.00072
		0.22154	0.38146	0.01968
		0.02481	0.04271	0.01820
	50	0.13684	0.41450	0.00790
		0.36572	0.63631	-0.01598
		0.05584	0.09852	0.08785
	100	0.13920	0.41394	0.00528
True R^2		0.37077	0.63937	-0.03126
= 0.8		0.04180	0.07210	0.06596
	200	0.14544	0.43157	0.00472
		0.38020	0.65492	-0.05555
		0.03001	0.05172	0.04057
	1000	0.14175	0.42041	0.00304
		0.37623	0.64793	-0.05167
		0.01432	0.02467	0.01921

Table 11 continued

Measure	N	Cragg/Uhler	Cragg/Uhler Unnormalized
	50	0.01387	0.01940
		0.06779	0.10450
		0.09680	0.09253
True R^2 = 0.2	100	0.01091	0.01672
		0.07344	0.10762
		0.07464	0.07203
	200	0.00920	0.01509
		0.07570	0.10860
		0.05917	0.05773
	1000	0.00442	0.00934
		0.06149	0.09346
		0.02538	0.02473
	50	0.05549	0.10506
		0.19508	0.29916
		0.13271	0.12540
True R^2 = 0.5	100	0.05708	0.10900
		0.21486	0.31494
		0.10500	0.09957
	200	0.06005	0.11280
		0.23001	0.32590
		0.08496	0.08154
	1000	0.04909	0.09851
		0.21854	0.31189
		0.03657	0.03532
	50	0.06848	0.19437
		0.24907	0.43645
		0.08069	0.06264
True R^2 = 0.8	100	0.07074	0.19612
		0.25912	0.44046
		0.06031	0.04619
	200	0.08030	0.20906
		0.28105	0.45635
		0.03645	0.02850
	1000	0.08214	0.21130
		0.28600	0.45945
		0.01849	0.01442

[a] The basic calculation is the error term (D) connected with each measure. The three numbers for the measures are mean of D^2, mean of D and standard deviation of D.

REFERENCES

ALDRICH, J. H., NELSON, F. D. (1984): Linear Probability, Logit, and Probit Models. Beverly Hills: Sage University Press.

AMEMIYA, T. (1980): "Selection of Regressors," International Economic Review, 21, 331-354.

AMEMIYA, T. (1981): "Qualitative Response Models: A Survey," Journal of Economic Literature, 19, 1483-1536.

ANDERSON, P., BAUER, R. K., FELS, E. (1954): On the Accuracy of Short-Term Entrepreneurial Expectations, mimeo.

BISHOP, Y. M. M., FIENBERG, S. E., HOLLAND, P. W. (1975): Discrete Multivariate Analysis, Cambridge, Mass., London, England

CRAGG, J. G., UHLER, R. (1970): "The Demand for Automobiles," Canadian Journal of Economics, 3, 386-406.

CRAMÉR, H. (1946): Mathematical Methods of Statistics. Princeton

DHRYMES, P. J. (1986): "Limited Dependent Variables," in Handbook of Econometrics, Vol. III, ed. by Z. Griliches and M. D. Intriligator, Amsterdam: North-Holland.

EFRON B. (1978): "Regression and ANOVA with Zero-One Data: Measures of Residual Variation," Journal of American Statistical Association, 73, 113-121.

FOMBY, T. B., HILL R. C., JOHNSON, S. R. (1984): Advanced Econometric Methods. New York: Springer-Verlag.

GOLDBERGER, A. S. (1973): "Correlations Between Binary Choices and Probabilistic Predictions," Journal of the American Statistical Association, 68, 84.

GOODMAN, L. A., KRUSKAL, W. H. (1954): "Measures of Association for Cross Classifications," Journal of the American Statistical Association, 49, 732-764.

GOODMAN, L. A., KRUSKAL, W. H. (1974a): "Empirical Evaluation of Formal Theory," Journal of Mathematical Sociology, 3, 187-196.

GOODMAN, L. A., KRUSKAL, W. H. (1974b): "More About Empirical Evaluation of Formal Theory," Journal of Mathematical Sociology, 3, 211-213.

GREENE, W. H. (1990): Econometric Analysis. New York: Macmillan Publishing Company.

HAUSER, J. R. (1977): "Testing the Accuracy, Usefulness and Significance of Probabilistic Choice Models: An Information Theoretic Approach," Operations Research, 26, 406-421.

HILDEBRAND, D. K., LAING, J. D., ROSENTHAL, H. L. (1974a): "Prediction Logic: A Method for Empirical Evaluation of Formal Theory," Journal of Mathematical Sociology, 3, 163-185.

HILDEBRAND, D. K., LAING, J. D., ROSENTHAL, H. L. (1974b): "Prediction Logic and Quasi-Independence in Empirical Evaluation of Formal Theory," Journal of Mathematical Sociology, 3, 197-209.

JUDGE, G. G., GRIFFITHS, W. E., HILL, R. C., LÜTKEPOHL, H., LEE, T.-C. (1985): The Theory and Practice of Econometrics. New York: John Wiley and Sons.

KAWASAKI, S., McMILLAN, J., ZIMMERMANN, K. F. (1983): "Inventories and Price Inflexibility," Econometrica, 51, 599-609.

KAWASAKI, S., ZIMMERMANN, K. F. (1986): "Testing the Rationality of Price Expectations for Manufacturing Firms," Applied Economics, 18, 1335-1347.

LAVE, C. A. (1970): "The Demand for Urban Mass Transportation," Review of Economics and Statistics, 37, 320-323.

MADDALA, G. S. (1983): Limited-Dependent and Qualitative Variables in Econometrics. New York: Cambridge University Press.

McFADDEN, D. (1973): "Conditional Logit Analysis of Qualitative Choice Behavior," in Frontiers in Econometrics, ed. by P. Zarembka. New York: Academic Press, 105-142.

McKELVEY, R., ZAVOINA, W. (1975): "A Statistical Model for the Analysis of Ordinal Level Dependent Variables," Journal of Mathematical Sociology, 4, 103-120.

MORRISON, D. G. (1972): "Upper Bounds for Correlation Between Binary Outcomes and Probabilistic Predictions," Journal of the American Statistical Association, 67, 68-70.

NETER, J., MAYNES, E. S. (1970): "Correlation Coefficient with a 0,1 Dependent Variable," Journal of the American Statistical Association, 65, 501-509.

THEIL, H. (1966): Applied Economic Forecasting, Amsterdam.

VEALL, M. R., ZIMMERMANN, K. F. (1990a): Evaluating Pseudo R^2's for Binary Probit Models, mimeo. Forthcoming 1993: Quality & Quantity. International Journal of Methodology.

VEALL, M. R., ZIMMERMANN, K. F. (1990b): Goodness of Fit Measures in the Tobit Model, mimeo.

VEALL, M. R., ZIMMERMANN, K. F. (1992a): "Pseudo R^2's in the Ordinal Probit Model," Journal of Mathematical Sociology, 16, 333-342.

VEALL, M. R., ZIMMERMANN, K. F. (1992b): "Performance Measures from Prediction - Realization Tables," Economics Letters, 39, 129-134.

ZIMMERMANN, K. F. (1986a): "On Rationality of Business Expectations: A Micro Analysis of Qualitative Responses," Empirical Economics, 11, 23-40.

ZIMMERMANN, K. F. (1986b): "Multivariate Micro Prediction Analysis of Qualitative Models," in Methods of Operations Research, 53, ed. by K. W. Gaede, K. Ritter and H. Schneeweiß, 683-696.

Testing for Causation Between Two Variables in Higher-Dimensional VAR Models*

Helmut Lütkepohl
(Humboldt University, Berlin)

1. Introduction

Different concepts of causality in vector autoregressive (VAR) models have been proposed in the literature. For instance, Granger (1969) defines a variable y_2 to be causal for y_1 if the former is helpful in predicting the latter. Formally, denoting by $y_{1,t}(h|\Omega_t)$ the optimal h-step predictor at origin t based on the set of all the relevant information in the universe Ω_t, y_2 may be defined to be Granger-noncausal for y_1 if

$$y_{1,t}(h|\Omega_t) = y_{1,t}(h|\Omega_t \setminus \{y_{2,s}|s \leq t\}), \qquad h = 1,2,\ldots, \qquad (1.1)$$

where $\Omega_t \setminus A$ denotes the set containing all elements of Ω_t that are not in A. If y_1 and y_2 are generated by a bivariate VAR(p) process

$$\begin{bmatrix} y_{1t} \\ y_{2t} \end{bmatrix} = \sum_{i=1}^{p} \begin{bmatrix} \alpha_{11,i} & \alpha_{12,i} \\ \alpha_{21,i} & \alpha_{22,i} \end{bmatrix} \begin{bmatrix} y_{1,t-i} \\ y_{2,t-i} \end{bmatrix} + u_t \qquad (1.2)$$

* Parts of this research have been presented in seminars at Berkeley,San Diego, USC/UCLA and Stanford and at a workshop on "Applied Econometrics" in Munich. The author has greatly benefitted from comments of the participants and especially the discussant Walter Krämer. The paper was also presented at the World Congress of the Econometric Society 1990 in Barcelona. Financial support was provided in part by the Deutsche Forschungsgemeinschaft.

and the information set is $\Omega_t = \{(y_{1,s}, y_{2,s})'|s \leq t\}$, then (1.1) is equivalent to

$$\alpha_{12,i} = 0, \qquad i = 1, 2, \ldots, p. \tag{1.3}$$

Under standard assumptions, these restrictions are easy to test.

In economic systems there are usually more than two relevant variables and it is highly desirable to extend this concept to higher dimensional systems. Different possible extensions have been considered. In one approach the vector of all variables, say y_t, is partitioned into two subvectors so that $y_t = (y_{1t}', y_{2t}')'$. Then the definition (1.1) may be used for the two subvectors y_{1t}, y_{2t} rather than two individual variables. If $\Omega = \{y_s|s \leq t\}$ and y_t is a VAR process of the form (1.2), where the $\alpha_{kh,i}$ are now matrices of appropriate dimension, the restrictions for noncausality are the same as in the bivariate case. In other words, y_{2t} is Granger-noncausal for y_{1t} if $\alpha_{12,i} = 0$ for $i = 1, \ldots, p$ (e.g., Lütkepohl (1991, Sec. 2.3.1)). Of course, a set of variables being causal for another set of variables does not necessarily imply that each member of the former set is causal for each member of the latter set. Therefore another approach is sometimes persued in applied studies.

Suppose we have a three-dimensional system with VAR representation

$$y_t = \begin{bmatrix} y_{1t} \\ y_{2t} \\ y_{3t} \end{bmatrix} = \sum_{i=1}^{p} \begin{bmatrix} \alpha_{11,i} & \alpha_{12,i} & \alpha_{13,i} \\ \alpha_{21,i} & \alpha_{22,i} & \alpha_{23,i} \\ \alpha_{31,i} & \alpha_{32,i} & \alpha_{33,i} \end{bmatrix} \begin{bmatrix} y_{1,t-i} \\ y_{2,t-i} \\ y_{3,t-i} \end{bmatrix} + u_t \tag{1.4}$$

Then causality of y_2 for y_1 is sometimes checked by testing

$$H_0 : \alpha_{12,i} = 0, \; i = 1, \ldots, p \tag{1.5}$$

(e.g. Heri (1988), Dorbny & Gausden (1988)). Unfortunately these restrictions are not quite equivalent to (1.1). They are equivalent to equality of the predictors in (1.1) for $h = 1$, given $\Omega_t = \{y_s|s \leq t\}$. However, if (1.5) is satisfied, the information in past y_{2t} may still be helpful in predicting y_{1t} more than one period ahead. Intuitively this happens because y_2 may have an impact on y_3 which in turn may affect y_1. Thus, the definition of noncausality underlying (1.5) is not in line with an intuitive notion of the term.

Therefore it seems preferable to either derive restrictions on the VAR coefficients that correspond to the stronger causality concept underlying (1.1) or use a notion of causality which was more or less explicitly suggested by Sims (1980, 1981), Newbold (1982, pp. 708-709), Penm & Terrell (1986) and others in the framework of VAR analyses. Sims considered the responses of the variables to innovations in the system. One variable may be called noncausal for another variable if innovations in the former have no impact on the latter. Sims pointed out that, for stationary processes, the impulse responses are the coefficients of moving average (MA) representations of the system. Therefore testing for causality in the above sense involves testing zero constraints on MA coefficients. Since we also consider nonstationary VAR processes that do not possess MA representations it is preferable to talk about impulse response functions or coefficients here. The objective of this article is to discuss tests for zero constraints on the impulse responses and point out problems related to such tests.

The plan of the paper is as follows. In the next section the basic framework is laid out and the null hypotheses to be tested are formulated. In Section 3 tests are considered. Conclusions follow in Section 4. A proposition stated in Section 2 is proven in the Appendix.

2. The Basic Framework

Let $y_t = (y_{1t}, \ldots, y_{Kt})'$ be a K-dimensional, zero mean VAR(p) process so that

$$y_t = A_1 y_{t-1} + \ldots + A_p y_{t-p} + u_t, \tag{2.1}$$

where the A_i are $(K \times K)$ coefficient matrices and $u_t = (u_{1t}, \ldots, u_{tK})'$ is K-dimensional white noise with $E(u_t) = 0$ and positive definite covariance matrix $\Sigma_u = E(u_t u_t')$. If the process is stationary and

$$\det(I_K - A_1 z - \ldots - A_p z^p) \neq 0 \quad \text{for} \quad |z| \leq 1, \tag{2.2}$$

it has a Wold MA representation of the form

$$y_t = \sum_{i=0}^{\infty} \Phi_i u_{t-i}, \tag{2.3}$$

where $\Phi_0 = I_K$ is the $(K \times K)$ identity matrix and

$$\Phi_i = \sum_{j=1}^{i} \Phi_{i-j} A_j, \qquad i = 1, 2, \ldots \tag{2.4}$$

with $A_j = 0$ for $j > p$.

Some researchers interpret the elements $\phi_{kh,i}$ of the Φ_i matrices as responses of the k-th variable to variations in variable h, i periods ago (e.g., Backus (1986)). If these coefficients actually reflect the true responses of the system, variable h is noncausal for variable k ($\neq h$) if the hypothesis

$$H_0 : \phi_{kh,i} = 0 \quad \text{for} \quad i = 1, 2, \ldots \tag{2.5}$$

is true. Thus, one would like to test hypotheses of this type in order to investigate the causal relations within the system. If the system consists of two variables only, H_0 is equivalent to noncausality from variable h to variable k in Granger's (1969) sense (e.g., Judge et al.(1985, Chapter 16)).

If the process (2.1) is nonstationary so that the determinant in (2.2) has roots on the unit circle as, for instance, in co-integrated systems, the impulse responses may still be computed as in (2.4). Therefore, in the following the Φ_i's are assumed to be matrices defined as in (2.4) and not necessarily MA coefficient matrices.

Sims (1981) and others have argued that the response functions based on the Φ_i coefficients may not properly represent the actual reactions of the system to shocks in the variables if the components of u_t are correlated. For instance, if u_{ht} and u_{kt} are correlated, shocks in variable h may be likely to be accompanied by shocks in variable k so that the system may reflect such an occurrence while it does not give a proper picture of isolated shocks in one of the variables. Therefore Sims suggests orthogonalizing the residuals.

To obtain the resulting impulse responses let P be a lower triangular Choleski decomposition of Σ_u such that $\Sigma_u = PP'$ and define $\Theta_i = \Phi_i P = (\theta_{kh,i}), i = 0, 1, 2, \ldots$. In this setting $\theta_{kh,i}$ represents the response of variable k to an innovation of one residual standard deviation in variable h, i periods ago. Since $\Theta_0 = P$ is a lower triangular matrix, innovations in y_{1t} may have an instantaneous impact on $y_{2t}, \ldots, y_{Kt}$ while innovations in y_{2t} cannot have an immediate effect on y_{1t} but only on $y_{3t}, \ldots, y_{Kt}$ and so on. Thus the order of the variables is now of importance for the interpretation of the relationships within the system and must be chosen properly by the investigator. If the elements $\theta_{kh,i}$ of Θ_i are the actual impulse responses of the system, the null hypothesis of no causality from y_{ht} to y_{kt} may be expressed as

$$H_0 : \theta_{kh,i} = 0 \quad \text{for} \quad i = 0, 1, 2, \ldots \tag{2.6}$$

In Sims' (1980, 1981) terminology this hypothesis could be formulated in terms of forecast error variance proportions. Specifically H_0 in (2.6) is equivalent to the case where the proportion of forecast error variance of variable k that is accounted for by innovations in variable h, is zero for all forecast horizons. In a bivariate system, $\theta_{12,i} = 0$ for $i = 0, 1, \ldots$, is equivalent to Granger-noncausality from y_{2t} to y_{1t} and absence of instantaneous causality between the two variables (see e.g. Judge et al. (1985, Chapter 16)). Tests for the null hypotheses in (2.5) and (2.6) will be presented in the next section. To simplify that task useful characterizations of these hypotheses are given in the following proposition.

Proposition 1. Suppose y_t is a K-dimensional VAR(p) process as in (2.1). Then the following holds for $k \neq h$:

1. H_0 in (2.5) is equivalent to

$$H_0 : \phi_{kh,i} = 0 \quad \text{for} \quad i = 1, 2, \ldots, p(K-1).$$

2. H_0 in (2.6) is equivalent to

$$H_0 : \theta_{kh,i} = 0 \quad \text{for} \quad i = 0, 1, \ldots, p(K-1). \qquad \square$$

The virtue of this result is that the infinite number of constraints in (2.5) and (2.6) is reduced to finitely many zero restrictions. The proof of Proposition 1 is given in the Appendix. From that proof it becomes obvious that, for instance, $\phi_{kh,i} = 0$ for $i = 1, 2, \ldots, p(K-1)-1$ is in general not sufficient for (2.5) to hold. In this sense the proposition gives a minimal set of constraints. Up to this point zero constraints on the A_i and Σ_u are not excluded. Thus, some of the components of y_t may be exogenous variables. If zero constraints of this type are known to be present the restrictions given in Proposition 1 may not be minimal.

3. Testing for Causation

3.1 Tests Based on Individual Response Coefficients

Traditionally causality hypotheses of the types (2.5) and (2.6) are checked by determining the significance of individual impulse response coefficients (e.g., Runkle (1987)). Based on Proposition 1 this approach can be turned into a formal asymptotic test by using the asymptotic normal distribution of the impulse response coefficients. In order to explain this approach we concentrate on a test of (2.5). A test of the null hypothesis in (2.6) may be obtained in a similar way.

Suppose $\hat{\alpha}$ is an estimator of $\alpha = \text{vec}(A_1, \ldots, A_p)$ with asymptotic normal distribution

$$\sqrt{T}(\hat{\alpha} - \alpha) \xrightarrow{d} N(0, \Sigma_\alpha). \tag{3.1}$$

Then the resulting estimator $\hat{\phi}_{kh,i}$ of $\phi_{kh,i}$ also has an asymptotic normal distribution,

$$\sqrt{T}(\hat{\phi}_{kh,i} - \phi_{kh,i}) \xrightarrow{d} N(0, \omega^2_{kh,i}), \tag{3.2}$$

where $\omega^2_{kh,i} = g_{kh,i}\Sigma_\alpha g'_{kh,i}$ and

$$g_{kh,i} = \frac{\partial \phi_{kh,i}}{\partial \alpha'} = \sum_{n=0}^{i-1} j_h (A')^{i-1-n} \otimes j_k A^n J'. \tag{3.3}$$

Here

$$A = \begin{bmatrix} A_1 & A_2 & \dots & A_{p-1} & A_p \\ I_K & 0 & \dots & 0 & 0 \\ 0 & I_K & \dots & 0 & 0 \\ \vdots & \vdots & \dots & \vdots & \vdots \\ 0 & 0 & \dots & I_K & 0 \end{bmatrix} \quad (Kp \times Kp)$$

$$J = [I_K \quad 0 \dots 0] \quad (K \times Kp)$$

and j_k is the k-th row of J (see e.g. Lütkepohl (1990)).

Note that (3.2) holds under standard assumptions for stationary and co-integrated VAR processes (for the latter case see Lütkepohl & Reimers (1992)). Thus if $\omega_{kh,i}^2 \neq 0$, the t-ratio $t_{kh,i} = \sqrt{T}\hat{\phi}_{kh,i}/\omega_{kh,i}$ has an asymptotic standard normal distribution under H_0 in (2.5). Of course, $\omega_{kh,i}$ may be replaced by a consistent estimator. Hence, by Bonferroni's inequality, the probability for

$$|t_{kh,i}| \geq c_{\gamma/2p(K-1)} \tag{3.4}$$

for some $i \in \{1, 2, \dots, p(K-1)\}$ is less than or equal to γ. Here c_γ is the upper 100γ percentage point of the standard normal distribution. Thus, using Proposition 1, rejection of H_0 in (2.5) if (3.4) holds for at least one $i \in \{1, 2, \dots, p(K-1)\}$ gives a simple test with asymptotic significance level not greater than γ. This upper bound requires, however, that $\omega_{kh,i} \neq 0$ for all $i = 1, \dots, p(K-1)$.

Unfortunately the latter condition is not generally satisfied. Consider, for instance, the trivial case where $K = 3$ and y_t is a white noise VAR(0) process while a VAR(1) is fitted to the available data. Then, $A = A_1 = 0$ so that, by (3.3), $g_{12,2}$ is a (1×9) zero vector and hence $\omega_{12,2}^2 = 0$.

A further drawback of tests based on individual response coefficients may be reduced power due to the possible overstatement of their asymptotic significance level. Phrased in more positive terms: Rejection of the noncausality hypothesis by a test of this kind is strong evidence against the null hypothesis, provided, of course, the t-ratios have approximate standard normal distributions. To avoid the problem of reduced power it is desirable to look for a test with exact asymptotic level. Since testing for causality in the present sense involves testing a set of highly nonlinear restrictions on the VAR coefficients and estimation of the unrestricted VAR coefficients is easy, Wald tests are a possible choice. These tests are considered in the next subsection.

3.2 Wald Tests

Again we focus on tests of (2.5). The procedures and problems are similar for testing (2.6). Using the notation

$$\phi_{kh} = \begin{bmatrix} \phi_{kh,1} \\ \vdots \\ \phi_{kh,pK-p} \end{bmatrix}$$

and Proposition 1, the null hypothesis in (2.5) may be stated as

$$H_0 : \phi_{kh} = 0 \tag{3.5}$$

The corresponding Wald statistic based on (3.1) is

$$W_{kh} = T\hat{\phi}'_{kh}(\hat{\mathbf{g}}_{kh}\hat{\Sigma}_\alpha\hat{\mathbf{g}}'_{kh})^+\hat{\phi}_{kh}, \tag{3.6}$$

where D^+ denotes the Moore-Penrose generalized inverse of the matrix D,

$$\mathbf{g}_{kh} = \begin{bmatrix} g_{kh,1} \\ \vdots \\ g_{kh,pK-p} \end{bmatrix}$$

and carets denote estimators obtained on the basis of the estimator $\hat{\alpha}$ of α and a consistent estimator $\hat{\Sigma}_u$ of Σ_u. We have the following result e.g. from Andrews (1987):

Proposition 2. Suppose $h \neq k, H_0$ in (3.5) is true,

$$\sqrt{T}(\hat{\alpha} - \alpha) \xrightarrow{d} N(0, \Sigma_\alpha),$$

and $\text{rank}(\hat{\mathbf{g}}_{kh}\hat{\Sigma}_\alpha\hat{\mathbf{g}}'_{kh}) = \text{rank}(\mathbf{g}_{kh}\Sigma_\alpha\mathbf{g}'_{kh}) = r$ (w.p.1). Then $W_{kh} \xrightarrow{d} \chi^2(r)$. □

The rank condition in this proposition is a sufficient but not a necessary condition for an asymptotic χ^2-distribution. Unfortunately it is not always satisfied in the present context. To see this consider a three-dimensional stationary VAR(1) process with coefficient matrix

$$A_1 = \begin{bmatrix} \alpha_{11} & \alpha_{12} & \alpha_{13} \\ \alpha_{21} & \alpha_{22} & \alpha_{23} \\ \alpha_{31} & \alpha_{32} & \alpha_{33} \end{bmatrix}$$

and suppose we wish to test causation from y_2 to y_1. In this case $p(K-1) = 2$ and the null hypothesis (3.5) becomes

$$H_0 : \phi_{12} = \begin{bmatrix} \alpha_{12} \\ \alpha_{11}\alpha_{12} + \alpha_{12}\alpha_{22} + \alpha_{13}\alpha_{32} \end{bmatrix} = \begin{bmatrix} 0 \\ 0 \end{bmatrix}. \tag{3.7}$$

Hence, y_2 is noncausal for y_1 if any one of the following sets of conditions holds:

$$\alpha_{12} = \alpha_{13} = 0 \quad \text{and} \quad \alpha_{32} \neq 0, \tag{3.8}$$

$$\alpha_{12} = \alpha_{32} = 0 \quad \text{and} \quad \alpha_{13} \neq 0, \tag{3.9}$$

$$\alpha_{12} = \alpha_{13} = \alpha_{32} = 0. \tag{3.10}$$

The partial derivatives $\mathbf{g}_{12}$ are

$$\mathbf{g}_{12} = \begin{bmatrix} 0 & 0 & 0 & 1 & 0 & 0 & 0 & 0 & 0 \\ \alpha_{12} & 0 & 0 & \alpha_{11}+\alpha_{22} & \alpha_{12} & \alpha_{13} & \alpha_{32} & 0 & 0 \end{bmatrix}.$$

This matrix has rank 2 if (3.8) or (3.9) holds. In that case $\hat{\mathbf{g}}_{12}\hat{\Sigma}_\alpha\hat{\mathbf{g}}'_{12}$ is a (2×2) matrix which has full rank (w.p.1) and no problems occur. On the other hand, if (3.10) holds, $\mathbf{g}_{12}$ has rank 1 and consequently $\mathbf{g}_{12}\Sigma_\alpha\mathbf{g}'_{12}$

has rank 1 if the VAR(1) is fitted by multivariate least squares estimation. However, substituting estimates for the α_{ij}, rank$(\hat{\mathbf{g}}_{12}) = 2$ (w.p.1). Hence, rank$(\hat{\mathbf{g}}_{12}\hat{\Sigma}_\alpha\hat{\mathbf{g}}_{12}') = 2$. The problem here is that in such a case the (generalized) inverse of the estimator $\hat{\mathbf{g}}_{12}\hat{\Sigma}_\alpha\hat{\mathbf{g}}_{12}'$ will generally not converge to $(\mathbf{g}_{12}\Sigma_\alpha\mathbf{g}_{12}')^+$ (see Pötscher (1985, Lemma A3), Andrews (1987, Theorem 2)). Therefore the rank condition is imposed in Proposition 2. If the rank condition is not satisfied the statistic W_{kh} may have an asymptotic χ^2-distribution with fewer degrees of freedom or some other limiting distribution.

It is known that the Wald test is not invariant under different parameterizations of the restrictions under H_0 (Gregory & Veall (1985), Breusch & Schmidt (1988)). This fact is worth remembering in the bivariate case where the restrictions in (3.5) may be formulated in terms of zero restrictions on the VAR coefficients. A Wald test of those restrictions may be preferable to (3.6).

3.3 Other Procedures

In a situation where the Wald test is problematic it may be tempting to try Lagrange multiplier (LM) or likelihood ratio (LR) tests. Unfortunately they will suffer from similar problems. In particular, if rank$(\mathbf{g}_{12}) \leq Kp - p$ some restrictions are superfluous. Since the number of restrictions determines the number of degrees of freedom of the asymptotic χ^2-distribution of the LM and LR tests and since rank$(\mathbf{g}_{kh})$ is usually unknown, we have again the problem of unknown asymptotic distributions. In addition, LM and LR tests require the computation of constrained estimates which results in a nontrivial nonlinear optimization problem.

An alternative strategy for checking causal relations is to impose as many zero constraints on the VAR coefficients as possible on the basis of model selection criteria. Thus, subset VAR modelling as proposed by Hsiao (1979), Penm & Terrell (1984, 1986) or Lütkepohl (1991, Sec. 5.2.8) may be considered. Of course, an easy way to check whether particular zero restrictions on the VAR coefficient matrices imply the noncausality constraints in (2.5) or (2.6) is to compute the Φ_i and Θ_i matrices for $i = 0, 1, \ldots, p(K-1)$ from the estimated coefficients $\hat{A}_1, \ldots, \hat{A}_p, \hat{\Sigma}_u$ and check whether the relevant elements $\hat{\phi}_{kh,i}$ or $\hat{\theta}_{kh,i}$ are zero.

3.4 A Simulation Experiment

We have conducted a limited simulation experiment to investigate the relative performance of different procedures in small samples. In particular we have generated realizations of three-dimensional Gaussian VAR(1) processes of the typ

$$\begin{bmatrix} y_{1t} \\ y_{2t} \\ y_{3t} \end{bmatrix} = \begin{bmatrix} 1 \\ 1 \\ 1 \end{bmatrix} + \begin{bmatrix} 0.5 & 0 & \alpha_{13} \\ 0.7 & 0.3 & 0.25 \\ 0.5 & \alpha_{32} & 0 \end{bmatrix} \begin{bmatrix} y_{1,t-1} \\ y_{2,t-1} \\ y_{3,t-1} \end{bmatrix} + \begin{bmatrix} u_{1t} \\ u_{2t} \\ u_{3t} \end{bmatrix}, \qquad \Sigma_u = I_3,$$

for various combinations of α_{13}/α_{32} values and sample sizes $T = 30$ and 100. 1000 replications of the experiment were performed for each design. The proportions of rejections of the null hypothesis (3.7) of noncausality from y_2 to y_1 obtained by different procedures are recorded in Table 1. Two subset VAR strategies were employed. The first one, a top-down strategy, starts from a full VAR(1) model and, for each separate equation, the significance of the parameters is checked by a model selection criterion. A parameter is deleted if that helps to reduce the criterion. In contrast, the bottom-up strategy is similar to the one proposed by Hsiao (1979). It starts from a VAR(0) model and adds coefficients that help reducing a prespecified criterion. Again we proceed equation by equation. The model selection criteria used are Akaike's (1974) AIC, a criterion adapted from Hannan and Quinn (1979) called HQ and the SC criterion suggested by Schwarz (1978) (see Lütkepohl (1991, Sec. 4.3)).

Three of the four parameter sets shown in Table 1 correspond to noncausality from y_2 to y_1 (see (3.8)-(3.10)). For these cases the Wald test rejects less often than is indicated by the nominal significance level for both sample sizes. $\alpha_{13} = \alpha_{32} = 0$ corresponds precisely to the situation

Table 1
Percentages of Rejections of Noncausality from y_2 to y_1
in the Simulation Experiment

Sample size	α_{13}	α_{32}	Causal event	Wald test 10%	Wald test 5%	Subset VAR strategies bottom-up AIC	bottom-up HQ	bottom-up SC	top-down AIC	top-down HQ	top-down SC
T=30	0	0.2	$y_2 \not\rightarrow y_1$	5.6	2.7	27.4	19.9	11.4	30.2	22.1	12.9
	0.3	0	$y_2 \not\rightarrow y_1$	8.4	4.3	22.4	17.1	10.8	30.3	23.6	14.8
	0	0	$y_2 \not\rightarrow y_1$	5.1	2.2	21.2	16.2	9.3	25.2	19.8	10.2
	0.3	0.2	$y_2 \rightarrow y_1$	14.7	7.9	37.8	31.5	20.7	45.0	38.3	25.2
T=100	0	0.2	$y_2 \not\rightarrow y_1$	3.7	1.9	29.0	15.5	4.7	31.5	15.8	5.1
	0.3	0	$y_2 \not\rightarrow y_1$	5.2	2.8	21.5	10.4	4.3	31.0	15.9	7.0
	0	0	$y_2 \not\rightarrow y_1$	3.2	1.6	18.7	8.7	3.0	19.9	9.4	3.3
	0.3	0.2	$y_2 \rightarrow y_1$	29.7	18.5	91.8	84.3	69.5	93.0	84.8	68.9

in (3.10), where the asymptotic distribution is not a $\chi^2(2)$. We have still used the critical values from that distribution because in practice the true asymptotic distribution is unknown. For $T = 30$ the Wald test has very little power against the specific alternative considered in Table 1. The power improves markedly for increasing sample size, however.

For sample size $T = 30$ none of the subset strategies behaves very satisfactorily when AIC or HQ is used as model selection criterion. More precisely, the actual size of a test based on any of these subset strategies would be quite a bit in excess of what one would choose in a common statistical test. This happens although, in a sense, we are working under ideal conditions in that the true order of the process is assumed to be known. The performance of the HQ subset strategies improves somewhat for $T = 100$.

The SC criterion leads to more conventional rejection levels when the noncausality hypothesis is true. For $T = 100$, the size of the SC bottom-up strategy is comparable to a 10% level Wald test when y_2 is noncausal for y_1. On the other hand, the subset strategies have much better power than the Wald test against the specific alternative where $\alpha_{13} = 0.3$ and $\alpha_{32} = 0.2$.

Of course, this is too small an experiment to draw general conclusions. It largely confirms and illustrates the asymptotic considerations of Section 3.2. On the basis of those findings and the simulation results it seems reasonable to use the Wald test or a subset strategy in conjunction with the SC criterion. Although it does not have impressive power properties one would at least be on the save side with a Wald test by not rejecting more frequently than expected on the basis of the asymptotic significance level chosen.

4. Concluding Remarks

In a VAR model a variable may be called noncausal for another variable if an impulse in the former variable has no effect on the latter. Thus, in order to test the null hypothesis of noncausality, zero constraints on impulse response coefficients have to be tested. It is shown that it suffices to check a finite number of impulse response coefficients. We have discussed causality tests based on individual response coefficients and joint tests based on the Wald principle. Both types of tests have the drawback that their asymptotic size is unknown in general. In addition, tests based on individual response coefficients may have low power. We have also mentioned the possibility of using subset VAR modelling strategies in order to investigate causal events. In a very limited simulation experiment the performance of these strategies was strongly affected by the model selection criterion used.

There are also some methodological problems that must be kept in mind in applying tests of causality of the present type. Prominent among these problems is the nonuniqueness of the impulse responses of a VAR process. Therefore, in order to interpret the outcome of the tests properly, the researcher needs to choose the response functions that reflect the interrelationships between the variables appropriately. This may be a difficult task in practice because the choice must be based on a priori knowledge. The statistical tool-kit is of little help in solving this problem.

Appendix. Proof of Proposition 1

The notation of Section 2 will be used. In addition we define

$$A(z) = I_K - A_1 z - \ldots - A_p z^p$$

where z is a complex number. Since $A(0) = I_K$, $A(z)$ is invertible in a neighborhood of $z = 0$. In that neighborhood we get

$$A(z)^{-1} = \Phi(z) = \sum_{i=0}^{\infty} \Phi_i z^i = \left[\phi_{kh}(z) \right]_{k,h=1,\ldots,K} = \left[\sum_{i=0}^{\infty} \phi_{kh,i} z^i \right]_{k,h}$$

where the Φ_i are precisely the matrices defined in (2.4). Thus,

$$\Phi(z) = A(z)^* / \det(A(z)),$$

where $A(z)^* = (A_{kh}(z))_{k,h}$ is the adjoint of $A(z)$ and $A_{kh}(z)$ is the hk-th co-factor obtained by deleting the h-th row and k-th column from $A(z)$ and taking the determinant of the remaining matrix of polynomials. Obviously, $\phi_{kh}(z) \equiv 0$ is equivalent to $A_{kh}(z) \equiv 0$. The latter polynomial has degree at most $p(K-1)$. Thus, for $k \neq h$,

$$\begin{aligned}\phi_{kh}(z) &= \phi_{kh,1}z + \phi_{kh,2}z^2 + \ldots = A_{kh}(z)\gamma(z) \\ &= (A_{kh,1}z + \ldots + A_{kh,p(K-1)}z^{p(K-1)})(1 + \gamma_1 z + \ldots),\end{aligned}$$

where $\gamma(z) = det(A(z))^{-1}$. Hence, $\phi_{kh,1} = A_{kh,1}$ and $\phi_{kh,i} = A_{kh,i} + \sum_{j=1}^{i-1} A_{kh,j}\gamma_{i-j}$ for $i > 1$ with $A_{kh,j} = 0$ for $j > p(K-1)$. Consequently, $A_{kh,i} = 0$ for $i = 1, 2, \ldots, p(K-1)$ is equivalent to $\phi_{kh,i} = 0$ for $i = 1, 2, \ldots, p(K-1)$ which proves (1) of Proposition 1.

To prove (2), we note that

$$\Theta(z) = \Phi(z)P = A(z)^*P/\det(A(z)),$$

where P is a lower triangular matrix. Thus, (2) follows with similar arguments as (1).

Q.E.D.

References

Akaike, H. (1974), "A New Look at the Statistical Model Identification," *IEEE Transactions on Automatic Control*, AC-19, 716-723.

Andrews, D.W.K. (1987), "Asymptotic Results for Generalized Wald Tests," *Econometric Theory*, 3, 348-358.

Backus, D. (1986), "The Canadian-U.S. Exchange Rate: Evidence from a Vector Autoregression," *Review of Economics and Statistics*, 68, 628-637.

Breusch, T.S. & P. Schmidt (1988), "Alternative Forms of the Wald Test: How Long is a Piece of String," *Communications in Statistics, Theory and Methods*, 17, 2789-2795.

Dorbny, A. & R. Gausden (1988), "Granger-Causality, Real Factor Prices and Employment: A Re-appraisal with UK Data," *European Economic Review*, 32, 1261-1283.

Granger, C.W.J. (1969), "Investigating Causal Relations by Econometric Models and Cross-Spectral Methods," *Econometrica*, 37, 424-438.

Gregory, A.W. & M.R. Veall (1985), "Formulating Wald Tests of Nonlinear Restrictions," *Econometrica*, 53, 1465-1468.

Hannan, E.J. & B.G. Quinn (1979), "The Determination of the Order of an Autoregression," *Journal of the Royal Statistical Society B*, 41, 190-195.

Heri, E.W. (1988), "Money Demand Regressions and Monetary Targeting: Theory and Stylized Evidence," *Schweizerische Zeitschrift für Volkswirtschaft und Statistik*, 12, 123-149.

Hsiao, C. (1979), "Autoregressive Modeling of Canadian Money and Income Data," *Journal of the American Statistical Association*, 74, 553-560.

Judge, G.G., W.E. Griffiths, R.C. Hill, H. Lütkepohl & T.-C. Lee (1985), *The Theory and Practice of Econometrics, Second Edition*, New York: John Wiley.

Lütkepohl, H. (1990), "Asymptotic Distribution of Impulse Response Functions and Forecast Error Variance Decompositions of Vector Autoregressive Models," *Review of Economics and Statistics*, 72, 116 - 125.

Lütkepohl, H. (1991), *Introduction to Multiple Time Series Analysis* , Berlin: Springer-Verlag.

Lütkepohl, H. & H.-E. Reimers (1992), "Impulse Response Analysis of Co-Integrated Systems," *Journal of Economic Dynamics and Control*, 16, 53 - 78.

Newbold, P. (1982), "Causality Testing in Economics," in O.D. Anderson (Ed.), *Time Series Analysis: Theory and Practice I*, Amsterdam: North-Holland, 701-716.

Penm, J.H.W. & R.D. Terrell (1984), "Multivariate Subset Autoregressive Modelling with Zero Constraints for Detecting 'Overall Causality'," *Journal of Econometrics*, 24, 311-330.

Penm, J.H.W. & R.D. Terrell (1986), "The 'Derived' Moving-Average Model and its Role in Causality," in J. Gani & M.B. Priestley (Eds.), *Essays in Time Series and Allied Processes*, Sheffield: Applied Probability Trust, 99-111.

Pötscher, B.M. (1985), "The Behaviour of the Lagrangian Multiplier Test in Testing the Orders of an ARMA-Model," *Metrika*, 32, 129-150.

Runkle, D.E. (1987), "Vector Autoregressions and Reality," *Journal of Business & Economic Statistics*, 5, 437-442.

Schwarz, G. (1978), "Estimating the Dimension of a Model," *Annals of Statistics*, 8, 147-164.

Sims, C.A. (1980), "Macroeconomics and Reality," *Econometrica*, 48, 1-48.

Sims, C.A. (1981), "An Autoregressive Index Model for the U.S. 1948-1975," in J. Kmenta & J.B. Ramsey (Eds.), *Large-Scale Macro-Econometric Models*, Amsterdam: North-Holland, 283-327.

The Reduced Form of Recursive Models: Asymptotic Properties*

Hans Schneeweiß
(University of Munich)

0 Introduction

It is well-know that the OLS estimator $\tilde{\Pi}$ of the reduced form parameters Π of an interdependent econometric (simultaneous equations) model is inferior to an estimator $\hat{\Pi}$ which is computed in two stages: first estimate the structural parameters by an efficient method, e.g. by FIML or 3SLS, and then solve the system for the endogenous variables, Goldberger et al (1961), Dhrymes (1973), Court (1973). The asymptotic covariance matrix of $\tilde{\pi} = vec\,\tilde{\Pi}$ is greater or equal to the asymptotic covariance matrix of $\hat{\pi} = vec\,\hat{\Pi}$, in symbols:

$$V(\tilde{\pi}) \geq V(\hat{\pi})$$

in the sense that the difference $V(\tilde{\pi}) - V(\hat{\pi})$ is nonnegative definite[1].

Similar statements can be made for so called partially restricted form estimators, Kakwani/Court (1972), Sant (1978), Nagar/Sahay (1978).

[1] We will always denote the vectorization of a matrix A, denoted by a capital letter, by the corresponding small letter: $vec\,A = a$, where $vec\,A$ is constructed by stacking the columns of A one beneath the other.

There are also some small sample results: Knight (1977), Mc Carthy (1981), Swamy/Mehta (1981).

Note, however, that these results typically refer to interdependent models with no restrictions in the covariance matrix of the error variables. The recursive model, as promoted by Wold (1953,1964), cf. also Mosbaek/Wold (1969), is not explicitly taken into account.

The present paper tries to close this gap by treating exclusively the case of a recursive model. In this model an efficient estimation procedure for the structural parameters is OLS as applied to each structural equation separately. Therefore the proof of the inferiority of $\tilde{\Pi}$ versus $\hat{\Pi}$ is carried out by referring only to well-known properties of OLS asymptotic theory. At the same time the recursive structure of the model is exploited.

In sections 1 and 2 a simple two-equations recursive model is defined and the estimators $\tilde{\Pi}$ and $\hat{\Pi}$ are introduced. In section 3 the asymptotic covariance matrices for $\tilde{\pi}$ and $\hat{\pi}$ are computed, and section 4 proves the inferiority of $\tilde{\pi}$ within this model and gives necessary and sufficient conditions for the equivalence of $\tilde{\pi}$ and $\hat{\pi}$. Section 5 extends these results to the case of a general recursive model. The general proof relies significantly on the results of section 4 for the two-equations case.

1 The model

Consider the following two-equations recursive model[2]

$$(\bar{M}) \qquad \begin{aligned} Y_1 &= Y_2 B + X_1\Gamma_1 + U_1 = Z\Delta + U_1 \\ Y_2 &= X_2\Gamma_2 + U_2, \end{aligned}$$

where the matrices $X_i : T \times p_i$ and $Y_i : T \times q_i$ comprise the observable variables and the matrices $U_i : T \times q_i, i = 1,2$, unobservable error variables. $B : q_2 \times q_1$ and $\Gamma_i : p_i \times q_i, i = 1,2$, are the unknown parameter

[2]To be sure, $(\bar{M})$ consists of two *multivariate (matrix)* equations. In the proof of Theorem 3 this multivariate version of $(\bar{M})$ is needed.

matrices. By definition

$$\begin{aligned} Z &= (Y_2, X_1) \\ \Delta &= (B', \Gamma_1')'. \end{aligned}$$

X_1 and X_2 are nonstochastic matrices of full column rank, whereas U_1 and U_2 (and by implication Y_1 and Y_2) are matrices of random variables such that $E(U_2) = 0, E(U_1|U_2) = 0, E(u_2u_2') = \Sigma_2 \otimes I$ and $E(u_1u_1'|u_2) = \Sigma_1 \otimes I$, where $u_i = vec\, U_i, i = 1, 2$, and I is the $(T \times T)$-identity matrix.

We can always construct a nonstochastic $(T \times m)$ matrix W of full column rank such that

$$X_i = WA_i,$$

where $A_i : m \times p_i$ has rank $A_i = p_i$. Simply take W as any matrix the column space of which, $M(W)$, includes the columns of (X_1, X_2). The matrix is assumed to be given[3], and A_i is uniquely determined by W and $X_i : A_i = (W'W)^{-1}W'X_i$.

The reduced form of $(\bar{M})$, with respect to W, is found by substituting $X_i = WA_i$ in $(\bar{M})$ and solving $(\bar{M})$ for Y_1 and Y_2. It is given by

$$(\bar{R}_1) \qquad Y_1 = W\Pi_1 + V_1$$

$$(\bar{R}_2) \qquad Y_2 = W\Pi_2 + U_2,$$

where

$$\begin{aligned} \Pi_1 &= A_2\Gamma_2 B + A_1\Gamma_1 = \Psi\Delta \\ \Psi &= (A_2\Gamma_2, A_1) \\ \Pi_2 &= A_2\Gamma_2 \\ V_1 &= U_1 + U_2 B. \end{aligned}$$

$(\bar{R}_1)$ and $(\bar{R}_2)$ can be condensed into

[3]Note that W is allowed to span a larger space than (X_1, X_2).

$$(\bar{R}) \qquad\qquad Y = W\Pi + V$$

with $Y = (Y_1, Y_2), V = (V_1, U_2), \Pi = (\Pi_1, \Pi_2)$.

We obviously have (with $v = vec\, V$)

$$\begin{aligned}
E(vv') &= \Sigma_v \otimes I, \qquad I : T \times T, \\
\Sigma_v &= \bar{\Sigma}_1 + \bar{\Sigma}_2 \\
\bar{\Sigma}_1 &= (I, O)'\Sigma_1(I, O), \quad I : q_1 \times q_1, \quad O : q_1 \times q_2, \\
\bar{\Sigma}_2 &= (B, I)'\Sigma_2(B, I), \quad I : q_2 \times q_2.
\end{aligned}$$

2 Two estimators

One can estimate Π either directly by applying OLS to $(\bar{R})$ or indirectly in two steps: first estimate the model parameters Δ and Γ_2 from $(\bar{M})$ by OLS, then insert these estimates into Π. The second estimator is called the Recursive Least Squares (RLS) estimator. The first (OLS) estimator is given by

$$\tilde{\Pi} = (W'W)^{-1}W'Y.$$

The RLS estimator is given by

$$\hat{\Pi} = (\hat{\Pi}_1, \hat{\Pi}_2),$$

where

$$\begin{aligned}
\hat{\Pi}_1 &= \hat{\Psi}\hat{\Delta} \\
\hat{\Psi} &= (A_2\hat{\Gamma}_2, A_1) \\
\hat{\Gamma}_2 &= (X_2'X_2)^{-1}X_2'Y_2 = (A_2'W'WA_2)^{-1}A_2'W'Y_2 \\
\hat{\Delta} &= (Z'Z)^{-1}Z'Y_1 \\
\hat{\Pi}_2 &= A_2\hat{\Gamma}_2.
\end{aligned}$$

3 Asymptotic properties

In order to be able to derive the asymptotic properties for $\tilde{\Pi}$ and $\hat{\Pi}$ we suppose that a model of type $(\bar{M})$ is given for each $T = 1, 2, \ldots$ such that at each transition from T to $T+1$ a new row of variables is added to Y_i, X_i, W_i and $U_i, i = 1, 2$, while the remaining rows are left unchanged and the parameters as well as the matrices A_i are the same for all T. For each T, the last row of Z is denoted by z'_T.

The parameter matrix Π is vectorized as $\pi = vec\,\Pi$. Similarly $\tilde{\pi} = vec\,\tilde{\Pi}$ and $\hat{\pi} = vec\,\hat{\Pi}$.

The following assumptions will be made

(A_1) Let u'_{1T} and u'_{2T} be the last rows of U_1 and U_2, respectively, $T = 1, 2, \ldots$, then $\{u_{2T}\}$ is a series[4] of i.i.d. random vectors, and $\{u_{1T}\}$, given $\{u_{2T}\}$, is a series of conditionally i.i.d. random vectors.

(A_2) Σ_2 is nonsingular.

(A_3) $\lim_{T\to\infty} \frac{1}{T} W'W = M$, M nonsingular.

Theorem 1: Under the assumptions (A_1) to (A_3),

$$\begin{aligned}
\sqrt{T}(\tilde{\pi} - \pi) &\overset{d}{\rightarrow} N(o, V(\tilde{\pi})) \\
\sqrt{T}(\hat{\pi} - \pi) &\overset{d}{\rightarrow} N(o, V(\hat{\pi})) \\
V(\tilde{\pi}) &= \Sigma_v \otimes M^{-1} \\
V(\hat{\pi}) &= \bar{\Sigma}_1 \otimes [\Psi(\Psi' M \Psi + \Sigma)^{-1} \Psi'] \\
&\quad + \bar{\Sigma}_2 \otimes [A_2(A'_2 M A_2)^{-1} A'_2],
\end{aligned}$$

where $\Sigma = (I, O)'\Sigma_2(I, O)$ with $I : q_2 \times q_2$ and $O : q_2 \times p_1$.

Proof: (a) The asymptotic normality of $\tilde{\pi}$ follows from standard asymptotic theory of OLS. The asymptotic covariance matrix $V(\tilde{\pi})$ is just the limit $(T \to \infty)$ of the small sample covariance matrix of $\sqrt{T}\tilde{\pi}$:

---

[4] $\{a_T\}$ is a short notation for the series $a_1, a_2, \ldots$.

$$V(\tilde{\pi}) = \lim T\Sigma_v \otimes (W'W)^{-1} = \Sigma_v \otimes M^{-1}.$$

(b) In order to compute the asymptotic covariance matrix of $\hat{\pi}$ we partition $\hat{\pi} - \pi$ as follows

$$\hat{\pi} - \pi = \begin{bmatrix} vec\,(\Psi(\hat{\Delta} - \Delta)) + vec\,((\hat{\Psi} - \Psi)\Delta) + vec\,((\hat{\Psi} - \Psi)(\hat{\Delta} - \Delta)) \\ vec\,(A_2(\hat{\Gamma}_2 - \Gamma_2)) \end{bmatrix}$$

Using the fact that $(\hat{\Psi} - \Psi)\Delta = A_2(\hat{\Gamma}_2 - \Gamma_2)B$ and setting $[vec'\,((\hat{\Psi} - \Psi)(\hat{\Delta} - \Delta)), o']' =: r$, this can be written as

$$\hat{\pi} - \pi = vec\,[\Psi(\hat{\Delta} - \Delta)(I, O)] + vec\,[A_2(\hat{\Gamma}_2 - \Gamma_2)(B, I)] + r,$$

where $O : q_1 \times q_2$.

After multiplying this expression with $\sqrt{T}$ we get

(1) $\sqrt{T}(\hat{\pi}-\pi) = ((I,O)'\otimes\Psi)\sqrt{T}(\hat{\delta} - \delta) + ((B,I)'\otimes A_2)\sqrt{T}(\hat{\gamma}_2 - \gamma_2) + \sqrt{T}r$

with $\hat{\delta} - \delta = vec\,(\hat{\Delta} - \Delta)$ and $\hat{\gamma}_2 - \gamma_2 = vec\,(\hat{\Gamma}_2 - \Gamma_2)$. By asymptotic OLS theory $\sqrt{T}(\hat{\gamma}_2 - \gamma_2)$ converges in distribution to $N(o, V(\hat{\gamma}_2))$ with

$$V(\hat{\gamma}_2) = \lim T\Sigma_2 \otimes (X_2'X_2)^{-1} = \Sigma_2 \otimes (A_2'MA_2)^{-1}.$$

Consequently the second term of (1) converges in distribution to $N(o, V_2)$ with

$$\begin{aligned} V_2 &= ((B,I)' \otimes A_2)(\Sigma_2 \otimes (A_2'MA_2)^{-1})((B,I) \otimes A_2') \\ &= \bar{\Sigma}_2 \otimes (A_2(A_2'MA_2)^{-1}A_2'). \end{aligned}$$

The first term of (1) converges conditionally to a normal distribution in the following sense: Suppose that

$$\lim \frac{1}{T} \sum_{t=1}^{T} z_t z_t' = \lim \frac{1}{T} Z'Z =: M_Z$$

exists and is nonsingular. Then the conditional distribution of $\sqrt{T}(\hat{\delta}-\delta)$, given $z := \{z_T\}$, converges to $N(o, V(\hat{\delta}))$ with

$$V(\hat{\delta}) = \Sigma_1 \otimes M_Z^{-1}.$$

Consequently, the conditional distribution of the first term of (1), given z, converges to $N(o, V_1)$ with

$$\begin{aligned} V_1 &= ((I,O)' \otimes \Psi)(\Sigma_1 \otimes M_Z^{-1})((I,O) \otimes \Psi') \\ &= \bar{\Sigma}_1 \otimes (\Psi M_Z^{-1} \Psi'), \end{aligned}$$

provided M_Z exists and is nonsingular. But M_Z does exist with probability 1 and is nonsingular. In fact, since

$$Z = W\Psi + U$$

with $U = (U_2, O)$, where $O : T \times p_1$, we have

$$M_Z = \Psi' M \Psi + \Sigma,$$

and the nonsingularity of M_Z follows from the fact that, by assumption, Σ_2 and M, and consequently also $A_1' M A_1$, are nonsingular.

Therefore, with probability 1, the first term of (1) converges conditionally, given z, to $N(o, V_1)$, where V_1 is a constant matrix not depending on z.

Now, since the second term of (1) is a function of z, it follows, by an argument given in the appendix, that the first two terms of (1) converge to a joint normal distribution with mean zero and covariance matrix

$$\begin{bmatrix} V_1 & O \\ O & V_2 \end{bmatrix}.$$

The last term of (1), multiplied by $\sqrt{T}$, obviously converges to 0 in probability and can therefore be neglected asymptotically.

Combining these arguments we ultimately find

$$\sqrt{T}(\hat{\pi} - \pi) \overset{d}{\rightarrow} N(o, V(\hat{\pi}))$$

with $V(\hat{\pi}) = V_1 + V_2$, which proves the theorem.$\diamond$

4 Comparison of estimators

$\hat{\Pi}$ is a better estimator of Π than $\tilde{\Pi}$ in the following sense:

Theorem 2: Given the assumptions of Theorem 1. Then

$$V(\tilde{\pi}) \geq V(\hat{\pi}).$$

Proof: Writing $V(\tilde{\pi}) = (\bar{\Sigma}_1 + \bar{\Sigma}_2) \otimes M^{-1}$ we see that the theorem will be proved if we can show that

(a) $M^{-1} \geq \Psi(\Psi' M \Psi + \Sigma)^{-1}\Psi'$,

(b) $M^{-1} \geq A_2(A_2' M A_2)^{-1} A_2'$.

Now, (b) is equivalent to

$$I \geq N A_2 (A_2' N' N A_2)^{-1} A_2' N',$$

where N is a square root of M, i.e., $M = N'N$. But this last inequality is obviously true since the right hand side is a projection matrix.

Similarly, (a) is equivalent to

$$I \geq N\Psi(\Psi'N'N\Psi + \Sigma)^{-1}\Psi'N',$$

which again is seen to be true by the following argument: Let $\Sigma = G'G$ and for abbreviation set $N\Psi =: H$, then the r.h.s. of the above inequality is $H(H'H + G'G)^{-1}H'$ and is a principal minor of the projection matrix $(H', G')'[(H', G')(H', G')']^{-1}(H', G')$ and therefore is $\leq I$.$\diamond$

In the following corollary we give a criterion for the equality of $V(\tilde{\pi})$ and $V(\hat{\pi})$. For later use we prove a somewhat more general result.

Corollary 1: Given the assumptions of Theorem 1. Let b be any $(m \times 1)$-vector and $I : (q_1 + q_2) \times (q_1 + q_2)$ and set $(I \otimes b')[V(\tilde{\pi}) - V(\hat{\pi})](I \otimes b) =: F$.

(i) Then $F = O$ if, and only if, there exist $(p_i \times 1)$-vectors $c_i, i = 1, 2$, such that $b = MA_ic_i$.

(ii) In particular, $V(\tilde{\pi}) = V(\hat{\pi})$ if, and only if, A_1 and A_2 are non-singular.

(iii) In this case

$$\tilde{\Pi} = \hat{\Pi}.$$

Proof: (i) Using Theorem 1 we find that

$$F = \bar{\Sigma}_1 \otimes b'[M^{-1} - \Psi(\Psi'M\Psi + \Sigma)^{-1}\Psi']b + \bar{\Sigma}_2 \otimes b'[M^{-1} - A_2(A_2'MA_2)^{-1}A_2']b.$$

By the proof of Theorem 2 the matrices in square brackets are nonnegative definite. Therefore $F = O$ is equivalent to the two statements

(a) $b'M^{-1}b = b'\Psi(\Psi'M\Psi + \Sigma)^{-1}\Psi'b,$

(b) $b'M^{-1}b = b'A_2(A_2'MA_2)^{-1}A_2'b.$

Now let N be a square root of M, as in the proof of Theorem 2, and let P be a symmetric square root of Σ_2 and write $a := N'^{-1}b, \bar{A} := NA_2, A := NA_1, B := NA_2\Gamma_2P^{-1}$. Then (a) and (b) can also be written as

$$\text{(a)}\quad a'a = a'(B, A)\begin{bmatrix} B'B + I & B'A \\ A'B & A'A \end{bmatrix}^{-1}\begin{bmatrix} B' \\ A' \end{bmatrix}a,$$

(b) $a'a = a'\bar{A}(\bar{A}'\bar{A})^{-1}\bar{A}'a$.

Using a well-known formula for inverting partitioned matrices and multiplying the resulting partitioned matrices we find that (a) is equivalent to

$$a'S(I-D)Sa = o$$

with $S = I - A(A'A)^{-1}A'$ and $D = B(I + B'SB)^{-1}B'$. Note that S is a projection matrix. Now

$$D = B(I - B'S(I + SBB'S)^{-1}SB)B'$$

and therefore

$$SDS = S[SBB'S - SBB'S(I+SBB'S)^{-1}SBB'S]S = S - S(I+SBB'S)^{-1}S$$

and finally

$$S(I-D)S = S(I + SBB'S)^{-1}S.$$

Thus $a'S(I-D)Sa = o$ is equivalent to $Sa = o$, which means that $a = Ac_1$ or

$$b = MA_1c_1.$$

Obviously (b) is equivalent to $a = \bar{A}c_2$ or

$$b = MA_2c_2,$$

which proves the first part of the corollary.

(ii) As for the second part, note that $V(\tilde{\pi}) = V(\hat{\pi})$ iff $F = 0$ for all b, which according to (i) means that every $(m \times 1)$-vector b can be written as $b = MA_i c_i, i = 1,2$. But this is equivalent to the statement that $rank\,(A_i) = m, i = 1,2$. But as also $rank\,(A_i) = p_i$ and $A_i : m \times p_i$, A_i is nonsingular.

(iii) To prove the last part of the corollary, first note that, with A_2 nonsingular.

$$\hat{\Psi} = (A_2\hat{\Gamma}_2, A_1) = (W'W)^{-1}W'(Y_2, WA_1) = (W'W)^{-1}W'Z$$

and so

$$\hat{\Pi}_1 = \hat{\Psi}\hat{\Delta} = (W'W)^{-1}W'Z(Z'Z)^{-1}Z'Y_1,$$

where $Z(Z'Z)^{-1}Z'$ is a projection matrix on $Z = (Y_2, WA_1)$. But since A_1 is nonsingular this is also a projection matrix on (Y_2, W). Therefore $W'Z(Z'Z)^{-1}Z' = W'$ and hence

$$\hat{\Pi}_1 = (W'W)^{-1}W'Y_1.$$

Similarly

$$\hat{\Pi}_2 = A_2\hat{\Gamma}_2 = (W'W)^{-1}W'Y_2.$$

Thus

$$\hat{\Pi} = (\hat{\Pi}_1, \hat{\Pi}_2) = (W'W)^{-1}W'Y = \tilde{\Pi}. \diamond$$

The following lemma, which also compares different estimators in the context of model $(\bar{M})$, will be useful for the next section.

Lemma: Under the assumptions of Theorem 1, suppose that in addition to $\hat{\Delta}$ there is a second estimator $\hat{\hat{\Delta}}$ of Δ, with $vec\,\hat{\hat{\Delta}} = \hat{\hat{\delta}}$, such that the conditional distribution of $\sqrt{T}(\hat{\hat{\delta}} - \delta)$, given $z = \{z_T\}$, converges to $N(o, V(\hat{\hat{\delta}}))$ with an asymptotic covariance matrix $V(\hat{\hat{\delta}})$ which does not depend on z and which satisfies

$$V(\hat{\delta}) \geq V(\hat{\hat{\delta}}).$$

Let $\hat{\hat{\Pi}}_1 = \hat{\Pi}\hat{\hat{\Delta}}$ and $\hat{\hat{\Pi}} = (\hat{\hat{\Pi}}_1, \hat{\Pi}_2)$ and set $vec\,\hat{\hat{\Pi}} = \hat{\hat{\pi}}$, then

$$\sqrt{T}(\hat{\hat{\pi}} - \pi) \to N(o, V(\hat{\hat{\pi}}))$$

and

$$V(\hat{\pi}) \geq V(\hat{\hat{\pi}}).$$

Proof: From the proof of Theorem 1 we see that we need only compare

$$V_2^* := [(I,O)'\otimes\Psi]V(\hat{\hat{\delta}})[(I,O)\otimes\Psi'] \quad \text{with} \quad V_2 = [(I,O)'\otimes\Psi]V(\hat{\delta})[(I,O)\otimes\Psi'].$$

But $V(\hat{\delta}) \geq V(\hat{\hat{\delta}})$ obviously implies $V_2 \geq V_2^*$, and this proves the lemma.◇

Corollary 2: Under the assumptions of the lemma, for any $(m \times 1)$-vector b,

$$(I \otimes b')[V(\hat{\pi}) - V(\hat{\hat{\pi}})](I \otimes b) = 0,$$

where $I : (q_1 + q_2) \times (q_1 + q_2)$ if , and only if,

$$(I \otimes b'\Psi)[V(\hat{\delta}) - V(\hat{\hat{\delta}})](I \otimes \Psi' b) = 0,$$

where $I : q_1 \times q_1$.

Proof: As in the proof of the lemma, $V(\hat{\pi}) - V(\hat{\hat{\pi}}) = V_2 - V_2^*$, and therefore

$$(I \otimes b')[V(\hat{\pi}) - V(\hat{\hat{\pi}})](I \otimes b) = [(I,O)' \otimes b'\Psi][V(\hat{\delta}) - V(\hat{\hat{\delta}})][(I,O) \otimes \Psi' b].$$

This expression is zero iff $(I \otimes b'\Psi)[V(\hat{\delta}) - V(\hat{\hat{\delta}})](I \otimes \Psi' b) = 0$.◇

5 Recursive models

We will now introduce the general recursive model as a generalization of the two-equations model $(\bar{M})$.

Let Y be a $(T \times q)$-matrix of endogenous variables and let $Y_i, i = 1, \ldots, g$, be $(T \times q_i)$-submatrices of Y with $\Sigma q_i = q$ such that Y can be partioned into $Y = (Y_1, Y_2, \ldots, Y_g)$. For $i = 1, \ldots, g$, let $Y_{(i)}$ denote a submatrix of Y which consists of a specific subset of the "columns" $Y_{i+1}, \ldots, Y_g$, i.e.

$$Y_{(i)} = (Y_{i_1}, \ldots, Y_{i_k}), \qquad i+1 \leq i_1 < \ldots < i_k \leq g.$$

$Y_{(i)}$ may also be empty $(k = 0)$. In particular, of course, $Y_{(g)}$ is empty. The recursive model can now be described by the following system of equations

$$(M) \qquad \begin{array}{rcll} Y_1 & = & Y_{(1)}B_1 & + \; X_1\Gamma_1 + U_1 \\ Y_2 & = & Y_{(2)}B_2 & + \; X_2\Gamma_2 + U_2 \\ & \vdots & & \\ Y_{g-1} & = & Y_{(g-1)}B_{g-1} & + \; X_{g-1}\Gamma_{g-1} + U_{g-1} \\ Y_g & = & & \; X_g\Gamma_g + U_g \end{array}$$

The X_i are full column rank $(T \times p_i)$-matrices of nonstochastic (exogenous) variables and the U_i are $(T \times q_i)$-matrices of random variables with $E(u_i|u_{i+1}, \ldots, u_g) = 0$ and $E(u_i u_i'|u_{i+1}, \ldots, u_g) = \Sigma_i \otimes I, i = 1, \ldots, g$, where $u_i = vec\, U_i$. The matrices B_i and Γ_i consist of unknown parameters.

As in the two-equations model $(\bar{M})$, we can construct a $(T \times m)$-matrix W of full column rank such that

$$X_i = WA_i,$$

where $A_i : m \times p_i$ has full column rank.

Substituting WA_i for X_i in (M) and solving for the endogenous variables yields the reduced form (with respect to W) of (M):

$$(R) \qquad Y = W\Pi + V.$$

The matrix Π can be estimated either directly from (R) by OLS or indirectly by estimating each equation of (M) by OLS and solving the system after the estimates have been inserted. The direct OLS estimator is denoted by $\tilde{\Pi}$, the indirect Recursive Least Squares (RLS) estimator by $\hat{\Pi}$. We denote $vec\,\Pi = \pi, vec\,\tilde{\Pi} = \tilde{\pi}, vec\,\hat{\Pi} = \hat{\pi}$.

In order to generalize Theorem 2 we introduce the concept of a series of models (M) depending on $T = 1, 2, \ldots$ just as in section 3. Assumptions (A_1) and (A_2) are generalized as follows, while (A_3) is taken over unchanged:

(A_1) Let u'_{iT} be the last row of $U_i, i = 1, \ldots, g, T = 1, 2, \ldots$ then $\{u_{iT}\}$, given $\{u_{i+1,T}, \ldots, u_{gT}\}$, is a series of conditionally i.i.d. random vectors.

(A_2) Σ_i is nonsingular, $i = 2, \ldots, g$.

(A_3) $\lim_{T\to\infty} \frac{1}{T} W'W = M$, M nonsingular.

Theorem 3: Under the assumptions (A_1) to (A_3)

$$\begin{aligned} \sqrt{T}(\tilde{\pi} - \pi) &\overset{d}{\rightarrow} N(o, V(\tilde{\pi})) \\ \sqrt{T}(\hat{\pi} - \pi) &\overset{d}{\rightarrow} N(o, V(\hat{\pi})) \end{aligned}$$

and

$$V(\tilde{\pi}) \geq V(\hat{\pi}).$$

Proof: The proof is carried out by induction. For $g = 1$ the assertion is obvious (Indeed, it is implied by Theorem 2 if only the second equation of $(\bar{M})$ is considered.) Suppose the theorem has been proved for the recursive system with $g-1$ equations. We will show that it is valid also for recursive systems (M) with g equations.

Consider the first $g-1$ equations of (M) and define new data matrices $Y^*_{(i)}$ and $X^*_i, i = 1, \ldots, g-1$, in the following way:

- If $Y_{(i)}$ contains Y_g, then $(Y^*_{(i)}, Y_g) = Y_{(i)}$ and $X^*_i = (Y_g, X_i)$.

- If $Y_{(i)}$ does not contain Y_g, then $Y^*_{(i)} = Y_{(i)}$ and $X^*_i = X_i$.

With these data matrices and corresponding parameter matrices B^*_i and Γ^*_i defined implicitly the first $g-1$ equations of (M) can be written as

$$(M^*) \qquad \begin{array}{rcl} Y_1 & = & Y^*_{(1)}B^*_1 \;\; + X^*_1\Gamma^*_1 + U_1 \\ & \vdots & \\ Y_{g-1} & = & X^*_{g-1}\Gamma^*_{g-1} + U_{g-1}. \end{array}$$

On the condition that Y_g is given and fixed, the X^*_i can be viewed as exogenous and (M^*) is again a recursive system, conditional on Y_g. Indeed, the conditional distribution of $U_1, \ldots, U_{g-1}$, given Y_g, satisfies the properties of a recursive model.

Now define

$$W^* = (Y_g, W)$$

and

$$A^*_i = \begin{bmatrix} I & O' \\ O & A_i \end{bmatrix} \quad \text{or} \quad A^*_i = \begin{bmatrix} O' \\ A_i \end{bmatrix},$$

depending on whether $Y_{(i)}$ contains Y_g or not, with $I : q_g \times q_g$ and $O' : q_g \times p_i$. Then A^*_i has full column rank and

$$X_i^* = W^* A_i^*.$$

The reduced form of (M^*) (with respect to W^*) is found by substituting X_i^* from the last equation in (M^*) and solving for $Y^* = (Y_1, \ldots, Y_{g-1})$. It is given by

$$(R^*) \qquad Y^* = W^* \Pi^* + V^*,$$

which can also be written as

$$Y^* = Y_g B^* + W \Gamma^* + V^*,$$

where B^* and Γ^* are defined implicitly.

To this equation add the last equation of (M), so that we get the system

$$(\check{M}) \qquad \begin{aligned} Y^* &= Y_g B^* + W\Gamma^* + V^* \\ Y_g &= X_g \Gamma_g + U_g. \end{aligned}$$

Obviously $(\check{M})$ is a two-equations recursive system of type $(\bar{M})$ with

$$\begin{aligned} Z &= (Y_g, W) = W^* \\ \Delta &= (B^{*\prime}, \Gamma^{*\prime})' = \Pi^*. \end{aligned}$$

The reduced form of $(\check{M})$, with respect to W, is identical to the reduced form (R) of the original recursive model (M).

Now we can define two estimators of Π^* and three estimators of Π.

1. $\tilde{\Pi}^*$ is the OLS estimator of Π^* computed from (R^*).
2. $\hat{\Pi}^*$ is the RLS estimator of Π^* computed from (M^*).
3. $\tilde{\Pi}$ is the OLS estimator of Π computed from (R).
4. $\check{\Pi}$ is the RLS estimator of Π computed from $(\check{M})$.

5. $\hat{\Pi}$ is the RLS estimator of Π computed from (M). It can also be computed from $(\check{M})$ when $\Delta = \Pi^*$ is estimated by $\hat{\Pi}^*$.

As before, we denote the vectorizations of these estimators by the corresponding small letters, and we use the symbol V to denote the asymptotic variances. Then by Theorem 1, as applied to system $(\check{M})$, $\sqrt{T}(\tilde{\pi}-\pi)$ and $\sqrt{T}(\check{\pi}-\pi)$ both converge to normal distributions (where $\check{\pi}$ corresponds to $\hat{\pi}$ in Theorem 1) and

$$V(\tilde{\pi}) \geq V(\check{\pi}). \tag{2}$$

Now consider model (M^*). Assumptions (A_1) to (A_3) of model (M) imply corresponding properties (A_1^*) to (A_3^*) for model (M^*): (A_1^*) and (A_2^*) are just (A_1) and (A_2) with g replaced by $g-1$, and (A_3^*) is the condition that

$$\lim \frac{1}{T} W^{*\prime} W^* = M^*$$

with probability 1, where M^* is positive definite. This condition is satisfied according to the following argument:

$$\begin{aligned}
\frac{1}{T} W^{*\prime} W^* &= \frac{1}{T}(Y_g, W)'(Y_g, W) \\
&= \frac{1}{T}(W A_g \Gamma_g + U_g, W)'(W A_g \Gamma_g + U_g, W) \\
&\underset{T \to \infty}{\longrightarrow} (A_g \Gamma_g, I)' M (A_g \Gamma_g, I) + (I, O)' \Sigma_g (I, O) =: M^*
\end{aligned}$$

and M^* is positive definite, because Σ_g and M are positive definite by assumptions (A_2) and (A_3).

Therefore, by the induction hypothesis, the conditional distributions of $\sqrt{T}(\tilde{\pi}^* - \pi^*)$ and $\sqrt{T}(\hat{\pi}^* - \pi^*)$, given Y_g, both converge to normal distributions such that

$$V(\tilde{\pi}^*) \geq V(\hat{\pi}^*). \tag{3}$$

Now, the conditional distribution given Y_g is the same as the conditional distribution given Z, as $Z = (Y_g, W)$ and W is nonstochastic. Since $\Pi^* = \Delta$ and therefore $\pi^* = \delta$, the two estimators $\tilde{\pi}^*$ and $\hat{\pi}^*$ correspond to $\hat{\delta}$ and $\hat{\hat{\delta}}$ of the lemma and, in particular, (3) can be written as $V(\hat{\delta}) \geq V(\hat{\hat{\delta}})$. According to the lemma, as applied to system $(\check{M})$, we therefore find

$$V(\check{\pi}) \geq V(\hat{\pi}) \tag{4}$$

because $\check{\pi}$ is the RLS estimator of π with $\hat{\delta} = \tilde{\pi}^*$ as estimator of the first stage, whereas $\hat{\pi}$ is the RLS estimator of π with $\hat{\hat{\delta}} = \hat{\pi}^*$ in place of $\hat{\delta}$.

Inequalities (2) and (4) taken together prove the theorem.$\diamond$

Finally we generalize the criterion of Corollary 1 to the present case of a recursive system.

Corollary 3: Given a recursive system as in Theorem 3.

(i) Let b be any $(m \times 1)$-vector and $I : q \times q$. Then

$$(I \otimes b')[V(\tilde{\pi}) - V(\hat{\pi})](I \otimes b) = 0$$

if, and only if, there exist $(p_i \times 1)$-vectors $c_i, i = 1, \ldots, g$, such that $b = MA_i c_i$.

(ii) In particular $V(\tilde{\pi}) = V(\hat{\pi})$ if, and only if, all the matrices $A_i, i = 1, \ldots, g$, are nonsingular.

(iii) In this case

$$\tilde{\Pi} = \hat{\Pi}.$$

Proof: We use the notations and arguments of the proof of Theorem 3.

(i) $(I \otimes b')[V(\tilde{\pi}) - V(\hat{\pi})](I \otimes b) = 0$ is equivalent to the following two statements taken together

(a) $(I \otimes b')[V(\tilde{\pi}) - V(\check{\pi})](I \otimes b) = 0$

(b) $(I \otimes b')[V(\check{\pi}) - V(\hat{\pi})](I \otimes b) = 0.$

According to Corollary 1, as applied to $(\check{M})$, (a) is equivalent to the existence of a vector c_g such that

$$b = MA_g c_g.$$

According to Corollary 2, as applied to $(\check{M})$, (b) is equivalent to

$$(I \otimes b'\Psi^*)[V(\tilde{\pi}^*) - V(\hat{\pi}^*)](I \otimes \Psi^{*\prime} b) = 0,$$

where $\Psi^* = (A_g\Gamma_g, I)$. By the induction hypothesis this is equivalent to the existence of vectors c_i^* such that

$$\Psi^{*\prime} b = M^* A_i^* c_i^*, \qquad i = 1, \ldots, g-1. \tag{5}$$

Now, we have two cases for A_i^*. In both of these cases (5) will be seen to be satisfied iff there exist vectors c_i such that

$$b = MA_i c_i, \qquad i = 1, \ldots, g-1.$$

Take, for instance, the case

$$A_i^* = \begin{bmatrix} I & O' \\ O & A_i \end{bmatrix}$$

Then (5) can be written more extensively as

$$\begin{bmatrix} \Gamma_g' A_g' b \\ b \end{bmatrix} = \begin{bmatrix} \Gamma_g' A_g' M A_g \Gamma_g + \Sigma_g & \Gamma_g' A_g' M \\ M A_g \Gamma_g & M \end{bmatrix} \begin{bmatrix} I & O' \\ O & A_i \end{bmatrix} \begin{bmatrix} d_i \\ c_i \end{bmatrix},$$

where c_i^* has been partitioned into $(d_i', c_i')'$ according to the partitioning of A_i^*. The unique solution of this system can be shown to be $d_i = 0$ and

$$b = MA_i c_i.$$

The same result, with $c_i = c_i^*$, will be obtained if the other case $A_i^* = (O, A_i')'$ pertains.

(ii) The proof of part (ii) is the same as in Corollary 1.

(iii) Suppose all the A_i are nonsingular. We will prove $\tilde{\Pi} = \hat{\Pi}$ again by induction, but this time by a different type of induction, viz., "from top to bottom" instead of the other way round. If we drop the first equation in the model (M), the system left over is again a recursive system:

$$(M^+) \qquad \begin{aligned} Y_2 &= Y_{(2)}B_2 + X_2\Gamma_2 + U_2 \\ &\vdots \\ Y_g &= X_g\Gamma_g + U_g. \end{aligned}$$

Its reduced form is given by

$$(R^+) \qquad Y^+ = W\Pi^+ + V^+,$$

where $Y^+ = (Y_2, \ldots, Y_g)$. Restricting (R^+) to $Y_{(1)}$, which is part of Y^+, we get

$$Y_{(1)} = W\Pi_{(1)} + V_{(1)}$$

with $\Pi_{(1)}$ a submatrix of Π^+ corresponding to $Y_{(1)}$.

To this equation now add the first equation of (M), which we had dropped before. The resulting system

$$(M_1) \qquad \begin{aligned} Y_1 &= Y_{(1)}B_1 + X_1\Gamma_1 + U_1 \\ Y_{(1)} &= W\Pi_{(1)} + V_{(1)} \end{aligned}$$

is analogous to $(\bar{M})$ with the reduced form

$$(R_1) \qquad \begin{aligned} Y_1 &= W\Pi_1 + V_1 \\ Y_{(1)} &= W\Pi_{(1)} + V_{(1)}, \end{aligned}$$

which is identical to the reduced form (R) restricted to $(Y_1, Y_{(1)})$. Now let $\tilde{\Pi}^+$ and $\hat{\Pi}^+$ be the OLS and RLS estimates of Π^+, respectively, where $\tilde{\Pi}^+$ is computed from (R^+) and $\hat{\Pi}^+$ from (M^+) or (M), which is the same, and let $\tilde{\Pi}_1$ and $\check{\Pi}_1$ be the OLS and RLS estimates of Π_1, respectively, where $\tilde{\Pi}_1$ is computed from (R_1) and $\check{\Pi}_1$ from (M_1) by using the OLS estimate $\tilde{\Pi}_{(1)}$. If instead of $\tilde{\Pi}_{(1)}$ the RLS estimate of $\Pi_{(1)}$, $\hat{\Pi}_{(1)}$, were used, the resulting estimate of Π_1 would be $\hat{\Pi}_1$, which is identical with the RLS estimate of Π_1 as computed from (M)[5] Now, by the induction hypothesis and since $A_2, \ldots, A_g$ are nonsingular, $\tilde{\Pi}^+ = \hat{\Pi}^+$ and consequently $\tilde{\Pi}_{(1)} = \hat{\Pi}_{(1)}$. By Corollary 1, since A_1 is nonsingular, $\tilde{\Pi}_1 = \check{\Pi}_1$, but because $\tilde{\Pi}_{(1)} = \hat{\Pi}_{(1)}$, we have $\check{\Pi}_1 = \hat{\Pi}_1$ and hence $\tilde{\Pi}_1 = \hat{\Pi}_1$. Since $\Pi = (\Pi_1, \Pi^+)$, we ultimately find that $\tilde{\Pi} = \hat{\Pi}$.$\diamond$

6 Conclusions

We proved the asymptotic efficiency of the OLS estimator of the reduced form of a recursive system as compared to its RLS estimator, which is computed by first estimating each equation of the recursive model by OLS and then solving for the endogenous variables. Both estimators have the same asymptotic covariance matrix if, and only if, the estimators themselves coincide, and this is the case if, and only if, each equation of the recursive model has essentially the same set of exogenous variables (more precisely: the matrices of the exogenous variables have the same column space).

When the recursive system consists of just two equations, explicit expressions for the asymptotic covariance matrices of the OLS and RLS estimators can be derived. This special case provides an important intermediate step in the proof of the corresponding results for the general recursive system.

---

[5]The various estimates mentioned above are $\tilde{\Pi} = (\tilde{\Pi}_1, \tilde{\Pi}^+) = (W'W)^{-1}W'(Y_1, Y^+)$, $\hat{\Pi} = (\hat{\Pi}_1, \hat{\Pi}^+) =$ RLS estimate of Π from (M), $\check{\Pi}_1 = \tilde{\Pi}_{(1)}\hat{B}_1 + A_1\hat{\Gamma}_1$, $\hat{\Pi}_1 = \hat{\Pi}_{(1)}\hat{B}_1 + A_1\hat{\Gamma}_1$, $\tilde{\Pi}_{(1)} = (W'W)^{-1}W'Y_{(1)}$, $\hat{\Pi}_{(1)} =$ submatrix of $\hat{\Pi}^+$ corresponding to $Y_{(1)}$.

It is interesting to note that similar results can be proved for the small sample covariance matrices of the OLS and RLS estimators, Kozák (1988), Schneeweiss (1989).

Appendix

The proof of Theorem 1 relies on a conditionality argument which in turn is based on the following lemma. I owe the rather general formulation of the lemma and its proof to P. Schönfeld, who came up with it in the discussion of this paper.

Lemma: Let $\{X_T\}$ and $\{Y_T\}$, $T = 1, 2, \ldots$, be two series of $p-$ and $q-$ dimensional random vectors all defined on the same probability space $(\Omega, \mathcal{F}, P)$ and let $\{\mathcal{F}_T\}$ be a series of sub σ-algebras of $\mathcal{F}$. Let P and Q be probability distributions on $\mathbb{R}^p$ and $\mathbb{R}^q$. Suppose the following conditions are satisfied:

(i) X_T is $\mathcal{F}_T$ measurable,

(ii) $X_T \xrightarrow{d} P$,

(iii) $Y_T|\mathcal{F}_T \xrightarrow{d} Q$ almost surely.

Then

$$(X_T, Y_T) \xrightarrow{d} P \times Q$$

Proof: Let F and G be the distribution functions of P and Q and let x and y be continuity points of F and G, respectively. Let $A_T = \{\omega | X_T(\omega) \leq x\}$ and $B_T = \{\omega | Y_T(\omega) \leq y\}$ and let I_A be the indicator function of $A \subset \Omega$. We have to prove that $P(A_T \cap B_T)$ converges to $F(x)G(y)$. Now,

$$\begin{aligned} P(A_T \cap B_T) \quad - \quad & F(x)G(y) = E(I_{AT} I_{BT}) - F(x)G(y) \\ &= E[E(I_{AT} I_{BT} | \mathcal{F}_T)] - F(x)G(y) \\ &= E[I_{AT} E(I_{BT} | \mathcal{F}_T)] - F(x)G(y) \qquad \text{because of (i)} \\ &= E[I_{AT}\{E(I_{BT}|\mathcal{F}_T) - G(y)\}] + G(y)[E I_{AT} - F(x)]. \end{aligned}$$

Both terms of the last line converge to zero, the first one because of (iii) and by Lebesgue's bounded convergence theorem, the second term because of (ii).◊

In the proof of Theorem 1 X_T and Y_T correspond to $\sqrt{T}(\hat{\gamma}_2 - \gamma_2)$ and $\sqrt{T}(\hat{\delta} - \delta)$, respectively, and $\mathcal{F}_T$ is the σ-algebra generated by $\{z_t\}$ and is the same for all T. (Alternatively we could have taken $\mathcal{F}_T$ as the σ-algebra generated by $(z_1, \ldots, z_T)$, i.e. by Z). P and Q are both normal distributions.

References

[1] Court, R.H. (1973), *Efficient estimation of the reduced form from incomplete econometric models*, Review of Economic Studies 40, 411–417.

[2] Dhrymes, P.J. (1973), *Restricted and unrestricted reduced forms: Asymptotic distribution and relative efficiency*, Econometrica 41, 119–134.

[3] Goldberger, A.S., A.L. Nagar, and H.S. Odeh (1961), *The covariance matrix of reduced form coefficients and of forecasts for a structural econometric model*, Econometrica 29, 556–573.

[4] Kakwani, N.C. and R.H. Court (1972), *Reduced-form coefficient estimation and forecasting from a simultaneous equation model*, Australian Journal of Statistics 14, 143–160.

[5] Kosák, J. (1988), *Application of Demidenko's approach to the solution of the prediction problem*, Economicko–Matematický Obzor 24, 68–80.

[6] Knight, J.L. (1977), *On the existence of moments of the partially restricted reduced form estimators from a simultaneous-equation model*, Journal of Econometrics 5, 315–322.

[7] Mc Carthy, M. (1981), *A note on the moments of partially restricted reduced forms*, Journal of Econometrics 17, 383–388.

[8] Mosbaek, E.J. and H. Wold (eds.)(1969), *Interdependent Systems. Structure and Estimation*, Amsterdam London: North–Holland Publ. Co.

[9] Nagar, A.L. and S. Sahay (1978), *The bias and mean squared error of forecasts from partially restricted reduced forms*, Journal of Econometrics 7, 227–244.

[10] Sant, D. (1978), *Partially restricted reduced forms: Asymptotic relative efficiency*, International Economic Review 19, 739–748.

[11] Schneeweiss, H. (1989), *The reduced form of recursive models: Small sample results*, Paper presented at the European Meeting of the Econometric Society in Munich.

[12] Swamy, P. and J. Mehta (1981), *On the existence of moments of partially restricted reduced form estimators: A comment*, Journal of Econometrics 17, 389–392.

[13] Wold, H. in association with Lars Juréen (1953), *Demand Analysis. A Study in Econometrics*, Stockholm: Almquist and Wiksell, New York: John Wiley and Sons.

[14] Wold, H. (1964), *Econometric Model Building*, Amsterdam: North–Holland Publ. Co.

Part II: Economic Applications

Testing the Stationary Search Model*

Christoph M. Schmidt
(SELAPO, University of Munich and CEPR, London)

1. Introduction

This paper uses tight parametric assumptions to model individual unemployment histories and confronts the resulting structural form with data from the Federal Republic of Germany. It thereby provides favorable evidence for the usefulness of models that deviate from the familiar reduced form approach in an attempt to give more economic structure to the analysis of individual unemployment spell durations. It follows the work of Kiefer and Neumann (1979), Lancaster and Chesher (1984), Lancaster (1985), and,

---

*This paper is a revised version of the first chapter of my doctoral dissertation at Princeton University. Financial support by the Industrial Relations Section, Princeton University, and by the Alfred P. Sloan Foundation for its Doctoral Dissertation Fellowship is gratefully acknowledged. Preliminary versions of this paper have been presented at the Princeton Labor Lunch series and at the EEA meeting in Lisbon, 1990. I thank Orley Ashenfelter, Angus Deaton, Richard Quandt, Klaus F. Zimmermann and in particular David Card for many helpful suggestions and advice. The analyzed data set was provided by the Zentralarchiv für Empirische Sozialforschung, Köln.

more recently, Jones (1988). The model allows derivation of the same log-linear simultaneous equation representation for elapsed durations and reservation wages of currently unemployed individuals and for completed durations and accepted wages of re-employed individuals.

Apart from constant terms the coefficients estimated for both groups of individuals should be identical. Jones (1988) provides estimates for a sample of unemployed individuals, but at the present time there is no evidence on the behavior of the model when data on both re-employed and unemployed individuals from the same environment are used. Here the model is estimated on subsamples of unemployed and re-employed individuals. At the present stage, emphasis is given to the qualitative robustness of the estimation results across these subsamples, not to the formulation of formal tests.

The paper is organized as follows. Section 2 introduces the model and derives the estimable log-linear specification first for currently unemployed individuals and then for re-employed individuals and discusses the issue of identification. Section 3 describes the data set and the variables used in the analysis. Section 4 discusses the appropriate econometric techniques, presents the estimation results and investigates their implications for the validity of the proposed model. Finally, section 5 sketches the limits of the analysis and possible improvements.

2. The Model

Suppose that the environment facing an unemployed individual is characterized by stationarity in the sense that he searches for a new job by drawing from a known offer distribution $F(w)$ according to a constant arrival rate, where wages w completely characterize jobs and the searcher is facing an infinite horizon. In particular, unemployment insurance (UI) benefits are paid indefinitely, a new job will last forever, and there is no uncertainty regarding economic variables. Moreover, think of only two states being possible, unemployment and employment, and ignore the possibility of leaving from unemployment into non-participation.

It is well known (see e.g. Lippman and McCall, 1976) that in this situation the individual's optimal policy is to reject all offers below a certain wage r, the reservation wage, and to accept all offers exceeding r. This reservation wage is constant over time, since in each instant of time the unemployed worker faces the same optimization problem. This has implications for the stochastic nature of the duration of the individual's unemployment spell: The probability of leaving unemployment in a short interval $(t, t+\delta t)$, conditional on still being unemployed at t, is also constant.

More formally, let the probability that a job offer arrives in the interval $(t, t+\delta t)$ be $\mu \cdot \delta t$, with μ being a constant, and consider the probability that a given offer exceeds the reservation wage r, $1-F(r)$. Then the probability of receiving and accepting a job offer in that interval is

$$\pi(r) \cdot \delta t = \mu \cdot (1-F(r)) \cdot \delta t \tag{1}$$

The constant $\pi(r) = \mu \cdot (1-F(r))$ is the *hazard rate*, which completely describes the stochastic properties of the underlying random variable *spell duration*. In a homogeneous population, specification of $F(.)$ as a parametric function would specify the form of $\pi(r)$ and thus would already suffice to yield an estimable model. In this paper I follow the example of Lancaster (1985) and Jones (1988) and postulate that arriving job offers follow a *Pareto distribution*. This distribution has a positive probability density only for values exceeding a certain cutoff value w^0 and its probability density function (pdf.) is given by

$$f(w) = \frac{\phi}{w} \cdot \left(\frac{w^0}{w} \right)^{\phi} \tag{2}$$

where $\phi > 0$ and $w > w^0$. Its coefficient of variation is $(\phi^2 - 2\phi)^{-1/2}$. The hazard rate can be written as

$$\pi(r) = \mu \cdot \left(\frac{w^0}{r} \right)^{\phi} \tag{3}$$

This hazard displays a constant elasticity with respect to the chosen reservation wage, $-\phi$. Constancy of the hazard implies that the duration of completed spells t, conditional on the chosen reservation wage r, is distributed exponentially with pdf. $g(t|r) = \pi(r) \cdot \exp(-\pi(r) \cdot t)$, which in the light of the given specification for $F(.)$ is

$$g(t|r) = \mu \cdot \left(\frac{w^0}{r} \right)^{\phi} \cdot \exp\left(-\mu \cdot \left(\frac{w^0}{r} \right)^{\phi} \cdot t \right) \tag{4}$$

Individual or match-specific heterogeneity provides a justification of the existence of a wage offer distribution as opposed to a single equilibrium wage. In a parametric reduced form model that captures individual differences in a proportional hazard, $\pi(r)$ would directly be taken as a function of exogenous variables. Here it is decomposed into two parts in order to enable us to focus on the relationship between reservation wages and durations directly.

It is assumed that the individuals' wage offer distributions given the reservation wage differ systematically according to measured personal characteristics, as captured in a vector of variables X, a conformable parameter vector β and a mean-zero error term u with variance σ_u^2 whose distribution does not depend on the observables X, and that reservation wages themselves vary systematically according to observable variables Z, a conformable parameter vector α and a mean-zero error term ε_2 with a given variance σ_2^2. In effect one can write

$$\mu \cdot (w^0)^{\phi} = \exp(X'\beta + u) \tag{5}$$

$$r = \exp(Z'\alpha + \varepsilon_2) \tag{6}$$

One of the main lessons of the literature on parametric models of unemployment duration is that the proper likelihood function for a sample of unemployment spells has to take into account whether the observations are on elapsed or completed spells, and how the individuals have been selected into the sample. This means in particular that in a situation where we have two samples of observations, say unemployed and re-employed workers, the derived estimates for both samples should be mutually compatible. The approach taken by this paper is to derive the estimable structure following from the model proposed above for unemployed and re-employed individuals, and to compare the estimation results across these samples.

Consider first the situation where we observe unemployment spells in progress and reported reservation wages. If the behavior of the inflow into unemployment is stable enough to assume that a spell is equally likely to start at any time and its elapsed duration at survey time is drawn from the same distribution regardless of the beginning of the spell (see Salant, 1977), we can interpret elapsed duration as the backwards recurrence time of the process (see Cox, 1962). Thus, if one samples randomly from the population of currently unemployed individuals, one can express the distribution of elapsed spell durations s at sampling time in terms of the distribution of completed spells.

In the specific case of the exponential distribution, elapsed durations are also distributed exponentially with hazard $\pi(X,r) = \exp(X'\beta + u)\cdot r^{-\phi}$ for a given reservation wage r, which is the same distribution as the distribution of completed spells. Since the moment generating function of $\log s$ is

$$M(q) = E(s^{q}) = \int_0^\infty u^{q}\cdot\pi(X,r)\cdot\exp(-\pi(X,r)\cdot u) = \frac{\Gamma(q+1)}{\pi(X,r)^{q}} \tag{7}$$

the derivative (evaluated at $q = 0$) of the cumulant generating function, i.e. of $K(q) = \log\Gamma(q+1) - q\cdot\log\pi(X,r)$, will yield the expectation of the logarithm of elapsed spell duration $\log s$ as

$$E(\log s\,|\,\pi(X,r)) = \frac{\Gamma'(1)}{\Gamma(1)} - \log\pi(X,r) \tag{8}$$

and, because the value of the digamma function $\Gamma'(s)/\Gamma(s)$ at $s=1$ equals the negative of Euler's constant, -0.5772, we have

$$E(\log s\,|X,r) = -0.5772 + \phi\cdot\log r - X'\beta - E(u\,|X,r) \tag{9}$$

Adding a mean-zero error term ε_1 capturing the unsystematic deviation of an observed random variable from its expectation gives the complete equation for $\log s$. Since $\log s$ follows an extreme-value distribution, the variance of ε_1 is given by $\sigma_1^2 = 1.6449$. In addition, ε_1 is uncorrelated with ε_2. Together with the postulated reservation wage equation

$$\log r = Z'\alpha + \varepsilon_2 \tag{6a}$$

we have a system of two recursive equations, with possible simultaneity introduced by correlation of the error terms u and ε_2.

Consider now the situation where we randomly select observations on completed spells and accepted wages in the new job. This situation will arise whenever one selects randomly out of the population of those leaving their spell of unemployment during a fixed time-interval, if the inflow into unemployment satisfies the stability properties mentioned above. Here we don't have to rely on the cancellation of interruption and length bias due to the assumption of an underlying exponential distribution as for elapsed durations, but on the other hand we can't observe the individual reservation wages directly.

Instead we observe the realization of a random variable accepted wage $\tilde{w}$, whose distribution is the distribution of the offered wage w conditional on this offer being higher than the reservation wage r. The pdf. of observed accepted wages is

$$h(\tilde{w}) = f(\tilde{w} \mid \tilde{w} > r) = \frac{f(\tilde{w})}{1 - F(r)} \tag{10}$$

Note in particular that the probability of observing a high accepted wage is time-independent because of the constancy of the reservation wage: longer spells make it more likely for many offers to arrive, but given that no previous offer exceeded the reservation wage, any new arriving offer is independent of these previous draws. From the discussion above, the completed spell duration t is distributed exponentially with pdf. $g(t) = \pi(X,r) \cdot \exp(-\pi(X,r) \cdot t)$. Following the previous argument we get

$$E(\log t \mid X,r) = -0.5772 + \phi \cdot \log r - X'\beta - E(u \mid X,r) \tag{11}$$

From the moment generating function of $\log \tilde{w}$,

$$M(q) = E(\tilde{w}^{q}) = \int_{r}^{\infty} \tilde{w}^{q} \cdot \frac{f(\tilde{w})}{1 - F(r))} d\tilde{w} = \frac{\phi}{\phi - q} \cdot r^{q} \tag{12}$$

we can derive the expectation of $\log \tilde{w}$ as the derivative of the cumulant generating function $K(q) = \log \phi - \log (\phi - q) + q \cdot \log r$ (evaluated at $q = 0$), and therefore

$$E(\log \tilde{w} \,|\, r) = \frac{1}{\phi} + \log r \tag{14}$$

This relation can also be expressed in terms of observable determinants of the reservation wage as

$$E(\log \tilde{w} \,|\, Z) = \frac{1}{\phi} + Z'\alpha \tag{14a}$$

Adding the mean zero error term τ with variance σ_τ^2, multiplying this equation by ϕ and subtracting it from the expected duration equation yields for the expected unemployment duration

$$E(\log t \,|\, \tilde{w},X) = -1.5772 + \phi \cdot \log \tilde{w} - X'\beta - E(u \,|\, \tilde{w},X) \tag{15}$$

In effect we find a log-linear simultaneous equation model with identical coefficients for completed spells and accepted wages in the case of re-employed individuals and for elapsed spells and reservation wages in the case of unemployed individuals, apart from constants and error terms.

The reservation wage equation is already a reduced form and identification of the duration equation is ensured by exclusion restrictions if the following argument holds. Any variables in X influencing the wage offer distribution also have an influence on the reservation wage chosen by a rational decision maker, and should therefore be included in Z, but not necessarily vice versa. If we succeed in finding at least one variable which influences the individuals' reservation wage choice while leaving the offer distribution unaffected, the first equation is identified. Natural candidates are variables relating to the cost of search like the number of dependent children or the level of unemployment support. The empirical part of this paper discusses several different choices.

3. Data and Sampling

The analyzed data were provided by the Zentralarchiv für Empirische Sozialforschung, Universität Köln. The survey was initiated by the Bundesminister für Arbeit und Sozialordnung, Federal Republic of Germany, and covers 2873 individuals. The actual interviews were conducted orally in February 1978 following prespecified questionnaires. 1637 of the respondents were chosen out of the population of those registered as unemployed as of November 1977 and 1236 individuals were chosen out of the population of those leaving the official unemployment register in a two week period in September/October 1977. All respondents were German citizens living in one of 25 regions in the Federal Republic of Germany which were selected as representative by the Bundesanstalt für Arbeit.

The data set provides extensive information on the individuals' demographic characteristics and their history in the labor market, in particular on their education, their previous position, and, if re-employed at survey date, their current position. All searching individuals were asked what minimum net monthly earnings they would require in order to induce them to take an offered position. In what follows their answer to this question is interpreted as their reservation wage. All analysis of "unemployed individuals" in this paper refers to those individuals that are registered as unemployed and claim to be actually searching for a job in order to avoid the problems arising from the apparent misstatement of unemployment in administrative data.

Here I concentrate on two subsamples of individuals. The first subsample contains 944 individuals that left the unemployment register during the sampling interval (September/October 1977) and were still employed at survey time (February 1978). The second subsample contains

573 individuals that were selected into the sample as unemployed in November 1977 and were still found unemployed at the time of the survey (February 1978). For the first group we have information on completed spells, for the latter group on elapsed spells at sampling time. Therefore, one can view these sample definitions as an attempt to recreate the information available at sampling time.

Several caveats have to be kept in mind, however. The derivation of the estimable structure for both subsamples rests on the assumptions on the stability of the inflow described above. Furthermore the sample definitions used necessarily discard potentially useful information. For example, some of those individuals included in the sample as unemployed in November 1977 have found a job by the time of the survey in February 1978. In this paper I make no attempt to analyze these individuals. The underlying assumption of exponential spells implies that there is no sample selection bias caused by the omission of this group in the analysis.

Similarly, no use is made of information on the length of individuals' employment spell durations following the transition into employment. Potentially the durations of employment and unemployment spells are linked, and this information may be important. Finally, monetary variables, in particular previous wages, have not been adjusted for inflation. Note, however, that due to underlying assumption of the constancy of reservation wages, the reservation wages at the time of the survey and those at the time of the interviews have necessarily to be the same.

Not all individuals included in the analyzed data set could actually be used in the investigation. I decided to eliminate all those individuals who had not been employed at some point in their lives, since for them no information on previous earnings - presumably our main indicator for the mean of the appropriate offer distribution - was available. Furthermore all handicapped individuals were excluded, since their treatment in the labor market is heavily influenced by federal laws (Ausgleichsabgabe). Finally, I excluded all persons who own a farm as source of additional earnings or who had been self-employed in their previous job, since their search behavior is difficult to interpret. A third group of excluded individuals are the nonparticipants, a fourth group are those re-employed individuals who returned to their previous employer after their unemployment spell, and a fifth group are those unemployed individuals waiting to start in a particular job.

Finally the exclusion of a sixth group was dictated by the choice of the wage variables: since I decided to use net monthly earnings I had to exclude all those individuals exclusively looking for part-time jobs, and I could not use those unemployed individuals who did not have a clear idea about their reservation wage. (942 individuals in the original data set stated to have a clear idea about the minimum net earnings envisaged, but asked for this amount 32 of them answered "don't know" and 14 didn't answer. Of the 453 individuals saying that they didn't have a very clear idea about minimum earnings, 337 actually stated an amount. I decided to retain all individuals in the data set who stated an amount, irrespective of their answer to the first question.) Moreover, all individuals with missing values for any of the relevant variables were excluded. As a result of these exclusions 374 individuals were left in the sample of re-employed workers, and 378 individuals were left in the sample of unemployed workers.

Table 1 reports descriptive statistics for the variables used in the empirical analysis. The logarithm of the *duration of the last* (elapsed or completed) *unemployment spell* in months at sampling time was slightly higher for individuals sampled from the stock of unemployed workers who were still found unemployed at survey time than for the flow of workers leaving the unemployment registers at sampling time. The logarithm of actual *net monthly earnings* in the current position (1209 DM) are, on average, lower than minimum acceptable net monthly earnings for unemployed individuals (1237 DM). Thus, the group of re-employed workers displays, on average, also lower reservation wages, since accepted wages are bounded from below by reservation wages.

Generally, workers in the unemployed sample tend to have lower education levels than those in the re-employed sample. *Years of schooling* display half a year difference, and there is an about 10 percentage point difference in the realization of an indicator for completed *vocational training* (apprenticeship or other). Three indicators of *labor market experience* document that re-employed workers have generally lower experience and an indicator for *mutiple unemployment spells* in the last 5 years preceding the survey shows that the experience of multiple unemployment spells is shared by only a fifth of the re-employed workers, but by almost a third of the unemployed workers.

Variables describing the *previous job* demonstrate that unemployed individuals had slightly lower *net monthly earnings* (1184 DM vs. 1197 DM), and that previous earnings were more dispersed for re-employed individuals. Unemployed workers also had a relatively low *tenure* in their previous job. Moreover, unemployed respondents worked more frequently in a position with low *qualification requirements* and the *job termination* was also more likely to be initiated by the employer.

Both samples display no difference in the sex distribution (about 53% male), but unemployed workers are, on average, 4 years *older*. Re-employed individuals are more likely to be *married*. The *number of children* below 14 years of age is higher for unemployed individuals and, thus, married unemployed workers tend to have more children.

Variables capturing the individuals' *financial situation* are an indicator for *eligibility for* the full amount of *unemployment insurance (UI) benefits* at the time the unemployment spell commenced and an indicator for *renting an apartment*. Both variables do not display differences in sample averages. In the Federal Republic of Germany unemployment benefits can only be collected when the individual registers as unemployed and basically take two different forms. If the unemployed individual is eligible for unemployment support (Arbeitslosengeld) he or she receives roughly 68% of average net earnings obtained before the start of the unemployment spell (this amount varies with the number of dependent children from 63% to 70%, and there exists an upper limit) for a time period which depends on the time he or she contributed to the insurance.

If the unemployed individual contributed to the unemployment insurance fund within the year preceding unemployment and does not qualify for Arbeitslosengeld or already has exhausted benefits, he or she is eligible for unemployment help (Arbeitslosenhilfe) which amounts to 58% of average net earnings in the period preceding unemployment. Individuals not qualifying for these types of unemployment benefits may receive welfare (Sozialhilfe), which is administered by a different government agency (Sozialamt). In addition to the described benefits the Arbeitsamt uses other kinds of financial benefits to support unemployed workers, like Winterhilfe, Überbrückungsgeld or the payment of training costs.

A remarkable pattern emerges in the analyzed data set. Only roughly 10% of the individuals finally contained in the analyzed data set did not receive the highest type of support, Arbeitslosengeld, when their spell commenced and only roughly another 10% had switched to the lower type of support, Arbeitslosenhilfe, during their spell. Only very few persons started out with Arbeitslosenhilfe, and all the other types of support (welfare, health insurance payments, additional payments by the employment agency) hardly played any role. Because of this extensive coverage, one can expect high multicollinearity in a regression involving the amount of support paid and net monthly earnings in the previous job, and this consideration lead to the choice of the simple measure described.

4. Empirical Results

The presentation of the empirical results concentrates on two issues. First, the system of equations is estimated for the two different subsamples. The main emphasis is given to the question of the robustness of the estimation results. Second, the validity of the underlying model is discussed in the light of these estimates. No formal tests for the equality of coefficients across subsamples are presented, although this is a subject for further research. The model and its variance structure are summarized in **Table 2**. The variance structure determines the appropriate choice of the estimation procedure for the system of equations.

By construction the error term τ in the (accepted) wage equation for re-employed individuals is uncorrelated with all observable exogenous variables Z, and similarly the error term ε_1 in the duration equation is uncorrelated with X and with the reservation wage r or the accepted wage $\tilde{w}$, respectively. By assumption any correlation between the observables X and the error terms u (in the re-employment hazard) and ε_2 (in the reservation wage equation), respectively, was excluded when relationships (5) and (6) were imposed. It is the possible non-zero covariance between ε_2 and u which requires some further thought.

Consider first the case where the covariance between ε_2 and u is zero. Here both the wage equation and the duration equation can be estimated consistently by performing Least Squares (LS) for each equation separately. LS estimates of the coefficients of the wage equation are reported in **Table 3**, LS estimates of the duration equation are presented in **Table 4**.

If there exists a nonzero correlation between ε_2 and u, the LS estimation of the duration equation turns out to be problematic. One scenario that argues for a positive correlation between the two error terms is the case where both potential employers and searching individuals observe an individual characteristic, unobserved by the econometrician, whose presence moves the respective wage offer distribution towards higher offers (positive u) and therefore influences the choice of the reservation wage in an upward direction (positive ε_2). A simple example could be the tendency to leave a good impression in interviews. In this case the reservation wage r, and thus the accepted wage $\tilde{w}$, will be negatively correlated with the error term in the duration equation and we can expect the estimate of ϕ to be downward biased.

In order to investigate the presence of this problem and to assess the size of a potential bias the duration equation was estimated by Two Stage Least Squares (2SLS). The results are reported in **Table 5**. Note that the LS estimates of the wage equation presented in Table 3 are identical to estimates derived by 2SLS, since the wage equation is already a reduced form. On a different note one might argue that a system estimator possibly improves the efficiency of the estimates. This consideration is not pursued here, but one should keep in mind that the special structure of the considered system of equations will introduce a specific type of heteroskedasticity whose properties should be incorporated into a system approach.

Finally, the choice of exclusion restrictions made in order to enable identification of the duration equation has to be discussed. I always excluded the indicator for living in a rented apartment and the number of children from the duration equation, in a first set of estimations alone, and in a second set together with the indicator of the extent of unemployment support. The wage equations were estimated with and without the measure of the previous wage included as a regressor. The latter specification should allow better comparison with studies that are based on data sets that do not provide information on previous wages.

Turning first to the estimated wage equations presented in Table 3, one can observe that both specifications seem to explain the formation of wages quite well. In general, specifications for reservation wages (columns (3) and (4)) show R^2 statistics a bit higher than for accepted wages (columns (1) and (2)). This fact is totally in accordance with the idea that accepted wages are influenced by an additional source of randomness. For both samples inclusion of monthly earnings in the previous job increases the explanatory power of the regression dramatically, and, in general, the magnitudes of all other regressors increase by a sizeable factor upon exclusion of previous earnings.

Looking at education, years of schooling and the indicator for completed vocational training both have significantly positive effects on the formation of reservation wages, but the latter is consistently insignificant for the wages of re-employed individuals. Moving to the individuals' history in the labor market, the time spent in the workforce should increase the available wage offers and thus reservation and accepted wages. Indeed the estimated coefficients increase with one minor exception with the extent of experience. However, for the first two dummies they tend to be insignificant and to start off negatively for the specifications including previous earnings.

Experience measures are inevitably correlated with age, and these somewhat disappointing results might be due to problems of multicollinearity.

Having had multiple unemployment spells tends to decrease reservation wages, but not significantly. The effect on accepted wages is also insignificant, but here the sign tends to be positive. The erratic behavior of this coefficient is not too surprising and will be discussed below together with its impact on spell durations. If tenure in the old position predominantly captures the amount by which previous earnings were induced by firm specific human capital, we would expect the coefficients of the three tenure indicators to be negative and decreasing. In fact, the behavior of the estimates is not totally unproblematic. In the majority of cases the coefficients are insignificant and the sign of the changes is contrary to the argument provided.

The indicator for unskilled work in the previous job turns out to be an excellent predictor for wages. Both accepted and reservation wages are significantly lower for those workers who previously held an unskilled position. Reservation wages also decrease significantly with the indicator capturing the reason for the last job termination, but for accepted wages the effect of this variable is insignificant and even positive. It seems that employers do not weigh the reason for termination as a signal, although individuals seem to expect that. It would be interesting to compare this finding with data from another time period when aggregate labor market conditions were different.

As to the group of demographic characteristics we see that age influences the reservation wage choice in the nonlinear fashion typically observed in earnings functions with a significantly positive linear effect and a significantly negative effect of the squared term that is of smaller order. Being male has a strong and significant positive effect, but it is somewhat puzzling to find married individuals with significantly lower wages, in particular since married individuals should be aware of the tax advantages they face and both reservation and accepted wages are expressed in net monthly earnings. One should keep in mind, however, that the labor supply decisions of the partner are not incorporated into the analysis. Reservation wages significantly increase with the number of children, whereas one might rather expect individuals to lower reservation wages since the presence of dependent children should make it more urgent to find a new job. Accepted wages, on the other hand, do not show this pattern.

Moving finally to the variables describing the individals' financial situation, the effect of living in an apartment is significantly positive, which could be explained by credit constraints imposed on houseowners. The coefficient of the indicator of reception of unemployment support to the full extent is insignificant and interestingly changes signs whenever one compares the same specification across sample definitions. One could argue, however, that the bad statistical performance of this regressor is unsurprising given the very high fraction of individuals in the data receiving the highest level of UI benefits.

One of the main implications of the theoretical model is the equality of coefficients across sub-samples of re-employed and unemployed individuals. As a general observation, several point estimates are quite different in magnitude and some show even different signs. It turns out, however, that these coefficients tend to be estimated relatively imprecisely. Overall the estimated coefficients seem to reveal the same causal relationships for both accepted and reservation wages.

The performance of the LS and 2SLS estimations of the duration equation turns out to be quite poor relative to that of the wage equation. Turning first to the LS estimates presented in Table 4 a few observations suffice. The R^2 statistics of all regressions are very low, although for most variables the behavior of the estimated coefficients is stable across samples. In general, the coefficients that vary most across samples are those that were also problematic in the wage equations discussed above.

In the discussion of the results derived by 2SLS reported in Table 5, the main emphasis should be given to the behavior of the estimated coefficient of the wage variable (reservation wage or accepted wage, respectively). This coefficient should be positive and large enough to represent a reasonable variation in the wage offer distribution. If there exists a positive correlation between the error terms affecting wage offers and reservation wages, u and ε_2, we would expect OLS estimates of this coefficient to be downward biased. Indeed this is apparently true.

The OLS estimate of the wage coefficient in the elapsed duration equation (unemployed workers) is small and positive, whereas the OLS estimate of the wage coefficient in the completed duration equation (re-employed) is actually negative. By comparison, the 2SLS estimates of these coefficients reported in Table 5 are uniformly positive and significant. They are of an order of magnitude sufficient to imply coefficients of variation of the wage offer distribution as small as 0.45 for unemployed workers.

This pattern confirms the earlier finding of Jones (1988) based on a sample of unemployed individuals. Moreover, the results are very similar for both re-employed and unemployed respondents. There are sizable differences in the magnitude of point estimates, however. Estimates for completed spells imply larger coefficients of variation of the wage offer distribution of up to 1.25. These results seem to reflect the additional source of randomness incorporated in accepted wages in contrast to reservation wages.

The negative coefficients of the variables capturing differences in education are quite weak both for elapsed and completed spells. While wage offers appear to be shifted by educational attainment, reservation wages reflect the variation in opportunities and there is at best at tendency to shorter spells for more educated individuals. Again the imprecision of the estimated experience coefficients suggests the presence of multicollinearity with age and will not be discussed further.

Different arguments can be offered to explain the large and significant negative effect of the indicator for multiple spells in the past that is observed for unemployed workers. In general, it will be difficult to distinguish between individuals who have been fired (frequently) in the past and individuals who changed firms (frequently) to enhance their career on the basis of the number of unemployment spells alone. Given the extensive coverage of the unemployment insurance system discussed above, there is an incentive to register as unemployed even for a relatively short spell. If multiple unemployment spells are a stigma, the individual might lower reservation wages considerably. In this case, however, one might have found a bigger negative effect of multiple spells in the estimates of the wage equation. An alternative explanation is that the experience of previous unemployment spells provides individuals with an advantage in searching.

The level of previous earnings significantly decreases spell duration for the unemployed workers. There are signs of multicollinearity between minimum acceptable earnings and previous earnings visible in these results, however, since their coefficients tend to outweigh each other. The coefficients of the tenure variables are estimated quite imprecisely, whereas having previously held an unskilled job turns out to be a good predictor of spell lengths for unemployed workers. The positive coefficient of the indicator for job termination by the employer is far more important for unemployed than for re-employed workers, but it is insignificant for both samples, similar to the results for the wage equations.

Men experience shorter unemployment spells, but this difference is only consistently significant for the re-employed sample. Age insignificantly influences spell duration in a nonlinear fashion, with a positive coefficient for age and a negative coefficient of smaller order for squared age. The effect of marital status is inconclusive, but it tends to decrease the length of elapsed spells, and to significantly increase that of completed spells. Finally, eligibility for UI benefits is estimated to significantly increase spell length for re-employed individuals, but to significantly decrease it for unemployed individuals.

Regarding the R^2 statistics the estimations based on observations of elapsed spells seem to have more explanatory power, but although completed spells in principle provide more information, the necessity to use accepted wages instead of reservation wages might explain this behavior. For all specifications the overidentifying restrictions were tested by Basmann's F - Test and the null hypothesis that the instruments are mutually consistent could never be rejected. For comparison, the respective 5% critical values given degrees of freedom n1 and n2=400 are: $F_{n1,400} = F_{1,400} = 3.86$ and for $F_{n1,400} = F_{2,400} = 3.02$. In the estimations it does not seem to matter whether the indicator of receiving unemployment benefits to the full extent is actually used as an instrument or not. This seems to indicate that in an unemployment insurance system with extensive coverage, the cost of search and consequently search behavior are mainly influenced by variables unrelated to unemployment support.

5. Concluding Remarks

This paper uses tight parametric assumptions to model individual unemployment histories in a structural form. Starting from a simple search model it is shown that individual spells are distributed exponentially with different hazard rates for heterogenous individuals. In contrast to the usual reduced form approach the choice of the reservation wage is directly incorporated into the analysis. In effect, a log-linear simultaneous equations system is derived that explains both reservation wages and elapsed spell durations of currently unemployed individuals in terms of exogenous variables. Moreover, it is demonstrated that apart from constant terms an identical structural form should be valid for accepted wages and completed spell durations for individuals who are re-employed at the time of the survey.

The empirical part of the paper uses data from the Federal Republic of Germany to estimate the parameters of this structural form both for a subsample of unemployed and a subsample of re-employed individuals. In this paper the main emphasis is given to the robustness of the estimation results across subsamples, not to the formulation of formal tests of the validity of cross-subsample restrictions. Although the results for both subsamples were remarkably similar and the model's empirical implications were not violated in an obvious way, some important differences across subsamples could be observed.

Mainly the results are reassuring, however. As a minimum this work confirms the finding that the choice of reservation wages indeed does matter for the length of individual unemployment experience and that there is a relationship between the duration of a spell and the chosen reservation wage that one cannot control for in a reduced form approach. The stable behavior of the results is especially remarkable if one realizes that not all information available in the data set has been used in the analysis.

Furthermore, this paper shows that in principle a formal test of the proposed model is possible, if one exploits the implications given by the model for different subsamples of observations in the data. This test will require proper account of the specific type of heteroskedasticity involved (possible following the approaches of Goldfeldt and Quandt, 1972, or Amemiya, 1977) and its development should be on the agenda for future work.

Despite the favorable evidence for the validity of the model one cannot overlook a few negative facts. The excellent performance of the estimated wage equations is not too surprising, given the well-documented success of empirical earnings equations. And this relationship was merely imposed, not derived out of an optimizing model. Moreover, irrespective of the estimation technique used, the duration equations perform relatively badly, even for cross-sectional data. In addition, one should note that the use of reported reservation wages for unemployed individuals as the counterpart of accepted wages for employed persons certainly requires some faith in the accuracy of the given answers.

Further extensions of this analysis model should concentrate on the treatment of unobserved heterogeneity and should allow for time-dependent reservation wages as in Lancaster(1985). A related line of work might attempt to understand the different magnitudes of the classical wage determinants like years of schooling in the different samples, possibly by allowing for different information structures for job searchers and potential employers.

Table 1: Descriptive Statistics

Variable	Re-employed	Unemployed
Sample Size	374	378
Log (Duration of Unemployment)	1.56 (0.94)	1.66 (1.02)
Log (Net Monthly Earnings)	7.00 (0.46)	7.06 (0.36)
Education:		
Years of Schooling	11.42 (1.95)	10.89 (1.74)
Vocational Training (1=yes)	81.0%	70.1%
Labor Market History:		
Experience 3 to 10 Years (1=yes)	39.9%	30.4%
Experience 10 to 20 Years (1=yes)	28.6%	28.3%
Experience over 20 Years (1=yes)	23.0%	34.7%
Multiple Unemployment Spells (1=yes)	19.8%	31.7%
Previous Job:		
Log (Net Monthly Earnings)	6.94 (0.57)	6.99 (0.42)
Tenure 1 to 3 Years (1=yes)	35.8%	24.6%
Tenure 3 to 10 Years (1=yes)	41.7%	31.7%
Tenure over 10 Years (1=yes)	6.4%	11.4%
Unqualified Work (1=yes)	49.7%	60.3%
Job Terminated by Employer (1=yes)	49.5%	62.7%
Demographics:		
Men (1=yes)	52.9%	53.7%
Age	31.34 (10.79)	35.55 (12.99)
Married (1=yes)	59.6%	54.0%
Number of Children	0.53 (0.84)	0.60 (0.98)
Financial Situation:		
Eligible for Full UI Benefits	91.7%	91.3%
Renting an Apartment (1=yes)	70.6%	69.8%

Table 2: The Model for Unemployed and Re-Employed

Re-Employed: Accepted Wages & Completed Durations:

$$\log \tilde{w} = 1/\phi + Z'\alpha + \varepsilon_2 + \tau$$

$$\log t = -1.5772 + \phi \cdot \log \tilde{w} - X'\beta - u + \varepsilon_1 - \phi \cdot \tau$$

Unemployed: Reservation Wages & Elapsed Durations:

$$\log r = + Z'\alpha + \varepsilon_2$$

$$\log s = -0.5772 + \phi \cdot \log r - X'\beta - u + \varepsilon_1$$

Covariance Structure:

$$u \sim (0, \sigma_u^2) \;,\; \varepsilon_1 \sim (0, 1.6449) \;,\; \varepsilon_2 \sim (0, \sigma_2^2) \;,\; \tau \sim (0, \sigma_\tau^2) \;,\; cov(\varepsilon_2, u) \neq 0$$

$$cov(u, \varepsilon_1) = cov(\varepsilon_1, \varepsilon_2) = cov(u, \tau) = cov(\varepsilon_1, \tau) = cov(\varepsilon_2, \tau) = 0$$

Table 3: Estimations of the Wage Equation

Variable	Re-employed		Unemployed	
	(1)	(2)	(3)	(4)
Sample Size	374	374	378	378
Education:				
Years of Schooling	0.0272**	0.0400**	0.0199**	0.0432**
	(0.0097)	(0.0105)	(0.0083)	(0.0098)
Vocational Training (1=yes)	0.0070	-0.0002	0.0787**	0.0659*
	(0.0468)	(0.0515)	(0.0303)	(0.0366)
Labor Market History:				
Experience 3 to 10 Years (1=yes)	0.0527	0.0980	-0.0961*	0.0686
	(0.0658)	(0.0722)	(0.0559)	(0.0659)
Experience 10 to 20 Years (1=yes)	0.0382	0.1107	-0.0784	0.1177
	(0.0842)	(0.0922)	(0.0752)	(0.0892)
Experience over 20 Years (1=yes)	0.2157**	0.2914**	-0.0485	0.2048**
	(0.1039)	(0.1139)	(0.0878)	(0.1038)
Multiple Unemployment Spells (1=yes)	0.0313	-0.0054	-0.0192	-0.0097
	(0.0454)	(0.0498)	(0.0290)	(0.0352)
Previous Job:				
Log (Net Monthly Earnings)	0.3241**	-	0.4670**	-
	(0.0372)		(0.0359)	
Tenure 1 to 3 Years (1=yes)	-0.0366	-0.0487	0.0368	0.0582
	(0.0496)	(0.0546)	(0.0324)	(0.0392)
Tenure 3 to 10 Years (1=yes)	-0.0294	-0.1049*	0.0381	0.0670
	(0.0537)	(0.0583)	(0.0344)	(0.0416)
Tenure over 10 Years (1=yes)	-0.0324	-0.0379	-0.0183	0.0076
	(0.0827)	(0.0910)	(0.0464)	(0.0562)
Unqualified Work (1=yes)	-0.1084**	-0.1527**	-0.0735**	-0.1350**
	(0.0361)	(0.0393)	(0.0280)	(0.0334)
Job Terminated by Employer (1=yes)	0.0076	0.0138	-0.0411*	-0.0413
	(0.0341)	(0.0376)	(0.0247)	(0.0300)
Demographics:				
Men (1=yes)	0.3225**	0.4635**	0.1573**	0.2857**
	(0.0380)	(0.0379)	(0.0277)	(0.0314)
Age	0.0018	0.0238*	0.0186**	0.0302**
	(0.0133)	(0.0144)	(0.0094)	(0.0113)
Age squared	-0.0001	-0.0004**	-0.0002**	-0.0004**
	(0.0002)	(0.0002)	(0.0001)	(0.0001)
Married (1=yes)	-0.0683*	-0.0424	-0.0441*	-0.0202
	(0.0360)	(0.0395)	(0.0259)	(0.0313)
Number of Children	-0.0275	-0.0307	0.0305**	0.0447**
	(0.0203)	(0.0224)	(0.0126)	(0.0152)

Table 3: Estimations of the Wage Equation

continued

Financial Situation:				
Eligible for Full UI Benefits	-0.0089	-0.0118	0.0155	0.0469
	(0.0593)	(0.0653)	(0.0426)	(0.0515)
Renting an Apartment (1=yes)	0.0833**	0.0961**	0.0505*	0.0675**
	(0.0356)	(0.0391)	(0.0260)	(0.0314)
Constant	4.3244**	5.9455**	3.1752**	5.7023**
	(0.2978)	(0.2560)	(0.2573)	(0.2044)
R-squared	0.5797	0.4895	0.6446	0.4768

Columns (1) and (2) report regressions of the logarithm of accepted net monthly earnings in the new job on explanatory variables for the sample of re-employed workers (equation (14a) in the text). columns (3) and (4) report regressions of the logarithm of minimum acceptable net monthly earnings (derived from the answer to the question "What are the minimum net monthly earnings you would require in order to accept a job offer?") on the same explanatory variables for the sample of unemployed workers (equation (6a) in the text). Standard errors are displayed in parentheses, a * indicates significance (two-tailed test) at the 10% level, a ** indicates significance (two-tailed test) at the 5% level.

Table 4: OLS Estimations of the Duration Equation

Variable	Re-Employed		Unemployed	
	(1)		(2)	
Sample Size	374		378	
log (Net Monthly Earnings)	-0.3296**	(0.1565)	0.2148	(0.2263)
Education:				
Years of Schooling	-0.0034	(0.0291)	-0.0037	(0.0362)
Vocational Training (1=yes)	-0.1280	(0.1390)	-0.0977	(0.1306)
Labor Market History:				
Experience 3 to 10 Years (1=yes)	0.3856**	(0.1937)	0.0043	(0.2431)
Experience 10 to 20 Years (1=yes)	0.0665	(0.2485)	-0.1788	(0.3260)
Experience over 20 Years (1=yes)	0.0674	(0.3078)	-0.5517	(0.3804)
Multiple Unemployment Spells (1=yes)	-0.0017	(0.1348)	-0.3782**	(0.1257)
Previous Job:				
Log (Net Monthly Earnings)	0.2167*	(0.1218)	-0.4078**	(0.1887)
Tenure 1 to 3 Years (1=yes)	0.1821	(0.1467)	0.1512	(0.1396)
Tenure 3 to 10 Years (1=yes)	0.2891*	(0.1594)	0.0902	(0.1475)
Tenure over 10 Years (1=yes)	0.2045	(0.2443)	-0.1024	(0.1994)
Unqualified Work (1=yes)	-0.0437	(0.1073)	0.0941	(0.1215)
Job Terminated by Employer (1=yes)	0.0804	(0.1014)	0.0923	(0.1066)
Demographics:				
Men (1=yes)	-0.1436	(0.1234)	0.0577	(0.1243)
Age	0.0747*	(0.0388)	0.1099**	(0.0407)
Age squared	-0.0008	(0.0005)	-0.0009*	(0.0005)
Married (1=yes)	0.1322	(0.1059)	-0.1883*	(0.1080)
Constant	0.6272	(1.0951)	0.8066	(1.3102)
R-squared	0.1196		0.1516	

Column (1) reports the regression of the logarithm of completed spell durations on explanatory variables, including the logarithm of accepted net monthly earnings in the new job, for the sample of re-employed workers (equation (15) in the text), column (2) reports the regression of the logarithm of elapsed spell durations on explanatory variables, including the logarithm of minimum acceptable net monthly earnings, for the sample of re-employed workers (equation (9) in the text). Standard errors are displayed in parentheses, a * indicates significance (two-tailed test) at the 10% level, a ** indicates significance (two-tailed test) at the 5% level.

Table 5: 2SLS Estimations of the Duration Equation

Variable	Re-Employed		Unemployed	
	(1)	(2)	(3)	(4)
Sample Size	374	374	378	378
log (Net Monthly Earnings)	2.2843	2.3655	3.3073*	3.4534*
	(1.4999)	(1.5165)	(1.7930)	(1.8197)
Education:				
Years of Schooling	-0.0792	-0.0823	-0.0652	-0.0714
	(0.0579)	(0.0586)	(0.0568)	(0.0577)
Vocational Training (1=yes)	-0.1398	-0.1288	-0.3058	-0.2970
	(0.1857)	(0.1878)	(0.2003)	(0.2031)
Labor Market History:				
Experience 3 to 10 Years (1=yes)	0.2207	0.1523	0.3096	0.3131
	(0.2751)	(0.2807)	(0.3469)	(0.3517)
Experience 10 to 20 Years (1=yes)	-0.0596	-0.1283	0.0698	0.1053
	(0.3396)	(0.3453)	(0.4263)	(0.4326)
Experience over 20 Years (1=yes)	-0.4738	-0.5799	-0.3738	-0.3626
	(0.5134)	(0.5222)	(0.4798)	(0.4865)
Multiple Unemployment Spells (1=yes)	-0.0727	-0.0839	-0.3119**	-0.3072*
	(0.1845)	(0.1865)	(0.1595)	(0.1617)
Previous Job:				
Log (Net Monthly Earnings)	-0.6418	-0.6671	-1.8845**	-1.9378**
	(0.5142)	(0.5199)	(0.8771)	(0.8898)
Tenure 1 to 3 Years (1=yes)	0.2642	0.2349	0.0152	0.0426
	(0.2015)	(0.2043)	(0.1888)	(0.1921)
Tenure 3 to 10 Years (1=yes)	0.3651*	0.3504	-0.0145	0.0261
	(0.2172)	(0.2197)	(0.1914)	(0.1955)
Tenure over 10 Years (1=yes)	0.3133	0.2845	-0.0096	0.0315
	(0.3322)	(0.3361)	(0.2514)	(0.2560)
Unqualified Work (1=yes)	0.2306	0.2658	0.3033	0.2998*
	(0.2118)	(0.2149)	(0.1918)	(0.1945)
Job Terminated by Employer (1=yes)	0.0689	0.0634	0.1931	0.2134
	(0.1356)	(0.1371)	(0.1435)	(0.1459)
Demographics:				
Men (1=yes)	-0.9854*	-1.0003**	-0.4319	-0.4884
	(0.5059)	(0.5114)	(0.3196)	(0.3257)
Age	0.0746	0.0845	0.0503	0.0389
	(0.0519)	(0.0527)	(0.0607)	(0.0619)
Age squared	-0.0006	-0.0007	-0.0002	-0.0001
	(0.0007)	(0.0007)	(0.0007)	(0.0007)
Married (1=yes)	0.3302*	0.3448*	-0.0953	-0.0758
	(0.1807)	(0.1828)	(0.1433)	(0.1457)

Table 5: 2SLS Estimations of the Duration Equation

continued

Eligible for Full UI Benefits (1=yes)	-	0.4231*	-	-0.3895*
		(0.2358)		(0.2300)
Constant	-10.694	-11.549*	-8.9572	-9.0163
	(6.5973)	(6.6843)	(5.8207)	(5.9008)
R-squared	0.0704	0.0770	0.1114	0.1153
Basmann's F	1.7589	0.2089	1.5758	0.1890
(Degrees of Freedom)	(2,374)	(1,374)	(2,378)	(1,378)

Columns (1) and (2) report the regression of the logarithm of completed spell durations on explanatory variables, including the predicted logarithm of accepted net monthly earnings in the new job derived from a regression as in column (1) of Table 3, for the sample of re-employed workers (equation (15) in the text), columns (3) and (4) report the regression of the logarithm of elapsed spell durations on explanatory variables, including the predicted logarithm of minimum acceptable net monthly earnings derived from a regression as in column (3) of Table 3, for the sample of unemployed workers (equation (9) in the text). Standard errors are displayed in parentheses, a * indicates significance (two-tailed test) at the 10% level, a ** indicates significance (two-tailed test) at the 5% level. Basmann's F is a test of overidentifying restrictions. The 5% critical values for 400 observations are $F_{1,400}$=3.86 and $F_{2,400}$=3.02.

References

Amemiya, T. (1977); A Note on a Heteroskedastic Model, *Journal of Econometrics*, vol.6, pp.365-370

Cox, D. R. (1962); *Renewal Theory*, London/New York

Goldfeldt, S. M. and Quandt, R. E. (1972); *Nonlinear Methods in Econometrics*, Amsterdam/London

Jones, S. R. G. (1988); The Relationship between Unemployment Spells and Reservation Wages as a Test of Search Theory, *Quarterly Journal of Economics*, vol.103, pp.741-765

Lancaster, T. (1985); Simultaneous Equations Models in Applied Search Theory, *Journal of Econometrics*, vol.27, pp.113-126

Lancaster, T. and A. Chesher (1984); Simultaneous Equations With Endogenous Hazards; in: Neumann, G. R. and N. C. Westergård-Nielsen; *Studies in Labor Market Dynamics*, Berlin et al.: Springer

Lippman, S. and McCall, J. (1976): The Economics of Job Search: A Survey, *Economic Inquiry*, vol.14, pp.155-190

Kiefer, N. M. and Neumann, G. R. (1979); An Empirical Job-Search Model, with a Test of the Constant Reservation-Wage Hypothesis, *Journal of Political Economy* , vol.87, pp.89-104

Salant, S. W. (1977); Search Theory and Duration Data: A Theory of Sorts, *Quarterly Journal of Economics*, vol.91, pp.39-57

Markup Differentials, Cost Flexibility, and Capacity Utilization in West-German Manufacturing*

Gebhard Flaig
(University of Augsburg)

and

Viktor Steiner
(ZEW, Mannheim)

I. Introduction

The empirical analysis of the relationship between pricing behaviour and market structure has a distinguished tradition in industrial economics. The size of markups of price over marginal or average costs has been the traditional indicator for market power in most empirical studies usually based on a cross-section of industries (for a survey see Schmalensee 1989). The standard explanation given for inter-industry differences in markups has usually been the existence of entry barriers arising from scale economies (see Scherer 1980 for a survey). Although no concurring opinion on the proper interpretation or even the existence of a positive relationship between

*) We thank Klaus Conrad, our discussant at the Second Munich Applied Econometrics Workshop, for helpful comments and Georg Licht for numerous useful discussions and for providing essential data. Helpful suggestions were also received from seminar participants at the University of Augsburg, the University of Munich and the Austrian Institute of Economic Research (WIFO), Vienna.

industry markups and market concentration seems to have emerged so far, it remains the basis for the predominance of the structure-conduct-performance paradigm in empirical industrial economics (see Schmalensee 1989 for a comprehensive survey). A related issue that has been extensively investigated within this approach is the cyclical variation in markups and prices and its dependence on market structure (see Scherer 1980, Ch. 13, Carlton 1989) although here too, judging from the literature, no unambiguous results seem to be available.

More recently, the relationship between imperfect competition and macroeconomic fluctuations in prices and output has been the topic of much empirical research (see, e.g., Gahlen, Buck and Arz 1985, Hall 1986, Nickell 1988, Carlton 1989). Several authors (Hall 1986, 1988; Domowitz et al. 1987, 1988), using a Solow productivity equation approach, have investigated the relationship between industry markups and concentration in U.S. manufacturing and found substantial market power in virtually all industries. Hall (1986) concluded that high markups over marginal costs can to a large degree be explained by chronic excess capacity, while Domowitz et al. (1988) attributed high markups over marginal costs to high overhead costs. The latter authors have also investigated the cyclical behaviour of markups in U.S. manufacturing and found strong evidence that markups behave procyclically, and the more so the higher market concentration is. Bils (1987) on the other hand found some evidence for procyclical marginal costs and countercyclical markups for U.S. manufacturing, without any effect from concentration.

The main problem with all of the studies cited is that they are only rudimentarily based on the modern theory of production and costs. They usually assume rather restrictive specifications for the production technology including constant returns to scale, Hicks-neutral technical progress and full flexibility of all factors of production. In particular, the assumption of constant returns to scale does not seem a terribly useful one considering the importance that increasing returns to scale occupy in much of recent research on productivity growth (see e.g. Romer 1986) and international trade (for surveys see Caves 1985 and Krugman 1989).

Our approach differs from previous studies primarily in that we allow for a considerably more general production structure. In particular, we account for both a non-homothetic production function incorporating non-constant returns to scale and the quasi-fixity of factors of production. Furthermore, in explaining industry markups we make extensive use of some modern concepts in applied production analysis such as short-run and long-run cost flexibility as well as an economically meaningful measure of capacity utilization. Compared to previous related studies, especially by Appelbaum (1982) for U.S. manufacturing and Borooah and van der Ploeg (1986) for the U.K., our empirical work is based on a much larger sample of manufacturing industries.

The first step in our modelling strategy is to estimate for each industry a three equation system consisting of a pricing equation and two demand equations for variable factors of production on industry time-series data. These equations are derived under the assumptions of short-run profit maximization with respect to the pricing decision and cost minimizing with respect to the input demands, respectively. In a second step, we follow the traditional structure-conduct-performance approach and correlate estimated price-cost margins with both the usual proxy variables for market structure and our derived measures for inter-industry differences in technology and capacity utilization.

The paper is structured as follows. In the next section the theoretical framework used to model pricing behaviour with special reference to the cost flexibility and capacity utilization measures used in the empirical model is explained in some detail. The subsequent section sets out the econometric specification of the restricted cost function and derives the estimating equations of our empirical model. The main results of the present study are summarized and discussed in section IV. In the concluding section the main conclusions of the paper are summarized. The appendix contains a short data description and some additional estimation results.

II. Theoretical Framework

Our empirical model is based on the proposition that pricing decisions in an industry can be described as the outcome of profit maximizing behaviour. We do not develop a fully formulated model of pricing behaviour of imperfectly competitive firms depending on market structure, but rather refer to the general proposition that profit maximizing firms equate short-run marginal costs to marginal revenue. In the recent literature there exist different approaches to identify and estimate the structural parameters of the cost and revenue functions as well as the conduct parameters determining pricing behaviour in oligopolistic markets (for recent surveys see Geroski 1988 and Bresnahan 1989). The traditional structure-conduct-performance approach has been partly replaced by the so-called "new empirical industrial organization" approach (Bresnahan 1989) which differs from the former in that, instead of correlating the traditional accounting profitability measures with concentration measures across industries, price-cost margins and their determinants are estimated econometrically using time series data for a single industry. In the present study, we follow this general approach. In particular, we try to estimate marginal costs and industry markups econometrically. This is achieved by specifying a rather general cost function which is capable of describing the technology for each industry in our sample as follows.

Let $Y = Y(X, Z, t)$ denote the industry production function characterizing how output Y depends on a vector of variable inputs X, a vector of quasi-fixed inputs Z, and a time index t representing the state of technology. It will be assumed that variable inputs can be fully adjusted within a year whereas, due to costs of adjustment, quasi-fixed inputs are not always at their long-run optimal level. If the production function satisfies certain regularity conditions, and if firms minimize variable costs $q'X$, where q' denotes a vector of exogeneously given prices of variable inputs, there exists a restricted cost function (Lau 1976) given by

$$(1) \quad G = G(q, Y, Z, t)$$

which is dual to the production function and contains all economically relevant information on the underlying technology. To qualify as a proper variable cost function G must be homogeneous of degree one and non-decreasing as well as concave in q, non-decreasing in Y, and non-increasing and convex in Z. The specification of variable costs as given by (1) assumes that adjustment costs with respect to quasi-fixed factors are external to the industry, which will be the maintained hypothesis of the present study (for the distinction of external and internal adjustment costs see Berndt, Morrison and Watkins 1981, and Morrison 1988a).

One of the main advantages of the dual approach to modelling the technology in an industry is that it allows for an straightforward derivation of input demand functions. For a given level of output and exogeneously given input prices the cost-minimizing demands for variable factors of production can be derived from the restricted cost function by applying Shephard's Lemma:

$$(2) \quad X_i = \frac{\delta G}{\delta q_i} \ .$$

The derived demand eq for variable factors are homogeneous of degree zero in all input prices and non-increasing in own input prices.

In the present study derived factor demand equations primarily serve as an important tool to identify and estimate the parameters of the cost function. As the properties of the demand functions in eq. (2) place quite a few restrictions on the parameters of the estimating equations, they can be used to check whether estimated marginal costs are economically meaningful. For example, a positive own-price elasticity of a variable factor would indicate nonsensical estimates for marginal costs.

Formulating the determination of pricing decisions within the restricted cost function approach offers two additional advantages over the more traditional approach. First, the effect of a change in output demand on marginal costs can properly be estimated. Secondly, the effect that a disequilibrium in the level of quasi-fixed inputs has on costs and prices can be modelled within a coherent framework. The first of these effects can be described by the concept of cost flexibility, the latter by an adequately defined measure of capacity utilization.

Cost flexibility measures the proportionate change in costs attributable to a proportionate change in output and is therefore given by the ratio of marginal costs to average costs. Its reciprocal is termed economies of size in the literature and serves in the dual cost function approach an analogous purpose as the concept of scale economies in the primal production function approach (for a more complete discussion of the relationship between these concepts see Chambers 1988, Chapter 2).

In case of quasi-fixed inputs this concept has to be extended to distinguish between different cost flexibility measures. The short-run elasticity of variable costs with respect to output, ε_{GY}, is defined by

$$\text{(3a)} \quad \varepsilon_{GY} = \frac{\delta G}{\delta Y}\frac{Y}{G} .$$

The short-run elasticity of total costs, C, with respect to output, ε_{CY}, is given by

$$\text{(3b)} \quad \varepsilon_{CY} = \frac{\delta C}{\delta Y}\frac{Y}{C} = \frac{\delta G}{\delta Y}\frac{Y}{G}\frac{G}{C} = \varepsilon_{GY}\frac{G}{C}$$

with total costs

$$\text{(4)} \quad C = G\,(q, Y, Z, t) + r\,'Z,$$

where the vector r denotes the one-period market prices (user costs) of the quasi-fixed factors. As we have only one quasi-fixed input in our empirical model, for notational convenience, we restrict the following analysis to this case, the generalization to more than one quasi-fixed inputs being straightforward.

The two short-run cost flexibility measures defined above are calculated for a given level of the quasi-fixed factor. The full (long-run) change in costs due to a change in output is given by the total differential of the cost function in eq. (4), i. e.:

$$\text{(5)} \quad \frac{dC}{dY} = \frac{\delta G}{\delta Y} + \frac{\delta G}{\delta Z}\frac{dZ}{dY} + r\frac{dZ}{dY}.$$

Some obvious manipulations yield the following expression for the long-run cost flexibility measure:

$$\text{(6)} \quad \frac{dC}{dY}\frac{Y}{C} \equiv \eta = \varepsilon_{GY}\frac{G}{C} + \eta_Z\left(\varepsilon_{GZ} + r\frac{Z}{G}\right)\frac{G}{C}$$

where ε_{GY} and ε_{GZ} denote the partial elasticity of variable cost with respect to output and the quasi-fixed input, respectively, and η_Z is the total (long-run) elasticity of the quasi-fixed input with respect to output.

The long-run optimal value of the quasi-fixed input is derived by minimizing the total cost function (4) with respect to this variable, which yields

$$(7) \quad \frac{\delta C}{\delta Z} = \frac{\delta G}{\delta Z} + r = 0,$$

where $S_Z \equiv -\delta G / \delta Z$ is the shadow-value of the quasi-fixed factor. Eq. (7) therefore affords an economically intuitive interpretation: At the optimum the effect of an additional unit of the quasi-fixed input in reducing variable costs must be equal to its one-period rental price. Solving this optimality condition for Z in terms of Y, q and r, we can derive the optimal value of the quasi-fixed factor and hence calculate η_Z .

From eq. (6) it is obvious that, at this optimal value Z^*, the long-run cost flexibility η is given by $\varepsilon_{GY} \cdot G / C^*$, where C^* is total costs at the optimum, i.e. $C^* = G + r \cdot Z^*$. The difference between the short- and long-run cost flexibility measure is given by

$$(8) \quad \varepsilon_{GY} - \eta = (\eta - \eta_Z) r \frac{Z}{G} - \eta_Z \cdot \varepsilon_{GZ}$$

which collapses to $\eta \cdot r \cdot Z^* / G$ at the long-run optimum.

As suggested by Berndt and Fuss (1986) and Morrison (1985, 1988b), an economically meaningful measure of capacity utilization (Γ) is given by the ratio of the short-run total cost flexibility to the long-run cost flexibility measures, i.e.:

$$(9) \quad \Gamma = \varepsilon_{CY} / \eta .$$

This capacity utilization measure indicates the cost consequences of not having adjusted the capital stock optimally in the short-run. Since $(\delta C / \delta Y) \cdot (Y / C) = \varepsilon_{GY} \cdot G / C$, we get from eq. (9) and eq. (6)

$$(9') \quad \Gamma = \left(\eta - \eta_Z \left(\varepsilon_{GZ} + r \frac{Z}{G} \right) \frac{G}{C} \right) / \eta$$

$$= 1 - (\eta_Z / \eta) \cdot \varepsilon_{CZ}$$

where

$$\varepsilon_{CZ} = \left(\varepsilon_{GZ} + r\frac{Z}{G} \right) \cdot \frac{G}{C}$$

denotes the elasticity of total costs with respect to Z. (Note that for a homothetic cost function this measure collapses to $\Gamma = 1 - \varepsilon_{CZ}$).

Therefore, at the output level where the shadow-value of the quasi-fixed factor is equal to its one-period rental price our capacity utilization measure equals one. It is above unity for all output levels where the shadow value of the quasi-fixed factor exceeds its user costs, and is below unity where the former falls short of the latter. Following suggestions by Morrison (1985, 1988b), our capacity utilization measure has been adjusted for scale effects, i. e. it depicts only the cost impact of a suboptimal level of existing fixed capacity, not the cost consequences of output variations resulting from economies of size.

Having outlined the cost side of the model, we now turn to the formulation of the marginal revenue function. As this part of the model is rather standard, we may be brief here. Static profit maximization implies the following optimality condition

$$(10) \quad \frac{\delta G}{\delta Y} = P\left(1 + \frac{\Phi}{\varepsilon}\right)$$

or

$$(10') \quad P = \frac{\delta G}{\delta Y} \cdot \Theta ,$$

where P is the price of industry output and $\Theta = 1/(1 + \Phi/\varepsilon)$ is the markup on marginal costs composed of the price elasticity of demand for industry output, ε, and a conduct parameter, Φ, characterizing competition in the industry. Under perfect competition $\Phi = 0$, implying $\Theta = 1$, whereas under pure monopoly $\Phi = 1$. For the probably more relevant case of oligopolistic behaviour Φ lies between these two extremes ($0 < \Phi < 1$) implying a markup that is larger than one.

Identification of ε and Φ could be obtained by appending an inverse demand function for industry output to the system of estimating equations (see Appelbaum 1982, Roberts 1984, Borooah and van der Ploeg 1986,

Conrad 1989). However, for the following reasons we have not attempted to identify these parameters. First, a priori reasoning and some empirical experimentation suggest that, at least for our rather diverse sample of industries, an output demand equation cannot satisfactorily be modelled as simply as it is done in the papers cited. To specify a general output demand equation that is appropriate for our relatively large sample of industries would call for a rather elaborate modelling of the demand equations based on a flexible functional form which is beyond the scope of the present study. Secondly, even if a demand function fits the data well it may nevertheless provide poor estimates of marginal revenue. Finally, in the present study we are primarily concerned with the assessment of market power in a basically descriptive sense which does not necessitate the identification of the price elasticity and conduct parameters, the interpretation of the latter, at least at this level of aggregation, being a rather adventurous task anyway (Geroski 1988, Bresnahan 1989).

In our empirical model we simply make industry markups dependent on time trends and the growth rate of industry output to capture possible cyclical effects in markups. Although estimating the pricing equation (10') does not allow us to identify the parameters ε and Φ, we can test against perfect competition in an industry which would imply $\Theta = 1$.

III. Econometric Specification

We try to estimate the model outlined in the previous section for the majority of West-German manufacturing industries (for a brief data description see the appendix) based on a given specification of the restricted cost function which has therefore to be formulated in a rather flexible way. We have chosen a variant of the Generalized Leontief functional form proposed by Diewert (1971) and extended by Morrison (1988 a), the latter allowing for the incorporation of quasi-fixed factors of production. In our model variable inputs are labour L and materials M with prices w and v. For the labour input variable we use total yearly hours actually worked in an industry. Although a somewhat restrictive assumption as this implies equal elasticities of workers and hours with respect to output, it allows us to treat labour as a variable input within the period under consideration. The only quasi-fixed input in the model is the stock of capital K. We assume that immediate adjustment of the capital stock to its optimal level is not economically feasible due to increasing costs of adjustment which we treat external to the industry (for alternative formal tests of this assumption see Kulatilaka 1985, Schankerman and Nadiri 1986, Conrad and Unger 1987). Hence, the variable or restricted cost function is specified as

$$(11)\quad G=Y\Big[a_{11}v+2a_{12}(v\cdot w)^{1/2}+a_{22}w+v\left(b_{11}Y^{1/2}+b_{12}/Y+b_{13}t^{1/2}+b_{14}/t\right)$$
$$+w\left(b_{21}Y^{1/2}+b_{22}/Y+b_{23}t^{1/2}+b_{24}/t\right)\Big]+(Y\cdot K)^{1/2}\cdot\left(c_1v+c_2w\right)\,.$$

The restricted cost function (11) is homogenous of degree one and concave in factor prices if $a_{12}>0$, and is non-increasing and convex in K if $\left(c_1v+c_2w\right)<0$. This specification is a second-order approximization to an arbitrary cost function and allows for fairly complex interactions between output, factor prices and the trend terms which represent the state of technology. In contrast, the term involving the capital stock is held somewhat simple as preliminary explorations have shown that our sample size does not allow more terms to be included in the cost function (for a more general formulation of the Generalized Leontief cost function see Morrison 1988, and for the underlying theory of flexible functional forms Diewert and Wales 1987).

Applying Shephard's Lemma to eq. (11), we get the following equations for the labour-output and materials-output ratios

$$(12)\quad \frac{M}{Y}=a_{11}+a_{12}\left(\frac{w}{v}\right)^{1/2}+b_{11}Y^{1/2}+b_{12}/Y+b_{13}t^{1/2}+b_{14}/t+c_1\left(\frac{K}{Y}\right)^{1/2}$$

$$(13)\quad \frac{L}{Y}=a_{22}+a_{12}\left(\frac{v}{w}\right)^{1/2}+b_{21}Y^{1/2}+b_{22}/Y+b_{23}t^{1/2}+b_{24}/t+c_2\left(\frac{K}{Y}\right)^{1/2}$$

The long-run optimal value for K is calculated using the optimality condition $r = -\delta G / \delta K$ and is given by

(14) $$K^* = Y(c_1 v + c_2 w)^2 / 4r^2$$

The short-run variable cost flexibility, ε_{GY}, and the elasticity of variable cost with respect to K, ε_{GK}, can easily be derived from the restricted cost function as given by eq. (11). As it is obvious from eq. (14), the long-run elasticity of capital with respect to output is 1. Given values for ε_{GY} and ε_{GZ}, it is straightforward to calculate the long-run cost elasticity from eq. (6) and the capacity utilization measure from eq. (9').

Finally, the pricing equation is given by

(15) $$P = \Big[v\left(a_{11} + b_{13} t^{1/2} + b_{14} / t\right) + w\left(a_{22} + b_{23} t^{1/2} + b_{24} / t\right) + 2a_{12}(v \cdot w)^{1/2} + \frac{3}{2} Y^{1/2}(b_{11} v + b_{21} w) + \frac{1}{2}(c_1 v + c_2 w) \cdot \left(\frac{K}{Y}\right)^{1/2} \Big] \cdot \left[\beta_0 + \beta_1 t + \beta_2 t^{1/2} + \beta_3 (\ln Y - \ln Y_{-1})\right]$$

where the first factor in square brackets denotes marginal costs as derived from eq. (11) and the second expression is the markup factor which includes two trend terms and the growth rate of industry output. Whereas the time trends should pick up long-term trends in factors affecting pricing behaviour, the latter variable is assumed to capture cyclical effects on pricing.

The system of estimating equations comprises the input demand equations given by (12) and (13) and the price equation (15). The model is estimated by nonlinear three stage least squares. All symmetry conditions and cross equation restrictions have been imposed on the estimating equations. To econometrically account for the potential endogeneity of the output variable, we instrument it by using the factor prices, the trend terms and lagged values of both the endogeneous variables and output as instruments.

IV. Results

Given the available data (see the appendix), the model was estimated for 25 out of 31 industries comprising the manufacturing sector of the West-German economy. (TSP 4.1. was used for estimation.) As the growth rate of industry output enters the pricing equation as an explanatory variable, we lose one observation. The estimation period is therefore from 1961 to 1985. As the main focus of the present study is on the pricing equation, the input demand equations being used to obtain reliable estimates for marginal costs only, discussion of estimation results from the input equations may be brief here. To save space we do not report parameter estimates for the input equations, but summarize output, own price and cross price elasticities in Table A1 in the appendix.

IV.1 Estimated Input Demand Equations and Marginal Costs

Before we briefly discuss the results with respect to the input demand equations, we note that for two industries (road vehicles and wood working) the convexity condition of the variable cost function with respect to the capital stock is not fulfilled. Our maintained model specification seems not an adequate description of technology in these industries which were therefore excluded from the subsequent analysis.

The elasticities in Table A1 in the appendix show the short-run response of input demand with respect to a change in factor prices and an exogeneous shift in output for a given capital stock, respectively. Thus, they do not account for possible second-round effects arising from adjustment of the capital stock to its long-run optimal level (see Morrison 1988a). Furthermore, we do not allow for the indirect effect a change in factor prices may have on the level of output. This would imply to model the output demand function for each industry explicitely, which is - as already explained - beyond the scope of the present study.

The time variation of the elasticities in Table A1 can be gleaned from their reported mean values and standard deviations over the estimation period. Furthermore, to give some information on the significance of the estimated elasticities, we report their absolute t-values for the year 1980, i.e. the year where prices in the model have been normalized.

With the exception of two industries (iron and steel, and wood working) the estimated elasticities of labour input with respect to output are within reasonable magnitudes. In most cases their time variation, as given by the reported standard deviations, is quite modest. Although these elasticities vary substantially between industries, as a rule they are rather smaller than one. In case of the two industries mentioned the estimated elasticities of labour input with respect to output are negative, although not significantly different from zero, at least for some years, which does not seem very plausible on a priori grounds. They are therefore excluded from the sample in the subsequent analysis.

The estimated own price elasticities are non-positive in all cases as it is required from the definition of a proper cost function. Although statistically different from zero in most cases, they tend to be rather small. These estimates do however confirm reasonably well with the few disaggregated results for West-German manufacturing (Hansen 1983, Nakamura 1984, Rutner 1984, Stark 1988).

The elasticity of intermediate inputs with respect to output is estimated at or above one in most cases. This result seems quite reasonable as it indicates that, with a given capital stock and with rather low employment elasticities, short-run adjustments to varying output levels are mainly brought about by variations in the level of intermediate inputs. This is also consistent with the fact that in our model labour and raw materials are substitutes in the production process. Empirically, in the majority of industries, the cross price elasticity is significantly different from zero. These results indicate that studies that assume strict proportionality between the demand for intermediate inputs and output and/or neglect substitution possibilities, as e.g. in the studies by Hall (1988) and Domowitz et al. (1988), cannot be relied upon to give sensible estimates of marginal costs.

For each industry the usual summary statistics, e.g. the Durbin-Watson statistics and the adjusted coefficients of determination, for the input equations and the price equation are summarized in Table A2 in the appendix. Although in a number of cases the DW statistic seems rather low and falls into the inconclusive region in some cases, only for two industries (iron and steel, wood working) our model was definitely rejected by the data. For further reference note that for the pricing equation the DW test statistics do not indicate that dynamic misspecification may be a serious problem for the industries not excluded from the sample.

To sum up the results with respect to the factor demand equations, it may be concluded that, with the exception of four industries (iron and steel, road vehicles, wood working and wood products) which are excluded from the subsequent analysis, marginal costs in individual industries seem to be quite adequately estimated by our specification.

IV.2 Time Profiles of Markups, Cost-Flexibility and Capacity Utilization

We may therefore turn to the main results of the present study which are summarized in the following Table 1. The table shows for each of the industries remaining in the sample estimates of means and standard deviations of the markup (Θ), the variable short-run (ε_{GY}) and long-run cost flexibility (η) and the capacity utilization measure (Γ) over the estimation period. In addition, the respective values of these variables and their test statistics for the year 1980 are given. The reported t-statistics test against the natural null hypothesis that each of these measures is equal to one. Before we comment on the variation of these measures over the estimation period, the results are assessed with respect to this year.

For the year 1980, the estimated markups are significantly larger than one in virtually every industry and within a reasonable range. Our estimates suggest that most industries in West-German manufacturing are characterized by a considerable extent of market power. Our estimated markups are between those reported for selected industries in the related studies by Appelbaum (1982) for the U.S. and Borooah and van der Ploeg (1986) for the U.K.. Furthermore, it may be interesting to note that these estimates are comparable to those obtained, though by a rather different

TABLE 1. **Markups, Cost elasticities and capacity utilization in selected industries**

INDUSTRY	Θ 1961-1985 μ	σ	Θ 1980[1)]	ϵ_{GY} 1961-1985 μ	σ	ϵ_{GY} 1980[1)]	η 1961-1985 μ	σ	η 1980[1)]	Γ 1961-1985 μ	σ	Γ 1980[1)]
14 Chemical products	1.498	0.100	1.358 (6.63)	0.793	0.024	0.809 (6.23)	0.748	0.021	0.732 (7.54)	0.867	0.054	0.915 (1.45)
16 Plastic products	1.290	0.145	1.160 (2.99)	0.941	0.059	0.998 (0.04)	0.888	0.023	0.907 (2.09)	0.934	0.023	0.966 (0.54)
17 Rubber products	1.279	0.034	1.305 (5.64)	0.877	0.019	0.864 (3.89)	0.833	0.036	0.804 (5.71)	0.899	0.015	0.906 (1.83)
18 Stones and clay	1.364	0.194	1.198 (3.43)	0.914	0.083	0.962 (0.85)	0.857	0.038	0.861 (3.44)	0.810	0.038	0.857 (3.04)
19 Ceramic goods	1.471	0.054	1.432 (4.19)	0.815	0.010	0.813 (3.33)	0.638	0.026	0.621 (6.72)	1.034	0.036	1.065 (0.56)
20 Glass	1.247	0.027	1.242 (5.18)	0.946	0.030	0.939 (1.73)	0.941	0.027	0.932 (1.54)	0.827	0.029	0.813 (3.62)
22 Non-ferrous metals	1.122	0.023	1.109 (1.59)	0.997	0.021	0.985 (0.25)	0.822	0.078	0.764 (5.59)	1.041	0.086	1.119 (1.11)
23 Foundries	1.218	0.031	1.246 (4.99)	0.910	0.035	0.878 (3.58)	0.627	0.123	0.509 (8.12)	1.226	0.181	1.414 (2.23)
24 Drawing plants etc.	1.296	0.022	1.286 (7.80)	0.915	0.038	0.898 (3.86)	0.871	0.053	0.833 (2.48)	0.869	0.033	0.910 (1.13)
25 Structural metal products	1.182	0.075	1.214 (3.20)	0.953	0.044	0.934 (1.43)	0.438	0.150	0.317 (4.40)	2.177	0.705	2.686 (1.20)
26 Mechanical engineering	1.167	0.034	1.187 (3.90)	0.958	0.050	0.912 (2.35)	0.849	0.055	0.796 (3.74)	0.985	0.016	0.998 (0.02)
31 Electrical engineering	1.223	0.018	1.227 (1.70)	0.927	0.015	0.914 (0.87)	0.654	0.062	0.593 (3.24)	1.284	0.087	1.366 (0.96)
32 Precision and optical instruments	1.457	0.048	1.432 (5.23)	0.843	0.016	0.843 (3.21)	0.710	0.093	0.628 (5.96)	1.072	0.132	1.207 (1.41)
33 Finished metal goods	1.245	0.024	1.222 (4.26)	0.935	0.010	0.932 (1.71)	0.748	0.061	0.690 (6.11)	1.093	0.063	1.158 (1.59)
34 Musical instruments, toys etc.	1.553	0.098	1.446 (6.13)	0.804	0.017	0.813 (4.47)	0.816	0.017	0.822 (3.70)	0.864	0.014	0.863 (1.88)
37 Paper manufacturing	1.171	0.023	1.175 (3.07)	0.957	0.031	0.949 (1.08)	0.814	0.095	0.720 (5.49)	0.913	0.077	1.001 (0.01)
38 Paper processing	1.257	0.015	1.264 (4.99)	0.938	0.043	0.908 (2.47)	0.993	0.035	0.970 (0.86)	0.821	0.036	0.792 (5.25)
39 Printing and duplicating	1.228	0.014	1.229 (1.59)	0.974	0.032	0.947 (0.48)	0.965	0.074	0.896 (0.62)	0.823	0.028	0.857 (0.59)
41 Textiles	1.156	0.043	1.131 (3.21)	0.988	0.030	0.958 (1.25)	0.864	0.056	0.794 (6.35)	0.926	0.024	0.946 (1.06)
42 Clothing	1.175	0.039	1.205 (3.64)	0.959	0.037	0.917 (1.99)	0.872	0.073	0.793 (5.93)	1.019	0.028	1.051 (0.69)
43 Food and beverages	1.052	0.047	0.914 (1.21)	1.117	0.071	1.065 (0.93)	1.128	0.078	1.065 (1.52)	0.867	0.009	0.866 (3.00)

1) absolute t-values for the hypothesis that the coefficient is one

method, by Domowitz et al. (1988) for two-digit U.S. manufacturing industries.

The short-run cost elasticity is only significantly smaller than one for half of all industries under consideration. In contrast, the long-run cost elasticity is estimated significantly below one in the great majority of industries. The latter result indicates that overall West-German manufacturing industries exhibit economies of size to a considerable extent. Imposing the homogeneity or homothecity assumption on industry cost functions as e.g. in the studies of Borooah and van der Ploeg (1986), Morrison (1988) and Conrad (1988) therefore seems (at least for West-German manufacturing) too restrictive an assumption. This, by the way, is also one of the results of various statistical tests by Conrad and Unger (1987) based on a translog variable cost function for a somewhat different sample of West-German industries.

Except for one industry, the estimates for our measure of capacity utilization seem within a reasonable range. For the year 1980 capacity utilization is not significantly different from one for the majority of industries which were therefore in equilibrium in the sense defined in the theoretical section. This conforms reasonably well with the result of the mentioned study by Conrad and Unger (1987) who, however, base their formal test on the whole observation period. For the structural metal products industry the estimated value for the capacity utilization measure seems absurdely high numerically, although it is insignificantly different from one. As the precision of this estimate is rather poor, this industry will be excluded from the subsequent analysis. From those seven industries (rubber products, stones and clay, glass, foundries, musical instruments and toys, processing of paper) which were not in long-run equilibrium in this year six industries were operating at excess capacity.

The behaviour of markups, costs and capacity utilization in West-German manufacturing over the estimation period can be assessed by looking at the estimated standard deviations of these variables reported in Table 1. However, a more impressive picture of the long-term development of these measures is given in the following Figure 1 where, for each industry

Figure 1 Markups, long-run cost flexibility and capacity utilization

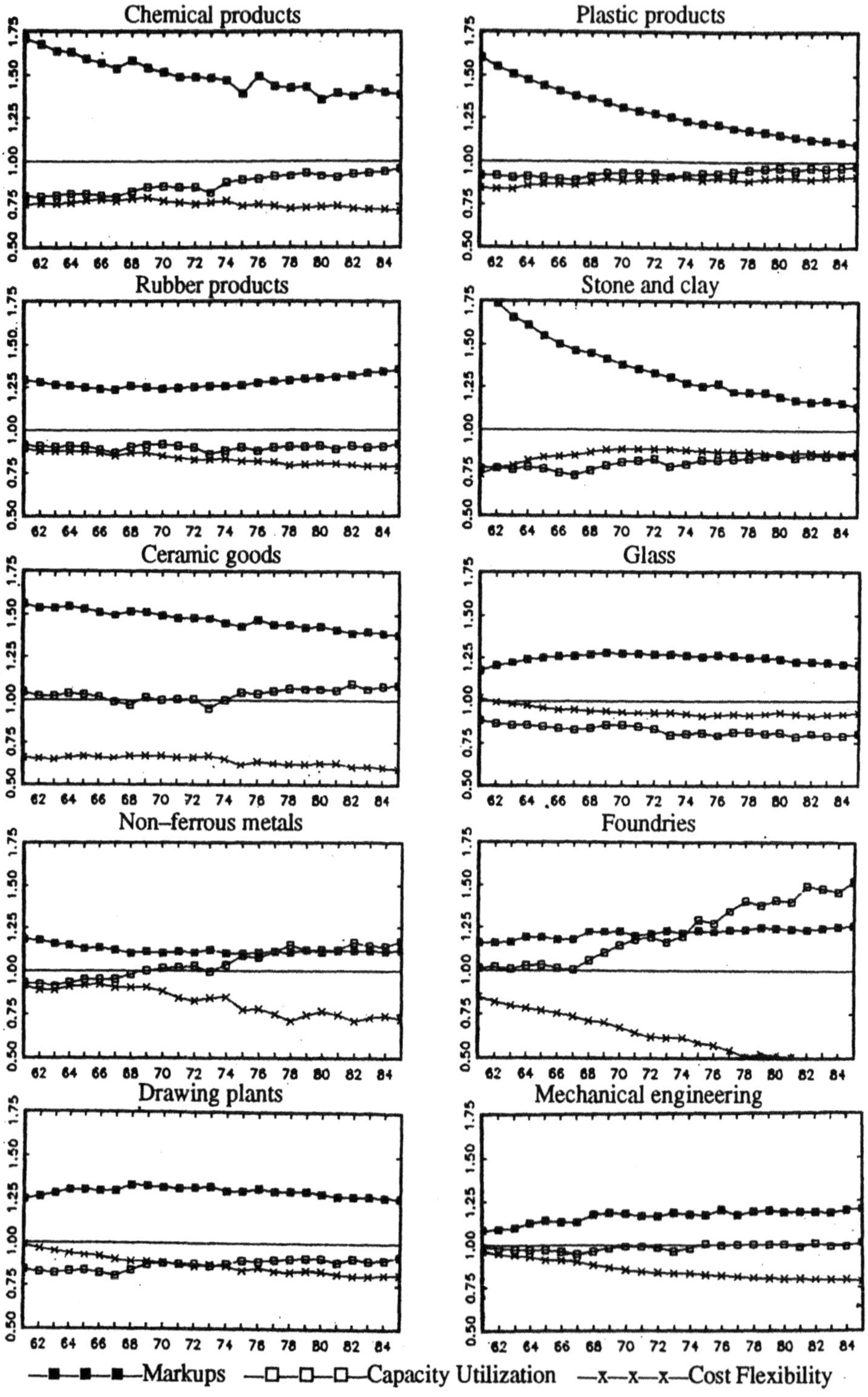

Figure 1 Continued

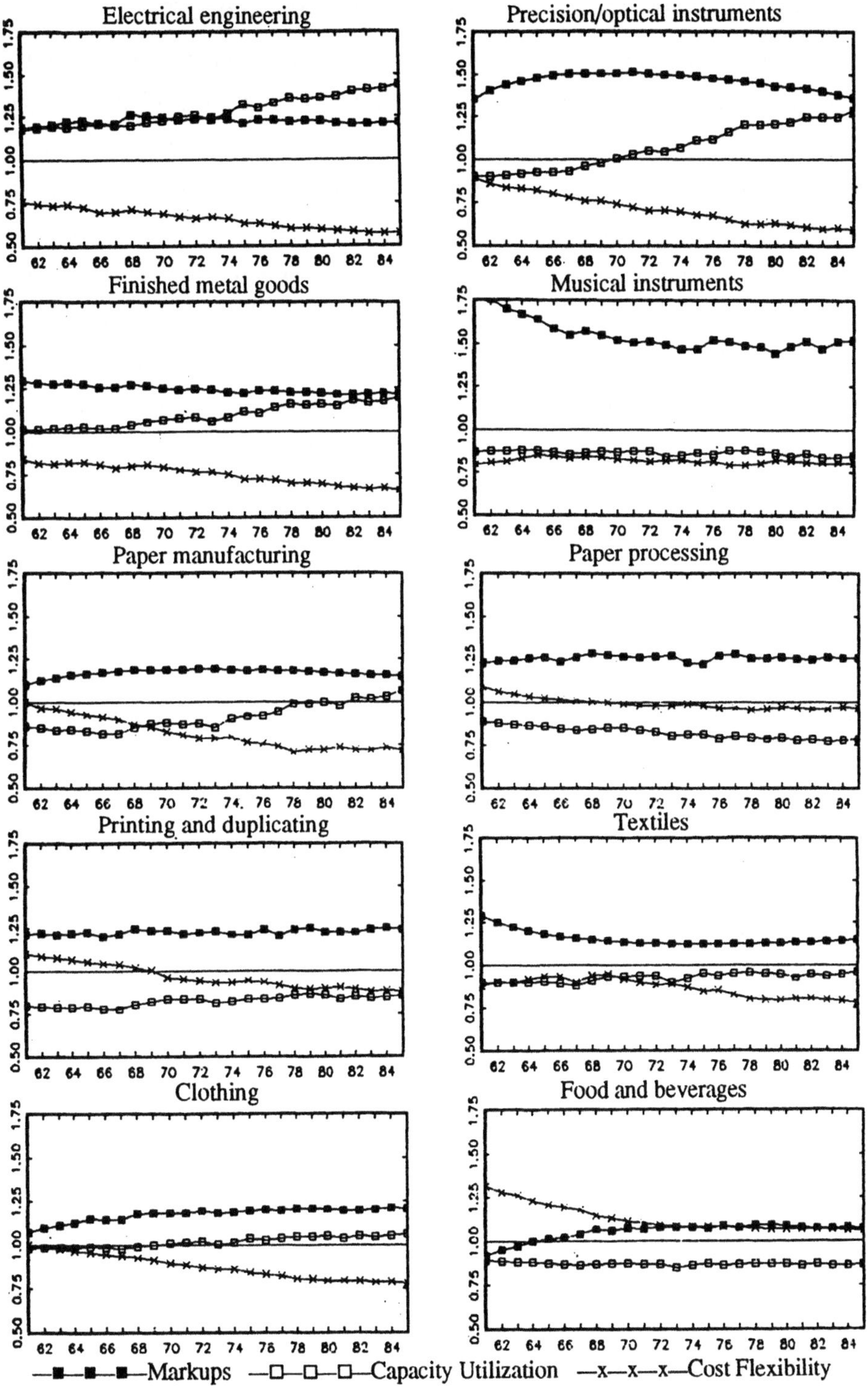

remaining in our sample, the markup, the long-run cost flexibility and the capacity utilization measure are plotted over the estimation period.

The general picture emerging from Fig. 1 can be summarized as follows. Except for those industries with very high markups at the beginning of the observation period (chemical products, plastic products, ceramic goods, stones and clay, musical instruments) which show a rather pronounced decline in markups, there seems to be no clear time trend in the levels of estimated industry markups. If anything, markups seem to be increasing on average. Prices well above marginal costs persist virtually in all industries for a relatively long period of time. This result indicates that high positive price-cost margins are not just a disequilibrium phenomena but rather a structural feature of the economy which can be attributed to the fact that for virtually all industries in our sample the elasticity of long-run cost with respect to output is considerably smaller than one. As this implies that marginal costs are lower than average costs, a positive markup is necessary to sustain an industry equilibrium.

With respect to the capacity utilization measure which captures short-run disequilibrium phenomena within our model specification, the conclusion from Fig. 1 would be that capacity utilization shows no or at most a modest positive trend in the great majority of industries. Although not particularly strong, our capacity utilization measure does show some cyclical variation in the recession years 1967 and 1973. In quite a few of the industries studied, there has been excess capacity over remarkable prolonged periods of time or even over the whole observation period. In stark contrast, over-utilization of capacity over longer time periods is only observed for a few dynamic industries such as electrical engineering, precision and optical instruments, and finished metal goods. The major exception that does not fit into the picture is the foundries industry which shows a very sharp rise capacity utilization measure.

IV.3 Flexibility of Prices, Marginal Costs and Markups

The analysis so far has been mainly restricted to the levels of markups and costs. A recurrent theme in the literature on industrial pricing has been how prices and/or markups respond to changes in the level of demand, and how these fluctuations are influenced by market concentration (see e.g. Scherer 1980, Carlton 1989). Most studies in this area are, however, blurred by their neglect to distinguish between changes in (marginal) costs and in markups leading to fluctuations in prices by implicitly assuming that (marginal) costs are constant (see e.g. Hall 1986, Domowitz et al. 1988). In contrast, the specification adopted in the present study enables us not only to directly estimate the elasticity of price with respect to output, but also allows for a proper identification of its components, i.e. the elasticity of marginal costs and the elasticity of the markup with respect to the level of output. The results of these calculations are summarized in Table 2.

Looking at the estimated price elasticities in Table 2 for the year 1980, the general conclusion that may be drawn from our results is that prices tend to be procyclical on average. This in itself is probably not a very controversial result as a lot of a priori reasoning may derive an upward sloping industry supply curve, the usual reason given for it being rising marginal costs. There is also some other supportive evidence for procyclical pricing behaviour in West-German manufacturing industries (see Arz 1989). However, as shown by the estimates for the elasticity of marginal costs for our reference year in Table 2, this seems not to be the case for the majority of industries under study. In fact, with the exception of two industries (glass and drawing plants), estimated elasticities at least for the reference year 1980 are either negative or not significantly different from zero.

This leaves the explanation for observed procyclical price fluctuations with procyclical markups. There is in fact strong evidence for quite a number of industries in our sample that markups are raised with increasing demand. This is also the result of a recent study by Domowitz et al. (1987, 1988) who have found, by extending the method developed by Hall (1988), evidence for procylical price-cost margins in U.S. manufacturing industries.

TABLE 2. Elasticities of price, marginal costs and markups with respect to output in selected industries

INDUSTRY	ϵ_{PY} 1961-1985 μ	σ	ϵ_{PY} 1980[1]	$\epsilon_{G'Y}$ 1961-1985 μ	σ	$\epsilon_{G'Y}$ 1980[1]	$\epsilon_{\theta Y}$ 1961-1985 μ	σ	$\epsilon_{\theta Y}$ 1980[1]
14 Chemical products	0.211	0.023	0.207 (2.40)	-0.042	0.037	-0.071 (1.07)	0.253	0.016	0.278 (3.86)
16 Plastic products	0.102	0.018	0.117 (1.94)	0.068	0.015	0.079 (1.31)	0.034	0.004	0.038 (0.99)
17 Rubber products	0.046	0.027	0.019 (0.29)	-0.003	0.026	-0.029 (0.45)	0.049	0.001	0.048 (0.97)
18 Stones and clay	0.049	0.115	-0.084 (1.00)	-0.056	0.128	-0.200 (2.67)	0.104	0.014	0.117 (3.28)
19 Ceramic goods	0.072	0.021	0.041 (0.81)	-0.048	0.024	-0.082 (1.65)	0.120	0.004	0.123 (3.79)
20 Glass	0.113	0.079	0.208 (4.16)	0.065	0.079	0.160 (3.46)	0.048	0.001	0.048 (1.47)
22 Non-ferrous metals	-0.124	0.043	-0.161 (1.36)	-0.027	0.042	-0.063 (0.83)	-0.100	0.002	-0.099 (1.24)
23 Foundries	-0.011	0.022	-0.045 (0.43)	-0.108	0.021	-0.140 (1.62)	0.097	0.003	0.095 (2.28)
24 Drawing plants etc.	0.150	0.081	0.238 (2.56)	0.064	0.081	0.152 (1.92)	0.086	0.001	0.086 (1.42)
25 Structural metal products	-0.237	0.061	-0.256 (3.86)	-0.189	0.060	-0.209 (4.87)	-0.048	0.003	-0.046 (0.83)
26 Mechanical engineering	0.016	0.022	0.001 (0.02)	-0.154	0.018	-0.166 (2.13)	0.171	0.005	0.168 (3.63)
31 Electrical engineering	0.116	0.027	0.087 (0.66)	-0.054	0.026	-0.081 (0.71)	0.169	0.003	0.169 (3.11)
32 Precision and optical instruments	-0.142	0.024	-0.193 (2.35)	-0.100	0.024	-0.151 (2.16)	-0.042	0.001	-0.042 (1.11)
33 Finished metal goods	0.136	0.036	0.100 (1.46)	0.050	0.037	0.009 (0.16)	0.085	0.002	0.087 (2.84)
34 Musical instruments, toys etc.	0.143	0.151	0.159 (1.91)	-0.036	0.160	-0.032 (0.42)	0.179	0.010	0.191 (4.29)
37 Paper manufacturing	-0.011	0.102	0.106 (1.56)	-0.022	0.103	0.095 (1.31)	0.012	0.001	0.012 (0.37)
38 Paper processing	0.211	0.040	0.246 (3.40)	0.032	0.041	0.069 (0.92)	0.178	0.002	0.177 (3.37)
39 Printing and duplicating	0.187	0.021	0.165 (1.30)	-0.008	0.020	-0.305 (0.25)	0.195	0.002	0.195 (2.93)
41 Textiles	0.063	0.303	-0.277 (2.26)	0.056	0.303	-0.283 (2.99)	0.006	0.001	0.007 (0.10)
42 Clothing	0.001	0.054	0.067 (1.40)	-0.104	0.051	-0.169 (4.72)	0.105	0.004	0.103 (3.48)
43 Food and beverages	0.247	0.058	0.313 (2.33)	-0.008	0.065	0.067 (0.67)	0.255	0.012	0.247 (2.65)

1) absolute t-values are in parentheses

IV.4 Inter-industry Differences in Markups

The results presented so far naturally evoke a host of questions on pausible explanations for the observed facts. Our main interest in this section is in possible explanations of inter-industry differences in markups and its relationship to market structure. Following established tradition in the industrial economics literature, we use both the Herfindahl-index of concentration *(HERF)* and the ten-firms concentration ratio *(CR10)* as indicators of market power. The Herfindahl-index is only available for the years 1977 to 1985. The particular *CR* measure was chosen because, compared to alternative *CR* measures, it is the most completely available measure for the observation period. In view of the very high correlation between the various concentration ratios, the choice of a particular measure does not seem very important anyway. Given the availability of these two measures and the fact that they change rather slowly over time, the years 1960, 1970, 1977, 1980 and 1985 were selected for the regressions in the following table.

TABLE 3. Determinants of inter-industry differences in markups

	Simple Pooling				Fixed Effects			
	I		II		I		II	
Constant	2.840	(19.19)	2.600	(23.11)		–		–
CR10	–0.035	(1.06)		–	–0.013	(0.10)		–
HERF		–	–0.023	(0.86)		–	0.019	(0.10)
IMQ	–0.084	(2.44)	0.016	(0.58)	–0.218	(2.87)	–0.230	–(2.66)
η	–1.687	(15.86)	–1.514	(17.76)	–1.535	(9.87)	–1.505	–(9.70)
$(\varepsilon_{GY} - \eta)$	–2.043	(12.85)	–1.759	(13.87)	–2.466	(7.79)	–2.410	–(6.82)
Γ	0.052	(0.57)	0.067	(0.88)	0.496	(2.67)	0.478	(2.74)
$\bar{R}^2$	0.83		0.87		0.77		0.69	
N	95		60		95		60	

Heteroscedasticity-consistent standard errors are in parentheses.

In Table 3 we report the results of some simple pooled cross-section time series regressions for the twenty remaining industries in our sample for these selected years. Each regression was run with the estimated markups from the previous section as the dependent variable and, alternatively, the *CR10* measure (Model I) and the Herfindahl index (Model II) as an explanatory variable by pooling the years available for the respective alternative. Following a priori reasoning and usual tradition in the industrial economics literature (Schmalensee 1989), we included the share of imports in an industry as a proxy variable for the competitive threat arising from international trade (see also Neumann et al. 1985) and three cost-based measures from our preceding analysis as explanatory variables in all regressions. To control for constant unobserved industry differences we have also estimated the various models by the standard fixed-effects within-group estimator. As heteroscedasticity seems a potential problem in cross section work of this kind, we have in each case calculated heteroscedasticity-consistent standard errors.

The rationale for the latter three variables is as follows. As explained above, long-term cost flexibility should be a very important predictor for differences in inter-industry markups. A significant negative correlation between these two variables can be considered a plausibility test of the estimated model. An alternative explanation for a negative correlation of the elasticity of (long-run) costs and markups with somewhat more intuitive appeal which is popular in the industrial economics literature is in terms of scale economies as barriers to entry. In our model the reciprocal of long-run cost elasticity defines the economies of size in an industry which, although not exactly equal to the elasticity of scale, may be seen as a proxy for barriers to entry. Our second cost-based variable is the difference between the short-run and long-run cost flexibility which, ceteris paribus, is the larger the more responsive variable costs are to an increase in the quasi-fixed factor (see eq. (8)). Finally, we have our capacity utilization measure which should account for disequilibrium effects on pricing behaviour.

Both the long-run cost flexibility and its difference to the short-run cost flexibility turned out highly significant in the regressions explaining the level of markups irrespective of the concentration measure and the estimation method used. It may be noted that the rather high explanatory power of these regressions, as measured by the coefficient of determination (corrected for degrees of freedom), is entirely due to these two variables. Although the capacity utilization measure shows a signifcant positive effect on the level of markups after unobserved industry effects have been controlled for, it is quantitatively less important. The traditional concentration measures have no significant effect on the level of markups irrespective of the particular model specification. This seems hardly surprising as the structure of production costs can be shown to play a key role in determining concentration in a number of theoretical models (see Davis 1988 for a survey, and Aiginger 1990 for a similiar argument in a related context). In contrast, the import share in an industry shows the expected negative coefficient after unobserved industry effects have been controlled for.

V. Conclusions

Our specification of the restricted cost function with capital as quasi-fixed factor of production allowed a satisfactory description of factor demand and pricing behaviour for the great majority of industries studied in this paper. For West-German manufacturing the following results have been established:

The hypothesis of perfect competition can be firmly rejected for all industries in our sample. In virtually all industries prices are considerably higher than marginal costs over the whole estimation period. Although the levels of markups differ quite substantially between industries, with the exception of a few industries which had exceptionally high margins at the beginning of the observation period markups have remained fairly stable over time.

The estimated long-run cost flexibilities are considerably smaller than one in virtually every industry indicating the importance of economies of size in West-German manufacturing. This structural feature of the West-German economy is the single most important explanation for the previous result of high industry markups.

In contrast to the former result, the short-run cost flexibility is significantly smaller than one only for about half of the industries studied. This quite clearly underpins the crucial role that accrues to the capital stock as a quasi-fixed factor of production. This corresponds reasonably well with our results with respect to the capacity utilization measure which reveals that a number of industries have been in disequilibrium with respect to the capital stock for substantial periods of time.

In the majority of industries under study prices behave procyclically, which is compatible with a priori reasoning and some of the available evidence. The reason for procyclical prices is, however, not to be found in increasing marginal costs which tend to be countercyclical on average, but in procyclical markups. The latter result is compatible with both some theoretical models of pricing behaviour and the recent empirical results for U.S. manufacturing.

Our pooled cross-section time series regressions suggest that traditional measures of market concentration such as the Herfindahl-index and the ten-firms concentration ratio cannot explain inter-industry differences in the level of markups after differences in economies of size have been statistically controlled for. Although differences in import competition seem modestly important to keep markups down, the inter-industry markups are predominantly determined by our derived cost flexibility measures.

APPENDIX

Data

The data refer to the manufacturing sector of the West-German economy over the period 1960 to 1985. Data for nominal gross output, nominal intermediate inputs and real value added have been taken from the yearly disaggregated national income accounts (Source: Statistisches Bundesamt (StaBu), Fachserie 18). Real gross output series have been obtained as follows: After correcting the producer price index for domestic and foreign sales at the industry level (Source: StaBu, Fachserie 17 and Fachserie M) for the change in the tax system in 1968 (when the sales tax was replaced by the value added tax), we obtained weights for the respective bundle of goods in each of our industries from the disaggregated input-output table for 1982 (StaBu, Fachserie 18, Reihe 2, Table 4.2). Then, price indices for industry gross output were calculated as a weighted sum of the domestic producer price index. An implicit price index for intermediate inputs for each industry was derived by dividing nominal intermediate inputs by the difference between real gross output and real value added. Yearly total hours at the industry level are average yearly hours actually worked per employee (Source: Institut für Arbeitsmarkt- und Berufsforschung Nurenberg, Kohler and Reyher 1988) multiplied by the number of employees in the respective industry. The capital stock and the user costs of capital which are fully compatible with the disaggregated national income accounts have kindly been made available by the IFO Institute Munich (see Gerstenberger et al. 1989). All variables have been normalized at the year 1980. Values for the Herfindahl-index and the CR10 for the years 1960, 1970, 1977, 1980 and 1985 have been obtained from Statistisches Bundesamt (1985) and Statistisches Jahrbuch (various issues), respectively.

Because of data problems six industries had to be excluded from the sample. For these industries there are either no consistent price indices (mineral oil refining, shipbuilding, aircraft and spacecraft, tobacco) or data is not available over the whole estimation period (office machinery and data processing equipment, leather and leather goods).

TABLE A1. **Elasticities of the input equations with respect to output and the wage rate.**

INDUSTRY	ε_{LY} 1961-1985 μ	σ	1980[2]	ε_{LW} 1961-1985 μ	σ	1980[2]	ε_{MY} 1961-1985 μ	σ	1980[2]	ε_{MW} 1961-1985 μ	σ	1980[2]
14 Chemical products	0.337	0.043	0.312 (2.46)	-0.163	0.041	-0.201 (2.78)	0.954	0.028	0.974 (31.09)	0.057	0.012	0.067 (2.76)
16 Plastic products	0.701	0.189	0.874 (5.53)	-0.225	0.051	-0.272 (3.40)	1.051	0.009	1.052 (23.96)	0.100	0.019	0.119 (3.42)
17 Rubber products	0.502	0.059	0.445 (4.07)	-0.097	0.015	-0.114 (1.88)	1.081	0.004	1.085 (29.86)	0.053	0.009	0.060 (1.86)
18 Stones and clay	1.309	0.147	1.109 (3.14)	-1.645	0.391	-2.043 (4.63)	0.720	0.188	0.900 (6.90)	0.767	0.109	0.863 (4.16)
19 Ceramic goods	0.650	0.069	0.589 (8.30)	-0.280	0.041	-0.327 (7.85)	1.003	0.060	1.051 (13.89)	0.321	-0.035	0.347 (7.90)
20 Glass	0.674	0.097	0.828 (8.94)	-0.139	0.030	-0.165 (2.07)	1.111	0.108	1.004 (20.37)	0.081	0.012	0.094 (2.07)
21 Iron and steel	0.046	0.236	-0.103 (0.50)	-0.015	0.004	-0.021 (0.11)	1.148	0.084	1.061 (20.36)	0.006	0.001	0.007 (0.11)
22 Non-ferrous metals	0.527	0.056	0.506 (2.40)	-0.131	0.039	-0.173 (3.08)	1.098	0.029	1.075 (16.22)	0.027	0.006	0.032 (3.02)
23 Foundries	0.575	0.045	0.559 (5.13)	0.018	0.002	0.021 (0.24)	1.155	0.043	1.107 (21.57)	-0.013	0.002	-0.015 (0.24)
24 Drawing plants etc.	0.481	0.100	0.612 (3.73)	-0.219	0.022	-0.244 (2.16)	1.106	0.083	1.026 (18.78)	0.097	0.013	0.110 (2.14)
25 Structural metal products	0.457	0.198	0.796 (4.68)	-0.216	0.048	-0.273 (1.70)	1.231	0.183	0.997 (21.79)	0.110	0.014	0.123 (1.70)
26 Mechanical engineering	0.685	0.022	0.683 (6.65)	-0.249	0.027	-0.273 (3.49)	1.115	0.077	1.050 (20.61)	0.145	0.019	0.165 (3.55)
28 Road vehicles[1]	0.816	0.054	0.861 (6.11)	-0.600	0.095	-0.724 (6.78)	1.033	0.061	0.980 (14.84)	0.245	0.042	0.287 (7.28)
31 Electrical engineering	0.569	0.088	0.653 (3.30)	-0.212	0.041	-0.250 (3.71)	1.140	0.061	1.081 (13.79)	0.129	0.031	0.160 (3.76)
32 Precision and optical instruments	0.621	0.126	0.753 (8.01)	-0.040	0.006	-0.046 (0.56)	1.005	0.100	0.912 (12.48)	0.030	0.005	0.035 (0.55)
33 Finished metal goods	0.500	0.039	0.456 (3.85)	0.031	0.004	0.036 (0.22)	1.172	0.024	1.192 (25.22)	-0.017	0.003	-0.019 (0.22)
34 Musical instruments, toys etc.	0.632	0.176	0.605 (7.91)	-0.251	0.023	-0.278 (4.84)	0.904	0.111	0.921 (14.93)	0.145	0.012	0.145 (4.55)
35 Wood working[1]	0.213	0.290	-0.066 (0.53)	-0.570	0.108	-0.687 (5.12)	0.919	0.038	0.884 (13.31)	0.162	0.036	0.190 (4.80)
36 Wood products	0.435	0.115	0.600 (3.47)	-0.060	0.013	-0.077 (0.41)	1.190	0.082	1.111 (20.19)	0.031	0.004	0.035 (0.41)
37 Paper manufacturing	0.821	0.334	1.103 (7.11)	-0.076	0.023	-0.092 (2.04)	1.011	0.127	0.900 (24.74)	0.024	0.005	0.029 (2.05)
38 Paper processing	0.612	0.051	0.642 (4.95)	-0.300	0.048	-0.327 (6.30)	1.075	0.075	1.015 (24.52)	0.117	0.017	0.131 (6.24)
39 Printing and duplicating	0.774	0.006	0.771 (3.68)	-0.218	0.043	-0.258 (3.49)	1.139	0.071	1.079 (8.52)	0.175	0.020	0.193 (3.46)
41 Textiles	0.666	0.238	0.386 (3.13)	-0.077	0.015	-0.092 (1.20)	1.127	0.122	1.201 (48.39)	0.033	0.006	0.039 (1.20)
42 Clothing	0.615	0.103	0.488 (4.43)	-0.250	0.040	-0.297 (4.27)	1.108	0.011	1.097 (35.31)	0.108	0.017	0.125 (4.28)
43 Food and beverages	0.722	0.288	1.066 (3.67)	-0.052	0.006	-0.057 (0.37)	1.183	0.127	1.065 (12.41)	0.009	0.001	0.011 (0.37)

1) The convexity condition of the variable cost function with respect to the capital stock is not fulfilled.
2) absolute t-values in parentheses

TABLE A2. Summary statistics for the input equations and the price equation.

INDUSTRY	L/Y		M/Y		P	
	DW	$\bar{R}^2$	DW	$\bar{R}^2$	DW	$\bar{R}^2$
14 Chemical products	1.91	0.759	1.68	0.999	1.91	0.992
16 Plastic products	1.33	0.881	1.47	0.997	1.14	0.998
17 Rubber products	1.73	0.931	1.54	0.994	0.94	0.997
18 Stones and clay	1.16	0.635	1.82	0.994	1.31	0.999
19 Ceramic goods	1.39	0.942	1.91	0.997	2.12	0.999
20 Glass	1.46	0.956	1.50	0.999	0.94	0.998
21 Iron and steel	1.05	0.620	0.75	0.987	1.48	0.993
22 Non-ferrous metals	1.09	0.405	1.16	0.999	1.93	0.994
23 Foundries	1.03	0.878	1.06	0.993	1.47	0.998
24 Drawing plants etc.	1.86	0.983	1.62	0.994	1.13	0.997
25 Structural metal products	1.80	0.934	1.01	0.992	1.13	0.998
26 Mechanical engineering	1.57	0.975	1.83	0.998	1.40	0.999
28 Road vehicles[1)]	0.78	0.861	1.07	0.996	0.77	0.997
31 Electrical engineering	1.34	0.886	2.16	0.997	1.50	0.993
32 Precision and optical instruments	0.97	0.914	1.41	0.999	1.07	0.994
33 Finished metal goods	1.58	0.925	1.06	0.997	1.42	0.999
34 Musical instruments, toys etc.	1.50	0.822	1.70	0.995	1.67	0.999
35 Wood working[1)]	0.98	0.498	1.39	0.997	1.41	0.993
36 Wood products	1.17	0.967	0.58	0.998	1.17	0.998
37 Paper manufacturing	1.79	0.874	1.44	0.996	1.64	0.996
38 Paper processing	1.52	0.970	1.55	0.995	1.71	0.997
39 Printing and duplicating	1.72	0.953	1.35	0.996	1.51	0.997
41 Textiles	1.61	0.941	1.62	0.998	1.40	0.996
42 Clothing	1.49	0.982	1.62	0.999	1.81	0.999
43 Food and beverages	0.91	0.948	1.90	0.999	1.31	0.997

1) The convexity condition of the variable cost function with respect to the capital stock is not fulfilled.

References

Aiginger, Karl, "Investitionsverhalten und Marktstruktur - Empirische Ergebnisse für Österreich", in B. Gahlen (ed.), Marktstruktur und gesamtwirtschaftliche Entwicklung (Heidelberg: Springer, 1990), 127-152.

Appelbaum, Elie,"The Estimation of the Degree of Oligopoly Power," *Journal of Econometrics* 19 (1982), 287-299.

Arz, Stefan, Preisflexibilität, Konzentration und Risikoeinstellung (Frankfurt am Main etc.: Peter Lang, 1989).

Berndt, Ernst R., Melvyn A. Fuss, "Productivity Measurement with Adjustments for Variations in Capacity Utilization and other Forms of Temporary Equilibrium", Journal of Econometrics 33 (1986), 7-29.

Berndt, Ernst R., Catherine Morrison and G. Campbell Watkins, "Dynamic Models of Energy Demand: An Assessment and Comparison", in E. R. Berndt and B. C. Fields (eds.), Modeling and Measuring Natural Resource Substitution (Cambridge, MA: MIT Press, 1981), 259-289.

Bils, Mark, "The Cyclical Behavior of Marginal Cost and Price", American Economic Review 77 (Dec. 1987), 838-855.

Borooah, V.K., and F. van der Ploeg,"Oligopoly Power in British Industry," *Applied Economics* 18 (1986), 583-598.

Bresnahan, Timothy F.,"Empirical Studies of Industries with Market Power," in R. Schmalensee and R.D. Willig (ed.), *Handbook of Industrial Organization Vol.II* (Amsterdam: North Holland, 1989), 1011-1057.

Carlton, Dennis W., "The Theory and the Facts of how Markets Clear: Is Industrial Organization Valuabe for Understanding Macroeconomics?", in R. Schmalensee and R.D. Willig (ed.), *Handbook of Industrial Organization Vol.I* (Amsterdam: North Holland, 1989).

Caves, Richard E., "International Trade and Industrial Organization", European Economic Review 28 (1985), 377-395.

Chambers, Robert G., Applied Production Analysis. A Dual Approach (Cambridge: Cambridge University Press, 1988).

Conrad, Klaus,"Kapazitätsauslastung und Wohlfahrtsverluste in der westdeutschen Stahlindustrie," in W. Franz, W. Gaab and J. Wolters (ed.), *Theoretische und angewandte Wirtschaftsforschung. H. König zum 60. Geburtstag* (Berlin, Heidelberg: Springer, 1988).

Conrad, Klaus, "Tests for Optimizing Behavior and for Patterns of Conjectural Variations", Kyklos 42 (1989), 231-255.

Conrad, Klaus and Ralph Unger, "Ex Post Tests for Short- and Long-Run Optimization", Journal of Econometrics 36 (1987), 339-358.

Davis, Stephan, "Concentration", in St. Davis and B. Lyons (ed.), Surveys in Economics: Economics of Industrial Organisation, Chapter 3, (London: Longman, 1988).

Diewert, W. Erwin and Terence J. Wales, "Flexible Functional Forms and Global Curvature Conditions", Econometrica 55(1, 1987), 43-68.

Domowitz, Ian, R. Glenn Hubbard, and Bruce C. Petersen, "Oligopoly Supergames: Some Empirical Evidence on Prices and Margins", The Journal of Industrial Economics 35 (June 1987), 379-398.

Domowitz, Ian, R. Glenn Hubbard, and Bruce C. Petersen, "Market Structure and Cyclical Fluctuations in U.S. Manufacturing", Review Econ. Statistics 70 (Feb. 1988), 55-66.

Gahlen, Bernhard, Andrew J. Buck and Stefan Arz, "Ökonomische Indikatoren in Verbindung mit der Konzentration", in G. Bombach, B. Gahlen and A. E. Ott (eds.), Indusstrieökonomik (Tübingen: Mohr-Siebeck, 1985), 127-166.

Geroski, Paul A., "In Pursuit of Monopoly Power: Recent Quantitative Work in Industrial Economics", Journal of Applied Econometrics 3 (1988), 107-123.

Gerstenberger, Wolfgang, Johannes Heinze, Marlies Hummel and Kurt Vogler-Ludwig, Sektorale Kapitalbildung in der deutschen Wirtschaft nach Eigentümer- und Benutzerkonzept (Munich: IFO Institute for Economic Research, 1989).

Hall, Robert E., "Market Structure and Macroeconomic Fluctuations", Brookings Papers on Economic Activity (2, 1986), 285-322.

Hall, Robert E., "The Relation between Price and Marginal Cost in U.S. Industry", Journal of Political Economy 96 (5, 1988), 921-947.

Hansen, Gerd,"Faktorsubstitution in den Wirtschaftssektoren der Bundesrepublik," *DIW-Vierteljahreshefte* zur Wirtschaftsforschung (1983), 169-183.

Kohler, Hans and Lutz Reyher, Arbeitszeit und Arbeitsvolumen in der Bundesrepublik Deutschland 1960-1986, BeitrAB 123, (Nurenberg: Institut für Arbeitsmarkt- und Berufsforschung, 1988).

Krugman, Paul R., "Industrial Organization and International Trade", in R. Schmalensee and R.D. Willig (ed.), *Handbook of Industrial Organization VolII* (Amsterdam: North Holland, 1989).

Kulatilaka, Nalin, "Tests on the Validity of Static Equilibrium Models", Journal of Econometrics 28 (1985), 253-268.

Lau, Lawrence J.,"A Characterization of the Normalized Restricted Profit Function," *Journal of Economic Theory* 12 (1976), 131-163.

Lyons, Bruce, "Barriers to Entry", in St. Davis and B. Lyons (ed.), Surveys in Economics: Economics of Industrial Organisation, Chapter 2, (London: Longman, 1988).

Morrison, Catherine J.,"Primal and Dual Capacity Utilization: An Application to Productivity Measurement in the U.S. Automobile Industry," *Journal of Business & Economic Statistics* 3 (1985), 312-324.

Morrison, Catherine J.,"Quasi-fixed Inputs in U.S. and Japanese Manufactoring: A Generalized Leontief Restricted Cost Function Approach," *Review of Economics and Statistics* (1988, a), 275-287.

Morrison, Catherine J.,"Capacity Utilization and Productivity Measurement: An Application to the U.S. Automobile Industry," in A. Dogramaci and R. Färe (ed.), *Applications of Modern Production Theory: Efficiency and Productivity* (Boston: Kluwer, 1988, b), 163-194.

Nakamura, Shinichiro,"A Dynamic Multisectoral Model of Production, Investment and Prices Based on Flexible Cost Functions," *DIW-Vierteljahreshefte zur Wirtschaftsforschung* (1986), 110-122.

Neumann, Manfred, Ingo Böbel and Alfred Haid, "Konzentration, Außenhandel und Marktergebnis" in G. Bombach, B. Gahlen and A. E. Ott (eds.), Industrieökonomik (Tübingen: Mohr-Siebeck, 1985), 169-189.

Nickell, Stephen, "Imperfect Competition and the Labour Market", in M. Beenstock (ed.), Modelling the Labour Market (London: Chapman and Hall 1988).

Roberts, Mark J.,"Testing Oligopolistic Behavior," *International Journal of Industrial Organization* 2 (1984), 367-383.

Romer, Paul M. "Crazy Explanations for the Productivity Slowdown", in S. Fischer (ed.), NBER Macroeconomics Annual 1987, 163-201.

Rutner, Dieter, Faktorsubstitution in den Produktionssektoren der Bundesrepublik Deutschland. Eine ökonometrische Analyse anhand des Translog-Modells, 1981-1980, (Frankfurt: Haag + Herchen Verlag, 1984).

Schankerman, Mark, and M. Ishag Nadiri,"A Test of Static Equilibrium Models and Rates of Return to Quasi-fixed Factors, with an Application to the Bell System," *Journal of Econometrics* 33 (1986), 97-118.

Scherer, F. M., Industrial Market Structure and Economic Performance (Chicago; Rand McNally, 1980).

Schmalensee, Richard, "Inter-Industry Studies of Structure and Performance," in R. Schmalensee and R.D. Willig (ed.), *Handbook of Industrial Organization Vol.II* (Amsterdam: North Holland, 1989), 951-1009.

Stark, Ernst, "Faktoreinsatzverhalten im verarbeitenden Gewerbe. Eine sektorale Analyse unter Verwendung eines Translog-Modells", Viertelsjahrshefte zur Wirtschaftsforschung (1/2 1988), 79-95.

Statistisches Bundesamt, Produzierendes Gewerbe. Fachserie 4, Reihe S.9., Konzentrationsstatistische Daten für den Bergbau und das Verarbeitende Gewerbe 1954 bis 1982 (Stuttgart: Kohlhammer, 1985).

Empirical Analysis of Optimal Firm Behaviour: Asymmetric Adjustment in Labour and Capital Demand in the Manufacturing Sector in the Netherlands and the U.K.*

Franz C. Palm
(University of Limburg, Maastricht)
and
Gerard A. Pfann
(University of Limburg, Maastricht)

1. Introduction

This paper overcomes one of the shortcomings of the linear rational expectations model for labour and capital demand. Since the dynamics of these models are often the result of quadratic adjustment costs, one can question the appropriateness of that specification which has been introduced by Holt et al. (1960) and used since then in many studies. In order to model the adjustment costs of two types of labour and capital, we use the more general asymmetric functional form that was put forward and tested in Pfann and Verspagen (1989) and in Pfann and Palm (1992).

---

* University of Limburg, P.O. Box 616, 6200 MD Maastricht, The Netherlands. Our thanks are due to Stephen Nickell, Gerd Hansen, Peter Kugler and Jürgen Wolters, and to the participants of the Econometric Seminar at CORE, Louvain and of the Workshop on Applied Econometrics, University of Munich for helpful comments and suggestions. We are grateful to Anthony Murphy for supplying the UK data. We would like to acknowledge the financial support of the Netherlands Organisation for the Advancement of Pure Research (N.W.O.) and the Royal Netherlands Academy of Arts and Sciences (K.N.A.W.).

Pfann and Verspagen (1989) and Pfann and Palm (1992) present empirical evidence on the asymmetry of adjustment costs for respectively aggregate employment in manufacturing in the Netherlands and for two types of labour in manufacturing in the Netherlands and the UK. Adjustment costs depend on the role of unemployment, labour market legislation, and union power (see Smith (1984), Burgess (1988), Burgess and Dolado (1989)) and (other) institutional constraints (see Bentolila and Bertola (1990)). Hamermesh (1989) finds that adjustment costs that do not depend on the size of the change in the workforce give rise to lumpy adjustment to a firm's moving target employment level.

The model presented here provides an alternative explantion for the "gestation" lag of the capital stock as mentioned by Kydland and Prescott (1982) and Rossi (1987). The paper makes three contributions. First, we briefly review the methodogological problems involved in the econometric analysis of Euler equations. In particular, we comment on the differences between analysing respectively linear and nonlinear first order conditions for optimal intertemporal economic behaviour. Second, we present a multivariate asymmetric adjustment costs model of the firm's labour and capital demand in which the symmetric linear rational expectations model (cf. Hansen and Sargent (1981), Epstein and Denny (1983), Kollintzas (1985)) is nested.

We investigate the impact of unanticipated shocks in wage costs, labour productivity or technology on factor input decisions. Third, we report empirical evidence for the model using UK and Dutch manufacturing time series. We examine the firm's demand for production and nonproduction workers and for capital allowing for differences in adjustment costs for the two types of labour (see Nickell (1986)) and capital. In this way we try to circumvent misleading (with regard to adjustment costs) explanations of factor demand dynamics (cf. Nickell (1984)) in terms of aggregation. We test for the presence of trends common to factor demand and factor prices using the Johansen (1988) test. We apply the GMM technique of Hansen (1982) to estimate the structural parameters of nonlinear first order conditions.

The paper is organized as follows. Methodological problems of the empirical analysis of Euler equations are reviewed in section 2. A multivariate labour and capital demand model in which adjustment costs are symmetric is presented in section 3. The impact of a structural break in the process of the forcing variables on the decision rules of the firm is discussed. In section 4 we empirically analyse this model using annual UK manufacturing data for the period 1955 to 1986 and quarterly Dutch manufacturing data for the period 1971.I to 1984.IV.

Capital and employment are simultaneously determined in the model. The forcing variables of the model are the real production and nonproduction wage costs and the real price of capital assets. The analysis of the data casts some doubts upon the stability of the long run relationship between factor inputs and real factor prices. However, the nonstationarity of the decision variables can be adequately explained by simultaneously allowing for common stochastic trends (real input prices) and deterministic trends (technological changes). The asymmetry in adjustment costs of capital appears to be similar in UK and Dutch manufacturing. According to the model, it is optimal for the firm to slow down the scrapping of capital during recessions and to invest during economic uprises in anticipation of higher profits. Finally, conclusions are drawn in section 5.

2. Econometric methodology

Optimal firm behaviour has been analysed along two lines in econometrics. In the past, many authors have assumed that the intertemporal objective function is quadratic in the decision variables or policy instruments. The associated decision rules are then linear. For a review of the literature, we refer to Cassings and Kollintzas (1991) and to Pfann (1990). The use of nonlinear models is of a more recent date.

First, a major advantage of linear first order conditions for intertemporal optimisation is that these conditions can be solved analytically for the policy instruments. The resulting decision rules are subject to testable restrictions. For instance, Palm and Pfann (1990) show that with a quadratic production function and quadratic adjustment costs, intertemporal expected profit maximisation over an infinite time horizon results in a multivariate linear first order autoregressive model with diagonal autoregressive matrix with current and all future expected values of the forcing variables being the explanatory variables of the decision variables. This finding has two important implications for the empirical analysis.

Once the order of the lag length of the processes for the forcing variables is determined, the order of the system is fully determined. Nondiagonal autoregressive matrices (interpreted as interrelation) can only result from nondiagonal dynamics in the forcing variables when their expected values in the decision rules have been replaced by expressions obtained from the processes of these variables.

Second, the closed form solution of the linear decision rules allows one to study the dynamics of the model, e.g. by checking analytically the value of the roots of the characteristic equations and/or by computing the coefficients of the moving average representation of the model. More details on these aspects can be found in Palm and Pfann (1990).

Third, as mentioned above, the parameters of the linear decision rules resulting from quadratic intertemporal optimisation are (non)linear functions of the basic parameters (called structural parameters) in the objective function. Generally, the system is subject to overidentifying (non)linear cross-equation restrictions. As long as the structural parameters are identified and invariant over the sample period, they can be directly estimated from the linear decision rules by e.g. the maximum likelihood (ML) method. Alternatively, a two stage procedure can be applied, first by estimating the system of decision rules as an unrestricted dynamic model, and second, by applying the method of asymptotic least squares (ALS) (see Gouriéroux, Monfort and Trognon (1985) and Kodde, Palm and Pfann (1990)), which minimizes the distance in a given metric between the unrestricted estimates of the parameters of the linear decision rules and these parameters expressed as functions of the structural parameters. If the unrestricted estimates have been obtained by ML (or an asymptotically equivalent estimator) and an optimal weighting matrix is used in the second stage, the resulting estimates will be asymptotically equivalent to ML estimates of the structural parameters. The minimum value of the distance criterion can be used to test the overidentifying restrictions on the decision rules implied by the theoretical model. In large samples, it has a χ^2-distribution with a number of degrees of freedom equal to the number of restrictions.

Also, standard tests for the order of the model, autocorrelation, autoregressive conditional heteroscedasticity (ARCH), exogeneity, Granger causality, structural stability and cointegration can be applied to the linear policy rules.

Fourth, under general conditions, these rules can be shown along the lines of Nickell (1985) to imply error correction behaviour on the side of the economic agent. Stated differently, the decision variables will be cointegrated with the forcing variables.

The econometric analysis of nonlinear first order conditions is usually more complicated than in the linear case. First, when the first order conditions for optimal behaviour are nonlinear in the decision variables, no closed form solution can be usually obtained. Numerical methods can be applied to study the dynamic behaviour of the Euler equations. Singleton (1988) presents methods for solving nonlinear models with rational expectations and discusses their use in estimating unknown parameters (see also Tauchen (1986), and the references in Singleton (1988)).

Second, to estimate the Euler equations, one cannot usually resort to the ML method. ML estimation requires distributional assumptions about random errors and a complete description of the stochastic environment.

Instead, the structural parameters can be estimated by the generalised method of moments (GMM) procedure put forward by Hansen (1982) and frequently applied since then. Hansen (1982) also gives a test of overidentifying restrictions based on GMM. Gallant (1987), and Newey and West (1987) developed likelihood ratio (LR), Wald and Lagrange multiplier (LM) tests based on the GMM method. Andrews and Fair (1988) give Wald, LR and LM statistics based on the GMM estimator to test structural stability. Eichenbaum, Hansen and Singleton (1988) put forward a LR-type test for structural stability, whereas Ghysels and Hall (1990a) developed a test for structural invariance based on out of sample prediction errors, where parameter estimates of one subsample are used to predict over another subsample.

Although GMM does not require strong distributional assumptions nor a complete description of the stochastic process, there are several points which are not yet satisfactorily solved. With the exception of Tauchen (1986), only asymptotic results are available for GMM. The finite sample results obtained by Tauchen (1986) indicate that the size of the bias in parameter estimation can be as large as the standard error. Hansen's test of overidentifying restrictions performs reasonably well in samples of 50 to 70 observations, although Tauchen finds a slight bias in favour of accepting the null hypothesis. Somewhat surprisingly for samples of the size 50 to 70, as the lag length in forming instruments is increased, the sampling distribution of parameter estimates becomes concentrated around strongly biased parameter values.

The problem of choice of the instruments to be used in GMM is not completely resolved. Hayashi and Sims (1983) obtain some results from asymptotic theory. Hansen (1985) derives a lower bound for the covariance matrix of GMM over the set of admissible instruments. But on the basis of the findings by Tauchen (1986), it might probably be wise in moderate sized samples to place most credence on the GMM estimates with the smallest instrument set.

With respect to the numerical properties, Eichenbaum and Hansen (1990) notice two limitations of GMM. In densely parametrised versions of the model, several local minima with similar value can occur. This finding probably points towards an identification problem. Also, it appeared to be difficult to get test statistics that are robust to the range of consistent estimates of the weighting matrix used in GMM estimation.

Finally, using results by Newey (1985), Ghysels and Hall (1990b) show that Hansen's test of overidentifying has no power against a class of local alternatives characterised by parameter drift. Alternative tests for structural stability based on GMM have already been mentioned above.

Third, for nonlinear models, some results on error correction and cointegration have been obtained by Escribano (1987). Singleton (1988) also discusses the nature and sources of secular, cyclical and seasonal fluctuations in aggregate series and of the relationships between the components of different series.

Although the issue of cointegration in nonlinear models is only partially resolved, nonlinear models derived from intertemporal optimisation will typically imply restrictions across the nonstationary components of the decision variables and therefore provide some guidance for the empirical analysis of long run relationships in nonlinear models.

3. Labour and capital demand under asymmetric adjustment costs

In the literature on the demand for production factors under uncertainty it has often been argued that the level of employment and the capital stock are determined simultaneously (e.g. Meese (1980), Epstein and Denny (1983), Pindyck and Rotemberg (1983a,b), Kokkelenberg (1984), Epstein and Yatchew (1985)).

We consider a representative firm which maximises the expected present value of profits over an infinite horizon assuming that real factor prices are given. In each decision period, the firm chooses a contingency plan for two types of labour L_{it}, $i = 1,2$ and for the stock of capital K_t, conditionally on currently available information. Marginal productivity (MP) of factor input X_{it} at time t is modelled as follows

$$MP(X_{it}) = \alpha_i - \Sigma_{j=1}^{3} \lambda_{ij} X_{it} + \xi_{it}, \quad i = 1,2,3, \tag{3.1}$$

where $X_{1t} = L_{1t}$, $X_{2t} = L_{2t}$ and $X_{3t} = K_t$, α_i and λ_{ij} are constant parameters and ξ_{it} denotes the impact of stochastic technological shocks. As a result of Young's theorem, we have $\lambda_{ij} = \lambda_{ji}$. The nonlinearity of the total product associated with (3.1) is due to the nonlinearity of the production schedule, not to monopolistic competition as assumed by e.g. Burda (1991). All three inputs are assumed to be quasi-fixed. The specification for the marginal adjustment costs of X_{it} is as follows

$$MAC_i(\Delta X_t) = \beta_i[\exp \beta_i\Delta X_{it} - 1] + \Sigma_{j=1}^{3} \gamma_{ij}(\Delta X_{jt}), \qquad i = 1,2,3, \qquad (3.2)$$

where γ_{ij} and β_i are constant parameters and $\Delta X_t = (\Delta X_{1t}, \Delta X_{2t}, \Delta X_{3t})'$. The specification of the adjustment cost function (AC) associated with (3.2) has been proposed by Pfann and Verspagen (1989). Regularity conditions require that $MAC_i(\Delta X_t) > 0$ (< 0) if $\Delta X_{it} > 0$ (< 0), $MAC_i(0) = 0$. Strict convexity is satisfied iff the Jacobian-matrix of MAC is positive definite. If β_i is negative, the costs of reducing factor i exceed those of an increase of factor i and a downward adjustment of factor i as a result of a change in the target level will take more time than an upward adjustment due to a change in the target level of the same size but in opposite direction.

If $\beta_i = 0$ and if the matrix $\Gamma = (\gamma_{ij})$ is positive definite, equation (3.2) corresponds to the quadratic AC function, being symmetric as $\gamma_{ij} = \gamma_{ji}$ by Young's theorem.

We assume that the firm faces linear variable costs that are proportional to factor input at each time t. In order to maximise the real present value of its expected profit stream the firm will make contingency plans for labour and capital satisfying the Euler conditions

$$MP(X_{it}) - MAC_i(\Delta X_t) - P_{it} + \tau E[MAC_i(\Delta X_{t+1}) + dP_{t+1} | \Omega_t] = 0, \qquad (3.3)$$

where $P_t = (W_{1t}, W_{2t}, Q_t)'$, W_{it} is the real wage cost of L_{it}, Q_t is the real price of capital, τ is a real discount rate, d is a diagonal (3x3)-matrix (0,

0, (1-δ))', δ denotes the depreciation rate of capital which we assume to be constant, and Ω_t is the information set available to the firm at time t. We used an a priori value for δ of 5 percent per year in the empirical analysis. Together with the transversality conditions, equations (3.3) define the firm's employment policy. However, current decisions are based on unobserved future expectations. Ideally, one would like to obtain an explicit closed form forward looking solution for (3.3). For linear first order conditions a closed form solution can be obtained (see e.g. Hansen and Sargent (1981), Kollintzas (1985)), whereas for nonlinear Euler equations this is only occasionally the case.

Explicit forward looking closed form solutions are useful to trace the effects of a structural change in the process generating the forcing variables in the model. In the asymmetric model, however, additional assumptions are needed on the distribution of forecast errors in order to identify the impact of an unanticipated structural change in the exogenous variables. Pfann (1990) shows that under normality, an unanticipated shock causing a step change in the optimal desired level of factor input yields a step change in both unconditional mean and variance of the expectational error of the firm. An unexpected exogenous shock that leads to a persistent change of the firm's forecast error variance without affecting the slope coefficient of employment (e.g. an increase in uncertainty about the future behaviour of forcing variables) yields a step change in unconditional mean and variance of the firm's expectational error. Consequently, an unexpected exogenous shock can be modelled by using dummy variables that account for these step changes. Autoregressive conditional heteroscedasticity due to increased uncertainty in the disturbance can be introduced to model a structural break in the variance.

4. Empirical analysis

In this section we present parameter estimates for the optimality conditions in (3.3). For the empirical analysis of the model we used seasonally unadjusted quarterly data for manufacturing in the Netherlands for the period 1971.I -1984.IV, and annual data for the manufacturing in the UK for the period 1955-1986. All prices are normalised by dividing by the output price index. All data have been divided by their sample mean. Definitions and data sources are given in appendix 1. Structural changes in the forcing variables, production and nonproduction real wage costs, W_{1t} and W_{2t}, respectively, and capital costs Q_t, may induce step changes in the factor demand levels and in their variances.

The learning in the presence of a structural change is modelled in accordance with the above mentioned arguments by including dummy variables in the present empirical analysis. The stochastic first order conditions (3.3) do not yield a complete solution to the maximization problem of the firm. In order to estimate the structural parameters of the Euler conditions we apply the GMM. The realised values of period t+1 are substituted for the unobserved expectations of one period ahead employment in (3.3) and a vector forecast error, u_{t+1}, of mean zero is added to the system (3.3) yielding

$$\begin{bmatrix}\delta_{01}\\ \delta_{02}\\ \delta_{03}\end{bmatrix} CONST + \begin{bmatrix}\delta_{11}\\ \delta_{12}\\ \delta_{13}\end{bmatrix} OC1 + \begin{bmatrix}\delta_{21}\\ \delta_{22}\\ \delta_{23}\end{bmatrix} OC2 - \begin{bmatrix}W_{1t}\\ W_{2t}\\ Q_t\end{bmatrix}$$

$$+ \begin{bmatrix}0\\ 0\\ \tau(1 \div \delta)\end{bmatrix} Q_{t+1} - \begin{bmatrix}\lambda_{11} & \lambda_{12} & \lambda_{13}\\ \lambda_{21} & \lambda_{22} & \lambda_{23}\\ \lambda_{31} & \lambda_{32} & \lambda_{33}\end{bmatrix} \begin{bmatrix}L_{1t}\\ L_{2t}\\ K_t\end{bmatrix}$$

$$+ \begin{bmatrix}\gamma_{11} & 0 & 0\\ 0 & \gamma_{22} & 0\\ 0 & 0 & \gamma_{33}\end{bmatrix} \begin{bmatrix}\Delta L_{1t} - \tau\Delta L_{1t+1}\\ \Delta L_{2t} - \tau\Delta L_{2t+1}\\ \Delta K_t - \tau\Delta K_{t+1}\end{bmatrix} \tag{4.1}$$

$$- \begin{bmatrix}\beta_1(\exp(\beta_1\Delta L_{1t}) - \tau\Delta\exp(\beta_1\Delta L_{1t+1}))\\ \beta_2(\exp(\beta_2\Delta L_{2t}) - \tau\Delta\exp(\beta_2\Delta L_{2t+1}))\\ \beta_3(\exp(\beta_3\Delta K_t) - \tau\Delta\exp(\beta_3\Delta K_{t+1}))\end{bmatrix} = \begin{bmatrix}u_{1t+1} - \xi_{1t}\\ u_{2t+1} - \xi_{2t}\\ u_{3t+1} - \xi_{3t}\end{bmatrix},$$

where the constant parameters δ_{ij} have replaced the productivity parameters α_1 and α_2 that are not identified due to a breakdown into a constant effect and oil shocks step changes. The variables OC1 and OC2 denote dummy variables which take the value 1 from 1973.IV (UK: 1974) and 1979.II (UK: 1979) respectively to the end of the sampling period, if the model is estimated in levels. For models estimated in first differences OC1 and OC2 are equal to one in 1973.IV (UK: 1974) and 1979.II (UK:

1979) respectively and zero otherwise. The composite error term, $u_{t+1} - \xi_t$, arises from forecast errors and productivity shocks. The productivity shock enters the equation because it is assumed to be realised when the decision is taken. Otherwise ξ_{it} would not appear in the disturbance term. Before proceeding with estimation we discuss the identification of the structural parameters. Normalisation with respect to prices results from the fact that variable real wage costs are assumed to be proportional to labour input. Moreover, contrary to linear closed form solutions, the real discount rate τ is identified in the first order conditions. However, in many applications τ is not very well determined from the Euler equations. One possible explanation for this empirical finding is the nonstationarity of the compound error term due to omitted nonstationary forcing variables (cf. Dolado (1987)).

First, we investigate the dynamic properties of the univariate series and their order of integration. Table 4.1 presents the results of unit root tests of the production factors L_{1t}, L_{2t} and K_t, and the real factor prices W_{1t}, W_{2t} and Q_t, where Q_t is the real price of capital. According to Fuller's test statistic τ_τ (see Fuller (1976), table 8.5.2) we do not reject the hypothesis that the univariate time series have one unit root. Also if we take account of the fact that some dummy variables are included in the model and therefore use the distribution given by Perron (1989), we reach the same conclusion.

TABLE 4.1 : UNIT ROOTS TESTS

Model : $V_t - V_{t-1} = a'Z_t + \alpha_1 V_{t-1} + \alpha_2 \Delta V_{t-1} + \varepsilon_t$

$V_t \in \{L_{1t}, L_{2t}, K_t, W_{1t}, W_{2t}, Q_t\}$

$H_0 : \alpha_1 = 0$

The Dutch manufacturing sector :

Z = (CONST, Q_2, Q_3, Q_4, OC1, OC2)*

{V_t : 1971.III - 1984.IV}

	L_{1t}	L_{2t}	K_t	W_{1t}	W_{2t}	Q_t
Fuller's $\hat{\tau}_\tau$	-2.48	-.04	-.15	-1.05	-2.16	-1.50
Adjusted R^2	1.00	1.00	1.00	.99	.99	.90
DW-statistic	2.08	2.32	2.01	2.15	2.21	1.95

The UK manufacturing sector :

Z = (CONST, TREND, OC1, OC2)*

{V_t : 1957 - 1986}

	L_{1t}	L_{2t}	K_t	W_{1t}	W_{2t}	Q_t
Fuller's $\hat{\tau}_\tau$	-1.96	-.34	-2.00	-.90	-.74	-1.20
Adjusted R^2	.98	.92	1.00	.99	.99	.90
DW-statistic	1.57	2.09	1.50	2.11	1.93	1.95

* Q_2, Q_3 and Q_4 are seasonal dummies, TREND denotes a linear trend, OC1 = 1 in 1973.IV and 1974, OC2 = 1 in 1979.II and 1979 for the Netherlands and the UK respectively and zero otherwise. No linear trend was included for UK capital and the real price of assets.

Second, we test for cointegration between the decision and forcing variables. When these series are cointegrated, the nonstationarity of L_{1t}, L_{2t} and K_t may well be modelled by the nonstationarity of W_{1t}, W_{2t} and Q_t. Then equation (4.1) can be interpreted as an error correction mechanism. Basically, according to the model, the adjustment to a linear long run relationship takes place in a nonlinear way. However, an important property of the concept of stationarity is that it is preserved under some nonlinear transformations (Escribano (1987)). Consequently, we test for long run equilibrium by computing linear cointegrating regressions. Results are given in table 4.2.

TABLE 4.2 : COINTEGRATION TESTS: THE FORCING VARIABLES ARE $\{W_{1t}, W_{2t}, Q_t\}$.

Cointegration regressions for the manufacturing sector in the Netherlands*

1971.I - 1984.IV

	CONST	OC1	OC2	TREND	W_{1t}	W_{2t}	Q_t	$\bar{R}^2$	CRDW	ADF
L_{1t}	0.67	0.00	0.04		-0.51	-0.70	(1.51)	0.97	0.41	-2.12
	(3.68)	(0.00)	(2.16)		(-2.62)	(-3.91)	(7.37)			
	1.64	-0.07	0.03	-0.01	0.73	-0.52	-0.49	0.99	0.95	-3.36
	(11.72)	(-5.65)	(2.80)	(-10.16)	(4.46)	(-5.17)	(-2.15)			
L_{2t}	0.56	0.14	0.03		-1.59	0.44	1.46	0.94	1.06	-3.20
	(2.92)	(7.52)	(1.77)		(-7.84)	(2.33)	(6.77)			
	1.56	0.07	0.02	-0.01	-0.31	0.62	-0.62	0.98	0.70	-3.78
	(10.39)	(5.40)	(2.08)	(-9.79)	(-1.78)	(5.63)	(-2.53)			
K_t	1.70	-0.04	-0.02		0.51	0.42	-1.58	0.97	0.77	-2.49
	(13.24)	(-3.43)	(-1.77)		(3.74)	(3.31)	(-10.89)			
	0.94	0.01	-0.02	0.01	-0.45	0.28	-0.01	1.00	0.92	-3.77
	(13.52)	(1.66)	(-2.85)	(15.92)	(-5.57)	(5.58)	(-0.11)			

Cointegrating regressions for the manufacturing sector in the UK*
1955 - 1986

	CONST	OC1	OC2	TREND	W_{1t}	W_{2t}	Q_t	$\dot{R}^2$	CRDW	ADF
L_{1t}	1.47	-0.10	-0.06		0.74	-0.97	-0.18	0.96	0.85	-3.80
	(4.09)	(-4.58)	(-2.10)		(2.87)	(-4.81)	(-0.41)			
	1.88	-0.15	-0.04	0.02	0.65	-1.30	-0.42	0.97	1.15	-5.01
	(4.66)	(-4.69)	(-1.61)	(1.92)	(2.60)	(-5.06)	(-0.96)			
L_{2t}	0.54	-0.16	-0.06		2.39	-1.89	0.03	0.73	1.03	-3.27
	(0.78)	(-3.53)	(-1.13)		(4.73)	(-4.78)	(0.04)			
	1.67	-0.28	-0.02	0.04	2.15	-2.78	0.04	0.79	1.28	-4.66
	(2.28)	(-4.81)	(-0.45)	(2.86)	(4.72)	(-5.94)	(2.86)			
K_t	-0.35	0.05	-0.02		0.78	0.02	0.54	0.99	1.66	-3.38
	(-1.47)	(3.47)	(-1.35)		(4.51)	(0.16)	(1.83)			
	0.33	-0.02	-0.00	0.03	0.63	-0.51	0.14	1.00	1.62	-4.03
	(-2.40)	(-1.88)	(-0.18)	(9.27)	(7.43)	(-5.90)	(1.00)			

* Asymptotic t-values are given within parentheses. OC1 = 1 for the period 1973.IV - 1984.IV and 1974-1986, OC2 = 1 for the period 1979.II - 1984.IV and 1979-1986 in the regressions for the Netherlands and the UK respectively. Seasonal dummies are not reported.

From the results, presented in table 4.2, we may draw the following conclusions. To make inference, we interpolate the critical value of the tables for the Cointegrating Regression Durbin- Watson (CRDW) statistic and the Augmented Dickey Fuller (ADF) statistics, applicable to our model. For the ADF statistics, we use the critical values of Phillips and Ouliaris (1990) and for the CRDW, we rely on the bounds for the critical values given in Sargan and Bhargava (1983) (SB). Some doubt is cast upon the existence of a long run equilibrium relationship between real factor prices and production employment and capital in the Netherlands, whereas the test of cointegration on nonproduction employment in the Netherlands and the UK manufacturing factor inputs seems to be only marginally significant. A possible explanation for this finding may be the coexistence of stochastic trends (real factor prices) and deterministic trends (e.g. technological innovations). Hence, we also test for cointegration when a linear deterministic trend is included in the regression equation. The inclusion of a trend removes the random walk behaviour from the long run equilibria. Consequently, a linear time trend was added to the first order conditions (4.1). We also performed Johansen's (1988) test for the number of cointegrating regressions. The results are reported in table 4.3.

TABLE 4.3 : JOHANSEN'S COINTEGRATION TEST*

The Netherlands

	Production workers	Nonproduction workers	Capital
r=1	34.21	31.68	38.96
r=2	17.44	14.30	19.00
r=3	3.79	3.59	-0.96**
r=4	1.60	0.42	-2.18**

The UK

	Production workers	Nonproduction workers	Capital
r=1	29.17	25.58	37.61
r=2	8.93	13.86	19.29
r=3	4.78	8.71	1.40
r=4	0.63	3.55	0.69

* Significance levels from Johansen (1988) are 35.6, 38.6 and 41.2 for α = 0.90, 0.95 and 0.975 respectively and M = 4.

** The negative values of the statistic are due to one out of four negative eigenvalues.

From the results in table 4.3, it is obvious that the test is not significant and that there is no evidence that more than one cointegrating relation between X_{it} and the factor prices W_{1t}, W_{2t}, Q_t and a linear trend exist. This conclusion relies of course on the finding that the variables involved are integrated of order one.

Note that in equation (4.1) we have restricted the matrix $\{\gamma_{ij}\}$ to be diagonal prior to estimation. The reason is twofold. First, it is consistent with the literature on dynamic factor demand. Second, due to the computational complexity and limited number of observations, only a small number of structural parameters can be estimated. Also the sets of IVs have been chosen in accordance with the information set Ω_t of the extended model.

The information set for the Netherlands has been extended by including a linear time trend, whereas the lagged levels of production and nonproduction employment and capital have been replaced by one period lagged first differences of these variables. The number of IVs in the information set for the Netherlands then equals 17. In the information set for the UK a linear trend has been included as well. The one and two periods lagged decision variables (L_1, L_2, K) have been replaced by one period lagged first differences, and the one period lagged first differenced real price of capital has also been added. Then the number of IVs for the UK is 12. GMM parameter estimates and model specification tests are given in table 4.4.

TABLE 4.4 : GMM ESTIMATES OF ADJUSTMENT COSTS PARAMETERS AND TESTS *

Manufacturing sector in the Netherlands

1971.IV - 1984.IV

Production workers		Nonproduction workers		Capital	
λ_{11}:	0.94 (2.80)	λ_{21}:	0.40 (0.60)	λ_{31}:	-0.01 (-0.04)
λ_{12}:	0.09 (0.33)	λ_{22}:	-0.06 (-0.15)	λ_{32}:	0.03 (0.25)
λ_{13}:	1.67 (1.11)	λ_{23}:	2.00 (0.93)	λ_{33}:	-0.34 (-0.51)
γ_{11}:	50.75 (3.07)	γ_{22}:	81.81 (1.85)	γ_{33}:	83.05 (2.73)
β_1 :	7.48 (5.85)	β_2 :	-9.08 (-3.74)	β_3 :	-9.48 (-5.22)

TESTS

SB : 1.82		SB : 2.32		SB : 2.26	
ARCH		ARCH		ARCH	
1	0.31	1	8.53	1	1.45
2	0.84	2	7.27	2	2.68
3	0.96	3	7.98	3	5.32
4	1.37	4	8.45	4	5.89

Overidentifying restrictions	:	$15.64 < \chi^2$ (.95;15)
Linearity	:	$15.35 > \chi^2$ (.95;3)
Structural stability after OC2	:	$40.92 < \chi^2$ (.95;33)

Manufacturing sector in the UK
1958 - 1986

Production workers			Nonproduction workers			Capital		
λ_{11}:	0.74	(0.70)	λ_{21}:	1.86	(1.08)	λ_{31}:	0.69	(0.74)
λ_{12}:	-0.75	(-1.16)	λ_{22}:	-1.38	(-1.24)	λ_{32}:	-0.54	(-0.66)
λ_{13}:	1.10	(0.97)	λ_{23}:	1.64	(0.91)	λ_{33}:	1.58	(0.70)
γ_{11}:	9.61	(1.95)	γ_{22}:	7.14	(1.23)	γ_{33}:	97.16	(1.47)
β_1 :	3.18	(3.85)	β_2 :	-2.47	(-2.71)	β_3 :	-11.06	(-2.63)

TESTS

SB :	1.95	SB :	1.81	SB :	1.59
ARCH		ARCH		ARCH	
1	1.77	1	0.69	1	0.58
2	1.57	2	0.94	2	2.47
3	2.77	3	1.48	3	3.31
4	4.91	4	1.49	4	3.22

Overidentifying restrictions	:	$17.48 < \chi^2$ (.95;9)
Linearity	:	$15.64 > \chi^2$ (.95;3)
Structural stability after OC1	:	$38.41 < \chi^2$ (.95;24)

* Asymptotic t-values are given within parentheses. Results conditional on a constant, two oil shock dummies, and for the Netherlands three seasonal dummies.

Estimating τ turns out to be difficult. No convergence was achieved when τ was estimated. Estimates of τ always turned out to be close to one. Consequently, τ was set equal to unity prior to estimation. Notice also that system (4.1) could be estimated as a sequence of linear GMM estimators by first fixing τ and β_i in the exponential term at an a priori value, then estimating the resulting linear system and iterating until convergence is achieved. A qualification should be made with respect to the asymptotic properties of the procedures we use. Given that the variables in the Euler equations were found to be integrated of order one, standard asymptotic theory may not apply to its full extent to the estimators and tests. However West (1988) has shown that for linear instrumental variables procedures with nonstationary regressors standard asymptotic properties are recovered when the nonstationary variables share a common root. As there is empirical evidence that input demand and factor prices are cointegrated, West's results possibly carry over to the nonlinear GMM estimator.

The SB statistic does not point at any significant nonstationarity in the residuals for the Netherlands. Hansen's (1982) J-statistic is reported to test the overidentifying restrictions of the IV orthogonality conditions. In the model for the Netherlands the overidentifying restrictions are not rejected. We compute Gallant's (1987) likelihood ratio (LR)-type statistic to test for symmetric linearity. Linearity, that is the importance of the asymmetric specification ($H_0 : \beta_i = 0, \; i = 1,2,3$) is rejected. There is no evidence in the data for the Netherlands that the parameters have undergone a structural change after OC2. However a significant first order ARCH statistic (see Engle (1982)) possibly indicates that a structural change occurred in the variance of the employment equation for nonproduction workers. The SB statistic points at the presence of nonstationarity in the residuals for capital in the UK (although the power of this test is low). The overidentifying restrictions and the structural stability are rejected at a 5 percent level, using the Chow-type test of

Andrews and Fair (1988), but not at a 1 percent level. Linearity is rejected for the UK data as well. The estimated value of UK's γ_{22} is unexpectedly low compared with γ_{11}. Although this result is not significant, it is inconsistent with the results presented in the previous section. In accordance with the empirical findings in Pfann and Palm (1992) hiring costs exceed firing costs for production workers ($\beta_1 > 0$), whereas firing costs exceed hiring costs for nonproduction workers ($\beta_2 < 0$). The estimate of the asymmetric adjustment costs parameter of capital, β_3, is negative for the Netherlands and for the UK. Therefore, scrapping of capital will take more time than building up new capital. The firm retains from scrapping capital during recessions, whereas the firm more quickly takes investment decisions during periods of an economic upswing.

5. Conclusions

In this paper we developed and analysed dynamic demand models for the profit maximising firm with asymmetric adjustment costs under uncertainty. In section 2, we discussed some aspects of the econometric methodology of modelling optimal decisions by firms.

In section 3, the model for a firm that employs production and nonproduction workers, uses capital stock and faces asymmetric adjustment costs has been presented. In section 4, the model has been applied and tested, using quarterly time series data of the manufacturing sector in the Netherlands for the period 1971.I - 1984.IV, and annual data for the manufacturing sector in the UK for the period 1955-1986.

To summarize, the following conclusions were reached.

1. There is no significant evidence for the existence of a long run relationship between factor inputs on the one hand and real factor prices on the other hand. There is however evidence for the coexistence of stochastic trends (real input prices) and deterministic trends (e.g. technological innovations).
2. Hiring costs exceed firing costs of production workers ($\beta_1 > 0$).
3. Firing costs exceed hiring costs of nonproduction workers ($\beta_2 < 0$).
4. Scrapping costs exceed investment costs of capital ($\beta_3 < 0$).

By and large, we may conclude that the asymmetric adjustment costs model is more appropriate for the data we analysed than the linear quadratic model. Our results also appear to be robust for both countries. The differences in the shape of the adjustment cost function indicate that disaggregation of labour into two categories is imperative in the present case.

A more extended comparison of time-to-build models of capital with asymmetric adjustment costs models will be the subject of future research.

Appendix 1A :

Sources of the quarterly Dutch manufacturing (SBI 2/3) data.

The base year of all prices and indices is 1980.

N^*, N_1, N_2: The total numbers (in thousands) of blue collar workers (N_1) and white collar workers (N_2) have been computed from quarterly indices of total manufacturing employment (N^*), obtained from the Centraal Bureau voor de Statistiek (CBS), Algemene Industrie Statistiek, and manufacturing total aggregate numbers and the ratio of blue and white collar workers have been interpolated from the CBS Loonstruktuur Onderzoek 1972 and the Arbeidskrachtentelling 1975, 1977, 1979, 1981 and 1983.

H_1, H_2: Average weekly working hours including overtime hours for blue collar workers (H_1) and white collar workers (H_2) have been obtained from the CBS Halfjaarlijkse Loononderzoek. These series are sixmonthly data which have been interpolated.

L_1, L_2: Total number of weekly hours worked by blue collar workers (L_1) and white collar workers (L_2) : $L_i = N_i * H_i$, $i = 1,2$.

Py: Producers price index of domestic sales, Producenten Prijsindexcijfers van de Binnenlandse Afzet van de Nederlandse Industrie (SBI 2/3) are unpublished data which have been kindly provided by CBS.

W^*, W_1, W_2: Gross hourly wage costs for blue collar workers (Pl_1) and white collar workers (Pl_2) have been computed from the CBS Halfjaarlijkse Loononderzoek, the CBS Driejaarlijkse Loonkosten Onderzoek,started in 1972, and the quarterly index of wage costs in current prices (W^*) obtained from the CBS Kwartaalonderzoek Verdiende Lonen. Real hourly wage costs (W_1,W_2) have been obtained by deflating Pl_1 and Pl_2 respectively by Py.

Y : Index manufacturing output in constant prices, obtained from CBS Nationale Rekeningen.

K, Q: Net capital stock (K) has been computed from annual manufacturing capital stock data which are used in the VINSEC model of the Centraal Plan Bureau (CPB), and from quarterly aggregate data of capital stocks used in the CPB model KOMPAS. The real price of capital has been obtained by deflating the price index of manufacturing investment goods in current prices (Pk) by Py.

R3L, YGB: Rate on three months loans to local authorities (R3L) and the yield of long term government bonds (YGB) for the Netherlands have been obtained from OECD Main Economic Indicators.

NUR: Rate of registered unemployment in the Netherlands (NUR) obtained from the Ministerie van Sociale Zaken en Werkgelegenheid.

Appendix 1B:

Sources of the annual UK manufacturing data.

The base year of all prices and indices is 1980.
The following main data sources were used.

BB:	Blue Book.
DEG:	Department of Employment Gazette.
ETAS:	Economic Trend Annual Supplement.
HABLS:	Historical Abstract of British Labour Statistic.
MM:	Mendis, L., and J. Muellbauer (1984), "British Manufacturing Productivity 1955-1983: Measurement Problems, Oil Shocks, and Thatcher Effects", CEPR Discussion Paper No. 34.

L_1, L_2: Total (full time and part time) number of production workers (L_1) and nonproduction workers (L_2) have been computed from theETAS total number of employees in UK manufacturing, and DEG employment shares.

Y, Py: Index of total manufacturing output (Y), and producers price index of home sales of all manufactured products (Py) have been obtained from ETAS.

W_1, W_2: Index of real weekly earnings of full time production workers (W_1) and nonproduction workers (W_2) have been obtained by deflating gross weekly earnings of manual and nonmanual workers respectively (pre- 1970 data: HABLS, from 1970 on data : New Earnings Survey in DEG) by Py.

K, Q: The gross capital stock at constant prices (K) has been obtained from BB for data from 1963 and from MM for pre-1963 data. The real price of capital (Q) has been obtained by dividing the series for manufacturing investment in current and constant prices obtained from ETAS and deflating this series by Py.

Pm: Producer price index of materials and fuel purchased by manufacturing industry (ETAS).

References

Andrews, D.W.K., and R.C. Fair (1988), "Inference in Nonlinear Econometric Models with Structural Change", Review of Economic Studies 55, 615-639.

Bentolila, S., and G. Bertola (1990), "Firing Costs and Labor Demand: How Bad is Eurosclerosis ?", Review of Economic Studies 57, 381-402.

Burda, M.C. (1991), "Monopolistic Competition, Costs of Adjustment, and the Behaviour of European Manufacturing Employment", European Economic Review 35, 61-79.

Burgess, S. (1988), "Employment Adjustment in UK Manufacturing", Economic Journal 98, 81-103.

Burgess, S., and J.J. Dolado (1989), "Intertemporal Rules with Variable Speed of Adjustment: An Application to UK Manufacturing Employment", Economic Journal 99, 347-365.

Cassings, S., and T. Kollintzas (1991), "Recursive Factor of Production Interrelations and Endogenous Cycling", International Economic Review 31, 417-440.

Dolado, J.J. (1987), "Employment, Price and Inventory in Manufacturing Industry", D. Phil.Thesis, University of Oxford.

Eichenbaum, M., and L.P. Hansen (1990), "Estimating Models with Intertemporal Substitution Using Aggregate Time Series Data", Journal of Business and Economic Statistics 8, 53-70.

Eichenbaum, M., L.P. Hansen, and K.J. Singleton (1988), "A Time Series Analysis of Representative Agent Models of Consumption and Leisure Choice under Uncertainty", Quarterly Journal of Economics, 51-78.

Engle, R.F. (1982), "Autoregressive Conditional Heteroskedasticity with Estimates of the Variance of UK Inflations", Econometrica 50, 987-1008.

Epstein, L.G., and M.G.S. Denny (1983), "The Multivariate Flexible Accelerator Model: Its Empirical Restrictions and an Application to US Manufacturing", Econometrica 51, 647-674.

Epstein, L.G., and A.J. Yatchew (1985), "The Empirical Determination of Technology and Expectations. A Simplified Procedure", Journal of Econometrics 27, 235-258.

Escribano, A. (1987), "Error-correction Systems: Nonlinear Adjustments to Linear Long-Run Relationships", CORE Discussion Paper 8730, University of Louvain, 29 pp.

Fuller, W.A. (1976), Introduction to Statistical Time Series, New York, John Wiley.

Gallant, A.R. (1987), Nonlinear Statistical Models, New York, John Wiley.

Ghysels, E., and A. Hall (1990a), "A Test for Structural Stability of Euler Conditions Parameters Estimated via the Generalized Methods of Moments Estimators", International Economic Review 31, 355-364.

Ghysels, E., and A. Hall (1990b), "Are Consumption-Based Intertemporal Capital Asset Pricing Models Structural ?", Journal of Econometrics 45, 121-143.

Gouriéroux, C., A. Monfort, and A. Trognon (1985), "Moindres Carrés Asymptotiques", Annales de l'INSEE 58, 91-122.

Hamermesh, D.S. (1989), "Labor Demand and the Structure of Adjustment Costs", American Economic Review 79, 674-689.

Hansen, L.P. (1982), "Large Sample Properties of Generalized Methods of Moments Estimators", Econometrica 50, 1029-1054.

Hansen, L.P. (1985), "A Method for Calculating Bounds on the Asymptotic Covariance Matrices of Generalized Methods of Moments Estimators", Journal of Econometrics, 30, 203-238.

Hansen, L.P., and T.J. Sargent (1981), "Linear Rational Expectations Models for Dynamically Interrelated Variables", in: R. Lucas and T. Sargent (eds.), Expectations and Econometric Practice, Minneapolis: University of Minnesota Press.

Hayashi, F., and C.A. Sims (1983), "Nearly Efficient Estimation of Time Series Models with Predetermined but Not Strictly Exogenous Instruments", Econometrica 51, 783-798.

Holt, C.C., F. Modigliani, J.F. Muth, and H.A. Simon (1960), Planning Production, Inventories and Work Force, Prentice-Hall, New Jersey.

Johansen, S. (1988), "Statistical Analysis of Cointegration Vectors", Journal of Economic Dynamics and Control 12, 231-254.

Kodde, D.A., F.C. Palm, and G.A. Pfann (1990), "Asymptotic Least Squares Estimation, Efficiency Considerations and Applications", Journal of Applied Econometrics 5, 229-243.

Kokkelenberg, E.C. (1984), "The Specification and Estimation of Interrelated Factor Demand under Uncertainty", Journal of Economic Dynamics and Control 7, 181-207.

Kollintzas, T. (1985), "The Symmetric Linear Rational Expectations Model", Econometrica 53, 963-976.

Kydland, F., and E. Prescott (1982), "Time to Build and Aggregate Fluctuations", Econometrica 50, 1345-1371.

Meese, R. (1980), "Dynamic Factor Demand Schedules for Labour and Capital under Rational Expectations", Journal of Econometrics 14, 141-158.

Newey, W.K. (1985), "Generalized Method of Moments Specification Testing", Journal of Econometrics 29, 229-256.

Newey, W.K., and K. West (1987), "Hypothesis Testing with Efficient Method of Moments Estimations", International Economic Review 28, 777-787.

Nickell, S.J. (1984), "An Investigation of the Determinants of Manufacturing Employment in the United Kingdom", Review of Economic Studies 51, 529-557.

Nickell, S.J. (1985), "Error Correction, Partial Adjustment and All That: An Expository Note", Oxford Bulletin of Economics and Statistics 47, 119-129.

Nickell, S.J. (1986), "Dynamic Models of Labour Demand", in O. Ashenfelter and R. Layard (eds.), Handbook of Labor Economics, Elsevier, Amsterdam.

Palm, F.C., and G.A. Pfann (1990), "Interrelated Demand Rational Expectations Models for Two Types of Labour", Oxford Bulletin of Economics and Statistics 52, 45-68.

Perron, P. (1989), "The Great Crash, the Oil Price Shock and the Unit Root Hypothesis", Econometrica 57, 1361-1401.

Phillips, P.C.B., and S. Ouliaris (1990), "Asymptotic Properties of Residual Based Tests for Cointegration", Econometrica 58, 165-193.

Pfann, G.A., and B. Verspagen (1989), "The Structure of Adjustment Costs for Labour in the Dutch Manufacturing Sector", Economics Letters 29, 365-371.

Pfann, G.A., and F.C. Palm (1992), "Asymmetric Adjustment Costs in Non-linear Labour Demand Models for the Netherlands and UK Manufacturing Sectors", CORE Discussion Paper nr. 9217, forthcoming in Review of Economic Studies.

Pfann, G.A. (1990), Dynamic Modelling of Stochastic Demand for Manufacturing Employment, Berlin, Springer-Verlag.

Pindyck, R.S., and J.J. Rotemberg (1983a), "Dynamic Factor Demands and the Effects of Energy Price Shocks", American Economic Review 73, 1066-1079.

Pindyck, R.S., and J.J. Rotemberg (1983b), "Dynamic Factor Demands under Rational Expectations", Scandinavian Journal of Economics 85, 223-238.

Rossi, P.E. (1987), "Comparison of Dynamic Factor Demand Models", 357-376, in Barnett W.A., E.R. Berndt, and H. White (eds.), Dynamic Econometric Modeling, Cambridge, Cambridge University Press.

Sargan, J.D., and A. Bhargava (1983), "Testing Residuals from Least Squares Regression for Being Generated by the Gaussian Random Walk", Econometrica 51, 153-174.

Singleton, K.J. (1988), "Econometric Issues in the Analysis of Equilibrium Business Cycle Models", Journal of Monetary Economics 21, 361-386.

Smith, D. (1984), "Short Run Employment Functions when the Speed of Adjustment Depends on the Unemployment Rate", Review of Economics and Statistics 66, 138-142.

Tauchen, G. (1986), "Statistical Properties of Generalized Method of Moments Estimators of Structural Parameters Obtained from Financial Data" (with comments), Journal of Business and Economic Statistics 4, 397-425.

West, K.D. (1988), "Asymptotic Normality, when Regressors have a Unit Root", Econometrica 56, 1397-1417.

Are Real Interest Rates Stable? An International Comparison*

Gebhard Kirchgässner
(University of St. Gallen and
Swiss Federal Institute of Technology, Zürich)

and

Jürgen Wolters
(Free University of Berlin)

1. Introduction

The question whether real interest rates are stable, has, with the exception of a very few papers, not been tackled so far. In empirical investigations, one has traditionally assumed that nominal and real interest rates are stationary. This was the basis for applying traditional econometric methods. In the last few years, however, quite a lot of empirical papers have found that nominal interest rates for various countries are not stationary but contain a unit root.[1] If this finding is correct, it can have implications for the stochastic structure of real interest rates and for the econometric methodology which one should apply. But also from a theoretical point of view, it is important to know the time series

---

* Paper presented at the Second Workshop on Applied Econometrics, Munich, January 11-12, 1990. Revised Version, March 1990. - We thank for helpful comments of the conference participants and we gratefully acknowledge financial support from the Deutsche Forschungsgemeinschaft by grant No. 322 147.

1. See, e.g. G. Kirchgässner and J. Wolters (1990).

behaviour of real interest rates. In general, the theoretical approaches at least implicitly assume stationary real interest rates.

This paper analyses domestic money market rates for the period of flexible exchange rates from January 1974 to December 1988 for the Federal Republic of Germany, Switzerland, the United States, France, and Britain together with the corresponding inflation rates. The applied methods are unit root and cointegration tests. As far as we know, there are only the papers by R. MacDonald and P.D. Murphy (1989), P. Kugler and K. Neusser (1990), A.K. Rose (1988), P.C. Schotman (1987, 1989), and R. Garcia and P. Perron (1989) which investigate the stationary behaviour of real interest rates. But all these papers do not deal in detail with the development of Swiss or German real rates and they differ in the applied test procedures.

The paper is organized as follows: the next chapter presents some theoretical and methodological considerations. Then, follows a short description of the data used. The fourth chapter contains the testing procedure for the unit root tests and the empirical results. The fifth chapter deals with the cointegration tests. We finish with some concluding remarks.

2. Some Theoretical Considerations

The starting point of all considerations on real interest rates is the following theorem formulated by I. Fisher (1930): the nominal interest rate (i) has as a linear approximation an orthogonal decomposition in the ex ante real rate (r) and the expected inflation rate (p^e):

$$i = r + p^{e}. \tag{1}$$

Both components on the right-hand side of equation (1) are not observable. In order to be able to work with this decomposition, one needs additional assumptions. Assuming that the expectations on inflation rates are formed rationally in the sense of J. Muth (1961), we can write

$$i_{k,t} = r_{k,t} + E_t(p_{t+k}), \tag{2}$$

where $i_{k,t}$ denotes the nominal interest rate of a bond with maturity k at time t, $r_{k,t}$ is the corresponding ex ante real rate and $E_t(p_{t+k})$ is the mathematical expectation of the inflation rate between time t and t+k. The forecast error ($u_{k,t}$) is stationary with $E(u_{k,t}) = 0$. It follows an MA(k-1)-process. This leads to a decomposition of the nominal interest rate in the ex post real rate $r_{k,t}^*$ and the inflation rate p_{t+k}:

$$\begin{aligned} i_{k,t} &= r_{k,t}^* + p_{t+k} \\ &= (r_{k,t} - u_{k,t}) + (E_t(p_{t+k}) + u_{k,t}). \end{aligned} \tag{3}$$

In contrast to the decomposition in (2), the components in (3) are negatively correlated.

The relation between nominal interest rates and inflation rates can be written more generally as

$$i_{k,t} = \alpha + \beta p_{t,k} + v_t. \tag{4}$$

The most restrictive assumption is: $r_{k,t} = \alpha$, i.e. at the ex ante real rate is constant, together with $\beta = 1$ and $v_t = -u_{k,t}$. But without knowing the expected inflation rate, it is empirically not testable since it is observationally equivalent to the assumption that the real interest rate follows an MA-process with maximal order k-1 and a constant expectation.

Now, we give up the traditionally made assumption of the stationarity of nominal interest rates and (expected) inflation rates[2)] and assume that nominal interest rates are integrated of order one. This means that the first differences of nominal interest rates are stationary and invertible. According to the theory of cointegrated processes by e.g. R.F. Engle and C.W.J. Granger (1987), we can draw the following conclusions: (i) If the (expected) inflation rate is stationary, the real rate is integrated of order one. (ii) If the (expected) inflation rate is integrated of order one but nominal interest rates and inflation rates are not cointegrated, then the real rate is non stationary. Then, the Fisher-hypothesis (4) can only hold as a short run relation. (iii) If the (expected) inflation rate is integrated of order one and cointegrated with the nominal interest rate, then the real rate is stationary and equation (4) holds as a long run relation. Here, we have not restricted the parameter β to one, because there are various theoretical explanations which lead to values for β less than one or larger than one. But in case the cointegrating parameter β differs from one, though the ex ante rate is stationary, the ex post real interest rate constructed as $r_{k,t}^* = i_{t,k} - p_{t+k}$ is non stationary.

If inflation rates are integrated of order one but differ from their expected rates only by a stationary process, conclusions based on cointegrating theory are correct for the observed and expected inflation rate and, therefore, also for the ex post and ex ante real rates. This gives us the possibility to test the stationarity assumption of ex ante real rates using observed inflation

2. See, e.g., M. Granziol and H. Schelbert (1983) or A. Thiemer (1987).

rates.

In testing, we can use two different procedures.

(i) We construct ex post real interest rates and apply unit root tests.

(ii) We test according to equation (4) the Fisher-hypothesis by using cointegration tests, which enables us to draw conclusions about the ex ante real rates.

But at first, in both cases, we have to test the necessary conditions. The order of integration for nominal interest rates and the inflation rates. Inflation rates must contain one unit root, the logarithms of prices have to possess a double unit root.

3. Data

We investigate domestic money market rates, inflation rates and ex post real interest rates for the U.S., the Federal Republic of Germany, Switzerland, France and Britain for the period of flexible exchange rates from January 1974 to December 1988.[3)] This period can be characterized as follows: Before 1980, exchange rates were flexible between the U.S. and Europe and also within Europe, though in the late seventies there were some attempts to stabilize exchange rates in Europe within the so-called 'snake'. During the period from 1974 to the end of 1979, there was a strong decline of the U.S. Dollar and the U.S. Federal Reserve followed a policy of interest rate targeting. Since 1980, exchange rates within Europe have been stabilized by

---

3. For the definition and sources of data, see the Appendix.

the 'European Monetary System'. With respect to the U.S. Dollar, this period was characterized by a sharp increase of its exchange rate until 1985 and an even stronger decline afterwards. Contrary to the seventies, the U.S. Federal Reserve placed its emphasis to control money growth on the development of the quantity of money and not on targeting interest rates at least until 1982. As different policy regimes can lead to different generating processes and different relations between economic variables, we perform all the tests also for the period from January 1980 to December 1988.

To measure price developments, we used the consumer price indices. All variables are seasonally adjusted with the multiplicative version of the Census X11-method.[4)] For the unit root tests, we used the logarithms of the seasonally adjusted price indices. Here, we investigated the levels and the first differences.

Since we have three month nominal interest rates in constructing ex post real interest rates, we also need three month inflation rates on an annual basis. With P being the price index, the inflation rate p is computed as

$$p_t = 400\,(\ln P_{t+2} - \ln P_{t-1}), \tag{5}$$

i.e. we have a moving average over three months of monthly inflation rates.

4. The seasonal movements in these data are not very strong. We found no indication for seasonal non-stationarities.

4. Results of Unit Root Tests

As a necessary condition for all further investigations, we have to find the order of integration for the individual time series. We apply the following testing procedure:[5] If the true model is a stationary series with a deterministic linear trend, then in the usual (augmented) Dickey-Fuller test equation without a trend term the coefficient of the lagged dependent variable tends toward one and its t-value towards zero.[6] This leads to the wrong conclusion of integration of order one. Therefore, if it is plausible to assume that the time series can contain a trend, then one should start the testing procedure with ordinary least squares (OLS) estimation of

$$y_t = \beta_0 + \beta_1 t + \rho y_{t-1} + x_t, \tag{6}$$

where the two alternatives used for x_t are

$$(i) \quad x_t = u_t + \alpha_1 u_{t-1}$$

and

$$(ii) \quad x_t = \sum_{j=1}^{p} \gamma_j \, \Delta y_{t-j} + u_t$$

to make it empirically white noise. To have empirically white noise residuals is very important since all tests used are very sensitive to remaining autocorrelations in the residuals.

5. For the following, compare also P. Perron (1988).
6. See P. Perron (1988, Theorem 1).

We do not apply the nonparametric approach by P. Phillips[7] since G.W. Schwert (1989) has shown in a Monte Carlo study that this procedure has drawbacks when the MA-process has a negative coefficient. This is the case with many of our data. The AR-specification (ii) can be seen as an approximation of the MA-process (i), therefore we have to use relatively high values for p ($\approx \sqrt{T}$).

We use the following test statistics for (6): t_τ and ϕ_3. They correspond to a t-test for $\rho = 1$ and an F-test for $\beta_1 = 0$ and $\rho = 1$. Both have as null hypothesis that there is a unit root without trend. As both statistics are invariant with respect to the true expectations μ of the series, the drift term can be arbitrary. The application of ϕ_3 is recommended since the limiting distribution of t_τ is not invariant to the coefficient of the trend term under the null hypothesis of a unit root. The test statistic ϕ_2 has as null hypothesis that there is a unit root without drift and trend.

Computation of these test statistics is done as follows: t_τ is the usual t-ratio of the OLS estimate of ρ in (6).[8] ϕ_3 and ϕ_2 are computed as common F-ratios.[9] Therefore, to calculate these statistics, one additionally has to estimate the restricted equations

$$\Delta y_t = \beta_0 + x_t \tag{7}$$

and

7. See, e.g., P. Perron (1988).

8. Critical values are given in W.A. Fuller (1976, Table 8.5.2).

9. Critical values can be found in D.A. Dickey and W.A. Fuller (1981, Table V and VI).

$$\Delta y_t = x_t. \tag{8}$$

If the null hypothesis can be rejected with the tests t_τ and ϕ_3, we can stop the procedure. If the null hypothesis is not rejected, this can be because of the poor power properties compared to the test statistics based on the regression model

$$y_t = \beta_0 + \rho y_{t-1} + x_t. \tag{9}$$

Before we can use the test statistics t_μ and ϕ_1, both testing for a random walk without drift, we have to verify with ϕ_2 that no drift exists because t_μ and ϕ_1 are not invariant with respect to the drift term.

The results for nominal interest rates for Switzerland (SSR), Germany (GSR), the U.S. (USR), France (FSR) and Britain (BSR) are presented in Table 1. They are very clear. There is strong evidence that nominal interest rates are integrated of order one with a vanishing drift parameter.[10)] There is one exception for USR with an MA(1) specification in the eighties. But this can be due to a more complicated generating process for the U.S. interest rates. Allowing for an AR(6) process does not lead to a rejection of the null hypothesis. In general, these findings are in line with the results by R. MacDonald and P.D. Murphy (1989) and A.K. Rose (1988) for other countries, too.

Unit root tests for price indices for Switzerland (SCPS), Germany (GCPS), the U.S. (UCPS), France (FCPS) and Britain (BCPS) are given in Table 2. Modelling the test equation with an AR(12) specification including the time

---

10. Additionally, we tested for unit roots in the first differences of nominal interest rates. In all cases, we have to reject the null hypothesis of a unit root.

Table 1: Unit Root Tests for Nominal Interest Rates

	USR		GSR		SSR		BSR		FSR	
	MA(1)	AR(6)	MA(1)	AR(6)	MA(1)	AR(6)	MA(1)	AR(6)	MA(1)	AR(6)
	1/1980 - 12/1988, 108 Observations									
$\hat{\rho}_\tau$	0.75	0.87	0.95	0.93	0.92	0.89	0.94	0.90	0.91	0.91
$\hat{t}_\tau$	-4.79**	-2.18	-1.61	-2.18	-2.03	-2.81	-1.60	-2.07	-2.46	-2.53
$\hat{\Phi}_3$	7.57*	2.40	1.61	2.48	2.14	4.00	2.74	3.20	3.23	3.33
$\hat{\Phi}_2$	5.08*	1.70	1.22	1.78	1.42	2.67	1.88	2.19	2.24	2.32
$\hat{\rho}_\mu$	0.91	0.96	0.97	0.98	0.95	0.92	0.93	0.93	0.97	0.98
$\hat{t}_\mu$	-3.04*	-1.21	-1.65	-1.42	-1.77	-2.47	-2.33	-2.42	-1.46	-1.02
$\hat{\Phi}_1$	3.00	0.88	1.14	1.19	1.46	3.06	2.88	3.03	0.98	0.66
	1/1974 - 12/1988, 180 Observations									
$\hat{\rho}_\tau$	0.93	0.97	0.96	0.97	0.96	0.94	0.95	0.93	0.96	0.96
$\hat{t}_\tau$	-3.20(*)	-1.44	-3.03	-2.64	-2.10	-3.01	-2.26	-3.02	-2.28	-2.23
$\hat{\Phi}_3$	3.36	1.08	3.69	3.89	2.13	4.71	2.98	4.76	1.98	2.50
$\hat{\Phi}_2$	2.24	0.72	2.77	2.72	1.43	3.14	1.99	3.17	1.33	1.68
$\hat{\rho}_\mu$	0.94	0.97	0.96	0.97	0.96	0.95	0.95	0.93	0.96	0.96
$\hat{t}_\mu$	-3.21*	-1.46	-3.40*	-2.79(*)	-2.03	-2.96*	-2.30	-3.08*	-2.26	-2.22
$\hat{\Phi}_1$	3.38	1.07	3.87(*)	4.08(*)	1.86	4.38(*)	2.93	4.73*	1.94	2.50

'(*)', '*' or '**' denote significance on the 10 percent, 5 percent or 1 percent level, respectively.

Table 2: Unit Root Tests for Price Indices (Logarithms of seasonally adjusted data)

	UCPS		GCPS		SCPS		BCPS		FCPS	
	MA(1)	AR(12)	MA(1)	AR(12)	MA(1)	AR(12)	MA(1)	AR(12)	MA(1)	AR(12)
	1/1980 - 12/1988, 108 Observations									
$\hat{\rho}_\tau$	0.93	0.96	0.98	0.98	0.98	0.98	0.92	0.95	0.99	0.99
$\hat{t}_\tau$	-7.80**	-3.28(*)	-2.78	-2.07	-1.36	-1.34	-8.46**	-3.81*	-2.45	-1.66
$\hat{\phi}_3$	27.62**	5.40	19.14**	4.01	6.19(*)	3.44	38.68**	7.27*	58.16**	7.30*
$\hat{\phi}_2$	59.01**	4.38(*)	31.89**	2.88	20.19**	3.12	93.40**	6.05*	134.63**	4.98*
$\hat{\rho}_\mu$	0.98	1.00	0.98	0.99	0.99	0.99	0.98	1.00	0.98	0.99
$\hat{t}_\mu$	-8.19**	-0.99	-8.49**	-2.84(*)	-4.69**	-2.60(*)	-8.30**	-1.13	-13.18**	-3.66
$\hat{\phi}_1$	66.88**	1.56	48.07**	4.36(*)	30.54**	4.63(*)	97.30**	2.23	200.83**	6.86**
	1/1974 - 12/1988, 180 Observations									
$\hat{\rho}_\tau$	1.00	0.99	1.01	1.00	0.99	0.98	0.99	0.99	1.01	1.00
$\hat{t}_\tau$	0.39	-1.67	1.63	-0.44	-0.50	-1.95	-2.67	-1.74	4.28	0.33
$\hat{\phi}_3$	16.53**	2.05	19.48**	0.92	2.35	1.93	34.32**	7.37*	48.35**	2.28
$\hat{\phi}_2$	93.49**	2.21	65.76**	1.37	26.70**	3.17	97.04**	6.07*	197.73**	1.96
$\hat{\rho}_\mu$	0.99	1.00	0.99	1.00	1.00	1.00	0.99	0.99	0.99	1.00
$\hat{t}_\mu$	-8.38**	-1.51	-7.50**	-1.36	-2.48	-0.54	-11.30**	-3.84**	-10.64**	-2.04
$\hat{\phi}_1$	138.87**	2.39	92.88**	2.07	40.24**	2.93	146.40**	9.10**	253.67**	2.74

'(*)', '*' or '**' denote significance on the 10 percent, 5 percent or 1 percent level, respectively.

trend variable does not lead to a rejection of the null hypothesis for the whole period according to the t-test. For the eighties, there is evidence for the alternative hypothesis only for the U.S. (10%) and Britain (5%). Excluding the time trend, the t-test rejects in some cases the null hypothesis although all coefficients are extremely close to one. On the other hand, using the MA(1) specification very often produces highly significant rejections of the null hypotheses for the F-tests. In this case, this can be interpreted as an indication that at least a double unit root exists. Performing F-tests, we estimate - in contrast to the t-test - under the null hypothesis. If there is more than one unit root, then Δy_t in (7) or (8) is itself non stationary. Using an MA-specification for x_t, the parametrization is not able to capture this non stationarity, in contrast to an AR-specification. Therefore, the residuals show a non stationary behaviour. In general, the results in Table 2 show that price indices possess at least one unit root but no drift.

For our investigation, the order of integration for the (monthly) inflation rates is much more important.[11)] These results are given in Table 3. For the inflation rate for the Federal Republic of Germany (DGCPS), we can in no case reject the unit root hypothesis without drift. The same result holds for the U.S. inflation rate (DUCPS) when we use an AR-specification. In the case of the MA-specification, the F-tests indicate deviations from the null hypothesis. Relatively mixed evidence appears for the Swiss inflation rate (DSCPS). For the whole period, all tests reject the null hypothesis with the AR-specification but not with the MA-specification. For the eighties, we

11. If the monthly inflation rate has a unit root, then the quarterly inflation rate constructed according to (5) also has a unit root and because of the averaging operator $(1+L+L^2)$, two conjugate complex roots on the unit circle in the MA part.

Table 3: Unit Root Tests for Monthly Inflation Rates (Seasonally adjusted data)

	DUCPS MA(1)	DUCPS AR(12)	DGCPS MA(1)	DGCPS AR(12)	DSCPS MA(1)	DSCPS AR(12)	DBCPS MA(1)	DBCPS AR(12)	DFCPS MA(1)	DFCPS AR(12)
	1/1980 - 12/1988, 108 Observations									
$\hat{\rho}_\tau$	0.69	0.86	0.30	0.50	0.03	0.19	0.92	0.74	0.03	0.04
$\hat{t}_\tau$	-2.48	-1.05	-2.02	-1.96	-3.00	-2.85	-0.65	-2.08	-0.77	-3.55*
$\hat{\phi}_3$	8.21*	2.43	5.24	2.02	11.10**	4.06	6.12(*)	3.84	2.22	6.32(*)
$\hat{\phi}_2$	5.53*	1.88	3.59	1.50	7.40**	2.74	4.40(*)	2.79	2.47	4.57(*)
$\hat{\rho}_\mu$	0.78	0.82	0.89	0.86	0.47	0.68	0.93	0.78	0.97	0.92
$\hat{t}_\mu$	-2.40	-2.18	-0.85	-1.24	-2.31	-1.78	-0.85	-2.75(*)	-0.32	-1.04
$\hat{\phi}_1$	7.23**	2.76	1.78	0.99	6.26*	1.62	6.68*	4.12(*)	1.77	1.02
	1/1974 - 12/1988, 180 Observations									
$\hat{\rho}_\tau$	0.78	0.83	0.88	0.71	0.46	0.57	0.66	0.46	0.96	0.76
$\hat{t}_\tau$	-2.37	-2.00	-0.71	-2.32	-2.71	-3.47*	-2.02	-3.93*	-0.35	-2.56
$\hat{\phi}_3$	6.63*	2.05	2.25	3.17	3.69	7.15*	8.31*	7.72*	1.72	3.32
$\hat{\phi}_2$	4.43(*)	1.39	1.21	2.52	1.64	5.16*	5.57*	5.16*	1.87	2.37
$\hat{\rho}_\mu$	0.86	0.89	0.94	0.82	0.53	0.59	0.91	0.84	0.99	0.91
$\hat{t}_\mu$	-1.92	-1.72	-0.59	-2.24	-2.64(*)	-3.78**	-1.12	-2.00	-0.24	-1.47
$\hat{\phi}_1$	4.68	1.52	0.82	3.13	1.58	7.74**	3.24	2.02	2.01	1.31

'(*)', '*' or '**' denote significance on the 10 percent, 5 percent or 1 percent level, respectively.

find significant deviations from the null only with the F-tests and the MA-specification. For the U.K. inflation rate (DBCPS) excluding the time trend, we find only very weak evidence against the null hypothesis for both periods. For France (DFCPS), the results of all tests support the unit root hypothesis.

Taking all results together, we have strong evidence that nominal interest rates and somewhat less evidence that inflation rates in these countries contain a random walk component without drift.[12)] In this case, it can be possible that nominal interest rates and inflation rates are cointegrated and if the cointegration coefficient is equal to one, that (ex post) real interest rates are stationary. Therefore, we perform unit root tests for the ex post real interest rates directly. The results are given in Table 4.[13)] The results for Germany (GSRR), the U.S. (USRR) and France (FSRR) are very clear. These rates show non stationary behaviour for both periods. The evidence for the Swiss real rate (SSRR) is mixed. For both periods, the results with the MA-specification are in line with the non stationarity hypothesis. But the findings with the AR-specification indicate stationary behaviour of the Swiss real rates. For the whole period, only the tests excluding the time trend show non stationary behaviour of the British real rate (BSRR), whereas in all other cases there is evidence for stationary behaviour at least at the 10 percent level.

---

12. With respect to the inflation rates, these findings are in contrast to the results by A.K. Rose (1988) whose tests with quarterly data lead to stationary inflation rates for all 18 countries considered, whereas - also with quarterly data - R. MacDonald and P.D. Murphy (1989) report in contrast to A.K. Rose (1988) that inflation rates for Belgium, Canada, UK and U.S.A. are integrated of order one.

13. In constructing real rates, we apply three month inflation rates. Therefore, we use a moving average process of order three in the test equations here.

Table 4: Unit Root Tests for Ex-post Real Interest Rates (Seasonally adjusted data)

	USRR		GSRR		SSRR		BSRR		FSRR	
	MA(3)	AR(12)	MA(3)	AR(12)	MA(3)	AR(12)	MA(3)	AR(12)	MA(3)	AR(12)
	1/1980 - 12/1988, 108 Observations									
$\hat{\rho}_\tau$	0.93	0.88	0.76	0.73	0.72	0.58	0.69	0.80	-0.78	0.80
$\hat{t}_\tau$	-1.17	-2.41	-1.19	-2.91	-0.83	-3.27(*)	-3.44(*)	-2.99	-1.61	-2.37
$\hat{\phi}3$	9.16**	5.15	5.34	5.43	6.37(*)	5.69(*)	6.99*	5.97(*)	3.50	4.10
$\hat{\phi}2$	6.13*	3.52	3.61	3.62	4.24(*)	3.84	4.75(*)	4.17(*)	2.64	3.23
$\hat{\rho}_\mu$	0.89	0.88	0.80	0.77	0.72	0.66	0.75	0.81	0.88	0.85
$\hat{t}_\mu$	-1.46	-2.41	-1.08	-2.49	-0.90	-3.16*	-3.32*	-3.47*	-1.63	-2.76(*)
$\hat{\phi}1$	3.04	3.02	3.13	3.09	6.17*	5.07*	6.99**	6.30*	3.60	4.55(*)
	1/1974 - 12/1988, 180 Observations									
$\hat{\rho}_\tau$	0.97	0.95	0.89	0.87	0.75	0.73	0.66	0.79	0.83	0.85
$\hat{t}_\tau$	-0.67	-1.37	-1.75	-2.80	-1.42	-3.49*	-3.76*	-3.29(*)	-1.90	-2.50
$\hat{\phi}3$	1.63	1.26	3.84	4.01	6.09(*)	6.34(*)	9.87**	5.42	4.84	3.14
$\hat{\phi}2$	1.19	0.91	2.63	2.78	4.08	4.32(*)	6.64**	3.67	3.47	2.36
$\hat{\rho}_\mu$	0.97	0.96	0.92	0.90	0.79	0.82	0.93	0.95	0.96	0.96
$\hat{t}_\mu$	-0.86	-1.53	-1.55	-2.33	-1.77	-3.04*	-1.98	-1.68	-1.26	-1.46
$\hat{\phi}1$	1.69	1.28	2.75	2.87	4.63(*)	4.78*	2.95	1.50	1.94	1.46

'(*)', '*' or '**' denote significance on the 10 percent, 5 percent or 1 percent level, respectively.

If one compares the results in Tables 3 and 4, one can observe that in quite a number of cases the null hypothesis of a unit root can be rejected for both inflation rates and ex post real interest rates, even though nominal interest rates seem to be clearly non stationary. But this is a contradiction. As explained above, if nominal interest rates are non stationary, either inflation or real interest rates have to be non stationary as well. Both together cannot be stationary. Thus, under the non stationarity assumption of the nominal interest rates, in such situations the null hypothesis of non stationarity cannot be rejected for both real interest and inflation rates, despite the statistical significance.

5. Results of Cointegration Tests

In this paper, we also concentrate on the investigation of the long run relations between nominal interest rates and inflation rates according to equation (4). In contrast to the construction of the ex post real interest rate, we do not restrict the parameter of the inflation rate to one. As we have concluded from the results in chapter 4 that nominal interest rates and inflation rates are integrated of order one, we can use the cointegration methodology according to R.F. Engle/C.W.J. Granger (1987) to test for a long run relation between these two variables.

First, we estimate by OLS the cointegrating equation

$$y_t = \alpha + \beta_1 x_t + u_t. \tag{10}$$

If y_t and x_t are cointegrated, this estimator has a lot of advantages.[14] The estimated parameter β_1 converges to β_1 at a rate proportional to the sample size T and not at a rate proportional to $\sqrt{T}$ as in the case with stationary variables. If one runs the reverse regression from x_t to y_t, then the inverse of the estimated slope parameter of this regression converges to β_1, too. This implies that the R^2, which is the product of the two estimated slope coefficients, converges to one. Thus, it does not matter which normalization is chosen. The consistency of the estimates of β_1 is not influenced by simultaneity or errors in variables problems. Especially in our context, where we apply the observed instead of the expected inflation rate, this is a very useful property. Moreover, the long run behaviour can be estimated correctly from a static regression; it is independent of the dynamic specification.

All tests for cointegration have as null hypothesis that y_t and x_t are not cointegrated. R.F. Engle and C.W.J. Granger have developed several testing procedures. Here, we only use two of them: (i) The null hypothesis of no cointegration can be rejected, if in (10) the Durbin Watson statistic (D.W.) is significantly different from zero. (ii) With the augmented Dickey-Fuller test (ADF), the null hypothesis can be rejected, if the OLS estimate of δ_1 in the following equation is significantly less than zero:

14. See R.F. Engle and C.W.J. Granger (1987) and J.H. Stock (1987).

$$\Delta \hat{u}_t = \delta_1 \hat{u}_{t-1} + \sum_{j=1}^{k} \gamma_j \Delta \hat{u}_{t-j} + \varepsilon_t \qquad (11)$$

Here, $\hat{u}_t$ are the estimated residuals from (10). To perform this test, we set k = 3. The critical values for this and the Durbin Watson test are given in R.F. Engle and C.W.J. Granger (1987, Table II, p. 547).

Tables 5a und 5b contain the results of the cointegration tests. Because of the properties mentioned above, we run the regressions in both directions. In no case the product of the two slope coefficients (β_1) is near to one. As we can see from the values of the R^2, it is far below. The t-ratios of β_1 are relatively high, but in this case we cannot use the usual critical values.[15)] In a Monte Carlo study, G. Kirchgässner (1988) has derived critical values. But only in the case of France for the eighties the reported empirical t-values are significant at the 10 percent level. Only for Switzerland (for both periods) the D.W. and the ADF test statistics are significant in the regression with the inflation rate (SIR) as dependent variable. The same holds for the corresponding equation for Germany and Britain in the eighties. In general, these results show that there is no cointegration between nominal interest rates and inflation rates. This is a further indication that (ex ante) real interest rates show a non stationary behaviour.

In a Monte Carlo study A. Banerjee et al. (1986) have shown that in the cointegrating equation (10) the estimate of β_1 may be heavily biased downwards even in large samples when the R^2 is low. To get rid of this problem

---

15. The correction given by K.D. West (1988) cannot be applied because the unconditional means of our non stationary variables are zero.

Table 5a: Tests for Cointegration of Nominal Interest and Inflation Rates
1/1980 - 12/1988, 108 Observations

Y	X	β_1	R^2	D.W.	ADF	β_2
USR	UIR	0.510 (7.62)	0.35	0.21	-1.49	1.113* (2.25)
UIR	USR	0.694 (7.62)	0.35	0.30	-2.82	-0.060 (0.12)
GSR	GIR	0.815 (11.88)	0.57	0.32(*)	-2.44	1.137** (7.32)
GIR	GSR	0.701 (11.88)	0.57	0.48*	-3.34*	0.559** (2.79)
SSR	SIR	0.284 (4.77)	0.18	0.22	-2.51	0.346 (1.27)
SIR	SSR	0.622 (4.77)	0.18	0.45*	-3.34*	0.717* (2.07)
BSR	BIR	0.371 (9.33)	0.45	0.25	-3.35*	0.489** (5.61)
BIR	BSR	1.215 (9.33)	0.45	0.32(*)	-4.08*	-0.176 (0.14)
FSR	FIR	0.553(*) (13.97)	0.65	0.29	-2.53	0.658** (5.78)
FIR	FSR	1.172(*) (13.97)	0.65	0.36*	-2.80	0.663 (1.00)

'(*)', '*' or '**' denote significance on the 10 percent, 5 percent or 1 percent level, respectively.

Table 5b: Tests for Cointegration of Nominal Interest and Inflation Rates
1/1974 - 12/1988, 180 Observations

Y	X	$ß_1$	R^2	D.W.	ADF	$ß_2$
USR	UIR	0.263 (5.10)	0.13	0.09	-1.62	1.111 (1.39)
UIR	USR	0.485 (5.10)	0.13	0.15	-2.07	-0.660 (0.83)
GSR	GIR	0.657 (9.44)	0.33	0.15	-2.42	0.801** (2.90)
GIR	GSR	0.508 (9.44)	0.33	0.30	-2.89	0.214 (0.65)
SSR	SIR	0.307 (6.29)	0.18	0.17	-2.62	0.439* (1.96)
SIR	SSR	0.592 (6.29)	0.18	0.45*	-3.63*	0.489 (1.52)
BSR	BIR	0.110 (4.49)	0.10	0.11	-2.70	0.131 (1.15)
BIR	BSR	0.922 (4.49)	0.10	0.17	-2.22	- 0.429 (0.27)
FSR	FIR	0.367 (8.23)	0.28	0.09	-2.32	0.492* (2.53)
FIR	FSR	0.751 (8.23)	0.28	0.15	-2.07	-1.017 (0.54)

'(*)', '*' or '**' denote significance on the 10 percent, 5 percent or 1 percent level, respectively.

they recommend to explicitly model the dynamics in the cointegrating equation. Therefore, we perform a test which has been proposed by M.R. Wickens and T.S. Breusch (1988). To do this, the cointegrating equation (10) is augmented by allowing for short run dynamics in the following way:

$$y_t = \alpha + \beta_2 x_t + \sum_{j=0}^{3} a_j \Delta y_{t-1} + \sum_{j=0}^{3} b_j \Delta x_{t-j} + \varepsilon_t. \qquad (12)$$

Applying OLS to (12) would produce inconsistent estimates since Δy_t appears on the right-hand side as regressor. One gets consistent estimates and correct standard errors in (12), if one uses y_{t-1}, y_{t-2}, y_{t-3}, y_{t-4}, x_t, x_{t-1}, x_{t-2}, x_{t-3}, x_{t-4} as instruments. The results of these tests are also shown in Tables 5a and 5b. In 50 percent of all cases the estimates of β_2 are larger than the estimates for β_1, but in 25 percent of all cases they are even negative. The number of significant coefficients increases when we apply the usual critical values for the t-test. Thus - although there seems to be more evidence in favour of cointegration - the results are not at all clear. This is in line with the findings by R. MacDonald and P.D. Murphy (1989) for Belgium, Canada, the U.K. and U.S. Using the Durbin Watson, the Dickey-Fuller and the augmented Dickey-Fuller tests they cannot reject the null hypothesis of no cointegration for the whole period of flexible exchange rates.

6. Summary and Concluding Remarks

In this paper, we investigate the stationary behaviour of nominal interest rates, inflation rates and ex post real interest rates for the period of flexible exchange rates from January 1974 to December 1988. We use money market rates for Switzerland, the Federal Republic of Germany, the U.S., France, and the U.K. The results of the unit root t- and F-tests indicate that all these variables are integrated of order one. The outcomes for the nominal interest rates are very clear, whereas for the inflation rates and the ex post real interest rates for some countries the evidence is somewhat mixed. Additionally, we test for cointegration of nominal interest rates and inflation rates. The empirical evidence for cointegration is rather weak. Thus, it seems that nominal interest rates and inflation rates tend to drift apart. This implies that the Fisher-hypothesis does not hold as a long run relation, maybe as a short run. The missing cointegration supports the results of the unit root tests for ex post real interest rates not to be stationary. Since institutional settings changed in 1980, we did all the tests for the period from January 1980 to December 1988, too. However, the results of the tests remain more or less the same.

Taking all results together, we find quite a lot of evidence that not only nominal, but also real interest rates are non stationary. This supports the results of R. Mac Donald and P.D. Murphy (1989) and also of A.K. Rose (1988), although with respect to the inflation rate our results differ from Rose's. However, in line with the authors mentioned, we only investigated bilateral relations. The application of multivariate methods can perhaps give further insights into the stationarity behaviour of real interest rates.

Appendix

Definition and Sources of Data

SSR: 3-month interbank rate
Source: Monatsberichte der schweizerischen Nationalbank

GSR: 3-month interbank rate
Source: Monatsberichte der Deutschen Bundesbank

USR: 3-month treasury bill rate
Source: Federal Reserve Bulletin

BSR: Treasury bill rate (91 days)
Source: Monatsberichte der Deutschen Bundesbank

FSR: 3-months interbank rate (Effets privés sous dossier à trois mois)
Source: Banque de France, Bulletin Trimestriel

SCPS:	Swiss consumer price index	1980 = 100
GCPS:	German consumer price index	1980 = 100
UCPS:	U.S. consumer price index	1980 = 100
BCPS:	U.K. consumer price index	1980 = 100
FCPS:	French consumer price index	1980 = 100

Source: OECD, Main Economic Indicators

All interest data are monthly averages. All price indices are seasonally adjusted with the multiplicative X11 - seasonal adjustment procedure.

References

BANERJEE, A., J.J. DOLADO, D.F. HENDRY, and G.W. SMITH (1986), Exploring Equilibrium Relations in Econometrics through Static Models: Some Monte Carlo Evidence, *Oxford Bulletin of Economics and Statistics*, 48, 253 - 277.

DICKEY, D.A., and W.A. FULLER (1981), Likelihood Ratio Test Statistics for Autoregressive Time Series with a Unit Root, *Econometrica*, 49, 1057 - 1072.

ENGLE, R.F., and C.W.J. Granger (1987), Cointegration and Error Correction: Representation, Estimation and Testing, *Econometrica*, 55, 251 - 276.

FISHER, I. (1930), *The Theory of Interest*, New York; German Translation: *Die Zinstheorie*, Gustav Fischer, Jena 1932.

FULLER, W.A. (1976), *Introduction to Statistical Time Series*, Wiley, New York.

GARCIA, R., and P. Perron (1989), An Analysis of the Real Interest Rate Under Regime Shifts, Princeton University, mimeo.

GRANZIOL, M., and H. Schelbert (1983), Ex ante Real-Zinssätze am Euromarkt, *Zeitschrift für Wirtschafts- und Sozialwissenschaften*, 103, 437 - 459.

KIRCHGÄSSNER, G. (1988), Validity or Collapse of Purchasing Power Parity Theory? Additional Empirical Results for the Seventies and Eighties, Beiträge des Fachbereichs Wirtschaftswissenschaften der Universität Osnabrück, Nr. 8802.

KIRCHGÄSSNER, G., and J. Wolters (1990), Uncovered Interest Party, Interest Rate Linkage, or Independance?, Empirical Results for 1961 - 1987, *Jahrbuch für Sozialwissenschaft*, 41 (1990), 289 - 311.

KUGLER, P., and K. Neusser (1990), Cointegration, Codependence and International Interest Rate Equalization, Universität Bern, mimeo.

MACDONALD, R., and P.D. Murphy (1989), Testing for the Long Run Relationship Between Nominal Interest Rates and Inflation Using Cointegration Techniques, *Applied Economics*, 21, 439 - 447.

MUTH, J. (1961), Rational Expectations and the Theory of Price Movements, *Econometrica*, 29, 315 - 335.

PERRON, P. (1988), Trends and Random Walks in Macroeconomic Time Series. Further Evidence from a New Approach, *Journal of Economic Dynamics and Control*, 12, 297 - 332.

ROSE, A.K. (1988), Is the Real Interest Rate Stable?, *Journal of Finance*, 43, 1095 - 1112.

SCHOTMAN, P.C. (1987), Long Run International Equilibrium Relations, Erasmus University, Rotterdam, mimeo.

SCHOTMAN, P.C. (1989), *Empirical Studies on the Behaviour of Interest Rates and Exchange Rates*, Dissertation, Erasmus University, Rotterdam, June 1989.

SCHWERT, G.W. (1989), Tests for Unit Roots: A Monte Carlo Investigation, *Journal of Business and Economic Statistics*, 7, 147 - 159.

STOCK, J.H. (1987), Asymptotic Properties of Least Squares Estimators of Cointegrating Vectors, *Econometrica*, 55, 1035 - 1056.

THIEMER, A. (1987), *Der Zusammenhang zwischen Realzins und Inflationserwartung*, Josef Eul, Bergisch Gladbach/Köln.

WEST, K.D. (1988), Asymptotic Normality, When Regressors Have a Unit Root, *Econometrica*, 56, 1397 - 1417.

WICKENS, M.R., and T.S. Breusch (1988), Dynamic Specification, the Long-Run and the Estimation of Transformed Regression Models, *Economic Journal*, 98, 189 - 205.

GPSR Compliance

The European Union's (EU) General Product Safety Regulation (GPSR) is a set of rules that requires consumer products to be safe and our obligations to ensure this.

If you have any concerns about our products, you can contact us on ProductSafety@springernature.com

In case Publisher is established outside the EU, the EU authorized representative is:

Springer Nature Customer Service Center GmbH
Europaplatz 3
69115 Heidelberg, Germany

Batch number: 10725973

Printed by Printforce, the Netherlands